GET YOUR FILM

UK film finance guide 2004

by Caroline Hancock and Nic Wistreich

with Adam P Davies of Investrum

very special thanks to
Jess Search, David Hancock, Tom Fogg, James MacGregor,
Stephen Salter, Jo Roberts, Lucy Bernstein, Clifford Thurlow,
Stephen Applebaum, Tony Pomfret & Andy Glynne

www.shootingpeople.org

About the authors

CAROLINE HANCOCK

Producer of *Darkhunters*, forthcoming horror feature from Gatlin Pictures. Currently working on personal film & writing projects, previously involved in arts management and exhibition organisation at the Brighton Media Centre.

NIC WISTREICH

Co-founder and publisher of UK film industry website Netribution.co.uk and former UK head of filmfestivals.com. Author of Film & TV Rights for MTI/DMG (1999) and Digital Asset Management for Informa (2001). When not working for Shooting People as Development Director, is a VJ and video artist with the polymedia collective 0.1.

ADAM P DAVIES

(author of Finance Options section in Chapter Two and Co-productions section in Chapter Six)
Qualified solicitor and co-founder of leading film finance consultancy, Investrum. In the past six years Adam has worked on over 100 films, including financing agreements for Gods and Monsters and Human Traffic, and talent agreements for the lead actors in Sexy Beast and Lock Stock and Two Smoking Barrels. Adam most recently worked as legal consultant on co-productions and international financing options for Grosvenor Park.

GET YOUR FILM FUNDED - UK FILM FINANCE GUIDE 2004

© 2003 Shooting People Ltd & Netribution Ltd. Reprinted 2003

DISCLAIMER

This publication is presented 'as is' without warranty of any kind. Whilst every effort has been made to maintain the accuracy of the information contained herein, the author, editor, contributors and/or publisher cannot accept liability whatsoever for incorrect or outdated information contained within. Furthermore, certain information presented in this publication may be based on the opinions and/or experiences of the author/contributors and cannot be taken as to be legally binding.

PUBLISHED BY

Shooting People Press
34 Keeling House
Claredale Street
London
E2 6PG

www.shootingpeople.org

ISBN 0-9544874-0-0

DISTRIBUTED BY

Wallflower Press
4th Floor,
26 Shacklewell Lane
London
E8 2EZ

www.wallflowerpress.co.uk

Printed and bound in Great Britain by Antony Rowe Ltd, Chippenham, Wiltshire

A catalogue record for this book is available from the British Library

Contents

Acknowledgements

With thanks to: Gwydion Lyn from 4 Minute Wonders; Katherine Müller from Arts & Business; Helen Dixon from Arts Connection; Libby Butler from Awards For All; Amy Minyard at BAFTA; Anna Wright from the B+ Awards; Kenneth D Baker; Steve Jenkins from BBC Acquisitions; Susy Liddell, Jane Wright, Charlotte Paget and Emma Parker from BBC Films; David Cormack from BECTU; Steve Mackler from Bedford Entertainment; Sarah Eccleston from the British Film Commission; Hugh Macleod and the staff from Britshorts; Alexandra Finlay from Channel 4 Acquisitions; David Smith from Cineworks; David White from City Eye Media Centre; Tim Clague; Colin Rogers from Cornwall Film Fund; Fred Brookes from Creative Advantage Fund; Calvin Taylor from Creative Yorkshire; Valerie Dixon from the Creativity Unit at the Dept of Culture Arts & Literature of Northern Ireland; Paul Johnson from the Croydon Media Awards; Mark Adamson and Alison Hughes from Cultural Business Venture; Chantel Burrell from the DCMS; Alice Bennett-Leyh from Depict!; Paul Welsh from Digicult; Jo Smith and Benjamin Nicholas from DNA Films; Ulwin Smartt from the DTI; James Eaves; Ros Davies from Edinburgh Film Focus; Duncan Rennie from Edinburgh Mediabase: Owen Thomas & May Miles Thomas from Elemental Films; Carol Clarke from Em-Media; Premila Sivanesan from the Enfield Film Fund; Geoffrey Brown from Culture 2000 at EUCLID; Nathalie Monteillet-Werle and Marije Plaum from Eurimages; Iris ME Kehr from the European Co-ordination of Film Festivals; Robert Jones; Paul Trijbits; Jenny Borgars; Ian Thomson; Caroline Cooper, Paul Hewlett, Yara Ocana, Tina McFarling, Vince Holden, Sophie Crabb, Anne Threlkeld, Chris Chandler, Alan Milne and Tracey McCarrick from the Film Council; Sanford Lieberson, Gill Henderson and Honnie Tang from Film London; Birgit Baehr from FilmFernsehFonds Bayern (Bavaran Film Fund); Helen Peetzen from the FilmFörderung Hamburg (Hamburg Film Fund); Peter Carlton, Robin Gutch, Tracey Josephs and Juliette Howell from Film Four; Leigh Thomas from First Light; Christine Berg from the Filmforderungsanstalt

(German Federal Film Board); David Nicholas Wilkinson from Guerilla Films; Hamish Walker from Glasgow Film Office; Rob Hull from Gone in 60 Seconds; Graham Ward, Robert Mumby, Fred Channing, Valerie Crockford, Kerry Machale, Rod Gilchrist, Neil Burley and Robert Galloway from the regional Government Offices; Clare Butler-Henderson from the Heritage Lottery Fund; Ben Hopkins; Barry Hutchinson; Sue Lewis from the Ignition Network; Sue Griffith from the Independent Television Commission; Eily Kilgannon from Irish Distillers; Louise Ryan from the Irish Film Board; Ceris Norris from Intermedia; Kim Fletcher and Hilary Dugdale from the Isle of Man Film Commission; Jacques Henry Bezy from Jameson Short Film Awards; Junko Takekawa from the Japan Foundation; Nicola Silver and Daniel Clarke from Kodak; Andrea Livingstone from the Kraszna-Krausz Foundation; Sarah Flint from Lighthouse; Leslie Lowes; Paul North and Rolf Dahmer, Mediamatch; Christine Haupt from Medien-und Filmgesellschaft Baden-Württemberg (MFG); Saul Metzstein; Nina Baxter from the Millennium Commission; Anna Burges-Lumden from NESTA; Carole Thomas from the Newham Film Fund; Carly Holliday and Helen Stearman from Northern Film & Media; Andrew Reid and Ann Dillon from the NIFTC; Phillip Hammond and Noirin McKinney from the Northern Ireland Arts Council; Lorraine Mahoney, Lorna Woods and Helen Bingham from North West Vision; Ann Marie O'Connor from the Oscar Moore Foundation; Pawel Pawlikowski; Alex Usborne from Picture Palace North; Jane Hooks from The Pool; Farrah Abushwesha from Rocliffe; Clare Pringle and Matt Neale from Rogers & Cowan; Becky Lloyd, Steve McIntyre and Kirsten Stewart from Scottish Screen; Nicky Dade, Darren Bender, Annabel Grundy and Laurie Hayward from Screen East; Gina Fegan, Lara Lowe and Pat Coxon from Screen South; Jane Slater, Steve Chapman and Sue Richardson from Screen West Midlands; Paul Staniland, Ren Herbert and Sally Joynson from Screen Yorkshire; Gilbert-Paul Jeannon from SEUPB; Rhodri Llyr ap Dyfrig, Anneli Jones and Judith Higginbottom from Sgrîn; Kate Gerova from Short Circuit; Sarah Jane Meredith, Emily Cooter and Clare Thalmann from South West Screen; Belle Doyle from the South West Scotland Screen Commission; Jacqueline Swanson; Piotr Szkopiak; Sarah Wren from the Tower Hamlets Film Office; Agnieszka Moody from the UK MEDIA Desk; Moira Campbell, Pikka Brasey & Philippa Goslet from Wanton Muse; Mark Herbert from Warp Films; Darren Ward; Ken Arnold from the Wellcome Trust; Paula Price-Davies from the Westminster Arts Council; Lucy Jones and John Mills at Willott Kingston Smith; Gareth Jones and Georgia Freeman from Winchester Entertainment; Harry Hicks from WJB Chiltern; Rachel Prior from Working Title Films; Anna Raynsford from Freud Communications on behalf of Working Title Films; the staff from YMPA.

Initials after interviews and case studies indicate: Tom Fogg (TF); Caroline Hancock (CH), James MacGregor (JM) and Nic Wistreich (NW). Photographs by TF and NW, except Piotr Szkopiak, Elemental Films and Johannes Roberts.

Full versions of many of the interviews in this book can be found at www.netribution.co.uk/features.

Extra special thanks to sponsors and editorial contributors: Willott Kingston Smith, WJB Chiltern, Dorsey & Whitney & Great British Films.

Foreword

The UK seems to have developed two film industries. There is the established industry, which can spend years developing a script before packaging it with named talent, paying a large crew a full wage and producing a sellable film that will probably be released, yet typically earns less than it cost. Then there are the ultra-indies, nurtured by Shooting People, Guerrilla Filmmakers Handbook and Raindance, who get into production through whatever means necessary. Films are shot on credit-card sized budgets with passionate commitment and resourcefulness from the production team, yet are rarely sold or released, let alone make their money back.

This book is targeted at both these sides of British film, because we think that each could learn a bit from the other. With the average UK film costing £3.5m and grossing £350,000 at the domestic box office, it's clear that – as the Film Council's Relph Report spells out (see page 28) – established UK producers need to shoot much cheaper films. The ultra-indie is an expert at this, and could comfortably shoot ten features for the average cost of one British film. But this is usually offset by a lack of script development and a shortfall in the skills needed to finance, target, package and sell a film to distributors and broadcasters.

Both these sides of filmmaking are at an interesting point. Ultra-indie production – fuelled by cheap DV cameras and desktop editing – is expanding, while properly financed production and distribution of UK films has fallen sharply since 2001 despite a massive rise in cinema admissions. If established producers continue making films for more than their realistic market value, and ultra-indies continue to ignore the demands of sales and distribution, the British industry at either level will struggle. Shooting People thinks that the more these two separate sides of film production work together – exchanging in both directions skills, talent and knowledge to reduce budgets and produce films that meet audience appetite – the stronger that the British film industry will become. The resurgence of Argentinian film over the past few years has shown that industry-wide invigoration and integration at a time of economic fallout can really push a country's film industry forward.

With this in mind we've pulled together in one book the financial contacts and information useful to a producer working at *any* level in the UK. From public money for video art and short films, right through to international co-productions, we've listed as many funding opportunities as we could find. Direct public financing for film appears in the Film Council, Nations and Regions and International chapters. Indirect public funds that can sometimes apply to film, as well as competitions and other schemes, are listed in Other Sources. Tax breaks, financing structures, production companies and sales agents are detailed in Finance & Investment. For producers starting out, the Big Picture primer on page 23 gives a background to the UK and the basic information needed before facing the industry, while the Support & Advice chapter at the back lists all the potential organisations you could contact for further help. To help navigate this myriad of funds, you can use the jumping off points in the Show Me the Money section that follows. Dotted throughout the book are dozens of interviews and case studies with filmmakers, buyers and fund heads to try to give a clearer picture of the range of activities and approaches in the UK.

This book has been talked about for years. In 2000 the BFI stopped publishing the Lowdown, and in an unofficial capacity Netribution.co.uk's funding section took over. Get Your Film Funded – the UK Film Finance Guide 2003, is born of that directory, originally compiled by Stephen Salter and now tirelessly researched and written afresh for Shooting People by Caroline Hancock. Film lawyer Adam P Davies of Investrum has produced finance, legal & international co-production articles, with further resources from Dorsey & Whitney, Willott Kingston Smith, WJB Chiltern & the Documentary Filmmakers Group. A big thank you to them, and everyone else who's helped bring this book to print – especially Cath and Jess at Shooting People for their tireless support.

I'm afraid that we still haven't found a magic funding formula. The only weapon a producer can arm themselves with to compete with the serious players, asides from a killer project, is knowledge. To a new producer, film finance is a confusing, often incoherent language and getting straight answers from anyone can – as we've found out in the making of this book – be a trial in itself. So while this book won't get your film financed for you, we hope that we've saved you some of the legwork.

Nic Wistreich

May 2003

PS - This is the first edition of what we intend to be an annually updated guide. We've been as exhaustive as we could but inevitably there will be some errors and oversights. Please do contact us with your comments and suggestions, corrections and additions by emailing us at- fundingbook@shootingpeople.org.

PPS - (added October 2003) the first print run of this book far outstripped our expectations and sold out within five months. This reprint has corrected a few glaring ommissions from the first edition, and updated some of the important info that was released shortly after first publication. Many thanks to Caroline Hancock, Becky Lloyd, Peter Carlton, Briony Hanson and Alan Denman for their help in this - and to all those who have bought the book so far.

Chapter 1
GETTING STARTED

Show Me the Money

Feature films

The potential revenues for a completed feature film come from a release cycle that would typically progress across each country of release as follows:

0 months	Theatrical release
3 months	Airline
4-6 months	Hotel PPV
6 months	PPV/VoD
6 months	Video rental
6-12 months	Video sale
18 months	Pay-TV (eg FilmFour)
36 months	Free-TV (eg BBC1)

With the right project, further revenues are available from soundtracks, merchandise, sponsorship and long term library sales if the film is part of a slate.

Feature films are financed in one of two ways:

100% financing. A studio or other backer gives 100% of the film's budget in return for full ownership of the film (and control over its production). Success in getting such deals, which are extremely rare especially in the UK, is based on the strength of the project, the track record of the producer and any key 'named' talent attached. Single party financing is not really an option for a first or second-time feature producer unless they surrender up all control, and as such is not covered in this book other than at the micro level where financing may come from a single private investor.

Multi-party financing. The independent producer typically raises finance from a host of sources – oversees distributors, TV–pre sales or private investors as well as 'soft money' such as tax breaks and public funds.

Multi-party financing options

Pre-sales. A distributor or broadcaster acquires an agreed set of rights to distribute or broadcast the film in a certain area in advance of the film being completed. For more information see page 54.

Negative pick-up. Where a distributor or studio promises to pay the film's budget on delivery of a completed picture in return for all rights. See page 55.

Co-prouducer. Makes an equity investment in a film, taking a share of future income. Some co-producers, such as BBC Films or FilmFour may also acquire UK TV and other rights at the same point. See page 80.

Gap financing. Banks occasionally provide a gap loan to match a shortfall between a film's budget and the total funds raised so far. See page 48.

Private equity. Section 42 and Section 48 offer private investors income tax relief on investment in feature films. See page 42.

Sales and leaseback. These offer UK producers a minimum 12.5% of their budget, at least until July 2005. Super-sale-and-leaseback also offers production investment in return for an equity stake at the same time. See page 44.

The Film Council. The three film council funds have a combined £20m annual pot for investing in British films and British international co-productions. See page 96.

Regional funds. Both the production company office address and the location of shooting allow producers to tap extensive regional investment. See page 116.

Oversees incentives. International co-productions allow UK producers to tap oversees sources of soft money such as tax breaks and public subsidy by partnering with foreign producers. See page 193 for incentives and 201 for public sources.

Product placement and sponsorship. Companies provide cash or in-kind services in return for screen-time or marketing associated with the film. See pages 74 & 76.

Venture Capital funds. VCs typically invest in high-risk, yet potential high-return product and if convinced on the strength of the team and slate may get involved. See page 70.

Friends and family. The first films from Stanley Kubrick, John Waters, Ed Burns and countless others where financed by close family.

Inventive alternatives. If all else fails there's always original funding sources that can be of greater publicity benefit than the money they raise, such as Robert Rodriguez allegedly offering himself for medical tests to finance *El Mariachi*. Rocliffe Productions invited friends and family to provide sperm to sell to a sperm bank to finance their short film *No Deposit, No Return*. By offering people the chance to give £20 instead they raised several thousand pounds, but of most value got press coverage including the Daily Star and Empire.

Budgets & structures

The first budget you draw up with a line producer should be a fully funded model that puts the director, producer, all crew and cast in at the appropriate fees and all post production in at industry standard prices. Unless you are already an established producer the chances are that you will now want to reduce this figure using all manner of favours and by forgoing or deferring some or all of your own fees and those of other key creatives. This will leave you with your cash budget – the money you need to actually shoot and finish the film including the delivery requirements needed to satisfy a sales agent or distributor.

For consistency throughout this book we've broken down the budgets of British film into four categories, based – not on Hollywood standard definitions – but the cash budgets used by the bulk of UK-financed productions:

Micro-budget - £100,000 and under
Ultra-low budget - £500,000 and under
Low budget - £2m and under
Mid budget - over £2m average £3.5m

MICRO-BUDGET - £100,000 AND UNDER

Example Finance Plan A: DigiBeta, ghost story, no named cast, inexperienced producer, director and writer all unpaid, intended to sell to DVD/Video

Development	Self-financed	nil
Production	Private Equity	£30,000
	Deferred Fees	£60,000
TOTAL		£90,000

Filmmakers at this level include Barry Hutchinson (Curse of the Bogwoman) – page 229; Kenneth D Barker (Kingdom) – page 73; Johannes Roberts (Diagnosis) - page 65; and Piotr Szkopiak (Small Time Obsession) - page 5.

ULTRA-LOW BUDGET - £500,000 AND UNDER

Example Finance Plan B: super16mm, Horror, one named British actor, producer and director with micro-budget experience on productions which have sold to distributors and has sales agent on board - intended for worldwide TV and DVD/video release.

Development	Private Equity	£10,000
Production	Private Equity	£160,000
	Advanced TV Sale	£20,000
	Sales agent as Co-Producer	£160,000
TOTAL		£350,000

Filmmakers at this level in the book: Ben Hopkins (Nine Lives of Tomas Katz) – page 7; Lab Ky Mo (9 Dead Gay Guys) - page 140; and Pawel Pawlikowski (Last Resort) – page xxx

LOW BUDGET - £2M AND UNDER

Example Finance Plan C: super16mm, Black Comedy, 2 x UK named cast, up-coming director and producer intended for print blow up for theatrical release

Development	Regional Lottery Funds	£10,000
	Private Equity	£10,000
Production	Isle of Man Film & TV Funds	£200,000
	Lottery New Cinema Fund	£280,000
	Bank loan based on distributor guarantees	£200,000
	Private Equity	£200,000
	Sale and leaseback	£100,000
TOTAL		£1,000,000

Filmmakers and producers at this level in the book: Owen & May Miles Thomas (Solid Air) – page 8; Gavin Emerson (Ratcatcher) – page 12; Amananda Posey (Fever Pitch) – page 86; Saul Metzstein (Late Night Shopping) – page 157; and Alex Usborne (Large) – page 14.

MID BUDGET - OVER £2M AVERAGE £3.5M

Example Finance Plan D: 35mm, Romantic Comedy, 1 x US named cast, 1 x UK named cast, experienced director and crew intended for theatrical release

Development	Lottery Development Funds	£10,000
	Private Equity	£10,000
	Foreign co-producer	£10,000
Production	Lottery Premiere Fund	£1,070,000
	Bank loan based on distributor guarantees	£540,000
	UK TV Pre-sale	£250,000
	UK TV Equity	£250,000
	Sale & Leaseback	£320,000
	Private Equity	£210,000
	Foreign co-producer	£1,110,000
TOTAL		£3,780,000

PIOTR SZKOPIAK | **SMALL TIME OBSESSION**

Micro to ultra-low - Shot for £40,000 / total budget £190,000 - Super16mm

Piotr Szkopiak's story is a microcosm of the issues facing ultra-low- budget UK indie filmmakers – he self financed his feature for £40,000, shot on Super16 and had the good fortune to get the strong support of a distributor who brought in £150,000 completion funds taking him through to a limited theatrical release. Yet without stars or a competitive marketing budget the film took just £5,533 at the UK box office.

"*Small Time Obsession* initially cost £40,000 to make. Half of that was my own money and the other half came from family and friends. My half of the money was savings from working as a freelance Avid editor for three years. I could save this much because I remained living at home and my family waived the rent. I accepted the fact that no one I didn't know was going to give money to an unknown, first-time director who wanted to use an unknown cast.

"I shot on Super16mm film, transferred everything to videotape, edited digitally on Avid and got a sound designer to do a TV quality stereo mix (with foley and everything). The beauty of editing digitally was that I did not have to cut my negative until I knew I had interest from a distributor. Why go to the expense of making a print unless you know you are going to get it shown? Anyway, I didn't have the money and Edinburgh does this great thing called Film UK. They list every UK film that has been made in the previous year, from a film like *Notting Hill* to the lowest of low budget video movies. They produce a booklet, which has all the films' details, and this is made available to all the buyers, sales agents and distributors at the festival. They then flick through the booklet and if there is something they like they can watch it in a special video viewing room, which stocks a couple of copies of every film. No pressure. This is where David Nicholas Wilkinson of Guerilla Films saw my film. He helped raise a further £150,000 to finish the film to 35mm print. All I had at this point was a virtual film if you like, it didn't exist in print form at all, just on Digibeta. The extra funding covered a re-cut, neg cut, blow-up, sound mix, music clearances, E&O insurance then telecines etc, etc, etc.

"The £150,000 came from a private investment in the form of venture capital. This was a unique situation because I went to them with a finished film and with a UK distributor already attached. Normally, if you went to them for initial funding, you would not have a leg to stand on because you cannot prove you have a market for your film. Having a distributor can change that situation. When approaching money or facilities, ask yourself why you would part with the money or why you would help a project like this one. Put yourself in their shoes. Look at it logically. Why should I give you £500,000 to make your film if you have never made a film before? Would you give someone £500,000 if they had never made a feature before?"

DISTRIBUTION

"All you really have if you are a small, independent film is word-of-mouth. You don't have the benefit of a multi-million dollar advertising campaign like all the US films. So, in comparison, we did REALLY well. In fact, per print, we were actually doing a lot better than most US films. This is what people tend to forget when they look at box office takings. £1,000 on one print is actually a better return than £10,000 on 100 prints. *Small Time Obsession* was released on four prints in London and around the country through ABC Cinemas and Warner.

"Its not that distributors do not want to spend money on distributing UK films, its just that they know they won't get their money back. That's a fact. Look at how you choose to go and see a film. When *Small Time Obsession* was released, there were about 25 other NEW films released that same month just in the cinema. Now, I love films but even I only see 3 or 4 films a month in the cinema. Furthermore, it costs the same amount of money to go see my film as it does *Gladiator*. Like it or not, you are in direct competition with *Gladiator* and, yes, you can offer something *Gladiator* doesn't but, again, without the advertising, you can't tell anyone what that is. All you have is word-of-mouth but that only spreads once people have seen the film.

"Unfortunately, you have been kicked out of the cinema because not enough people knew about the film to come see it on the opening weekend because you didn't have the advertising spend. As a result, the film gets low box office figures and then the next UK film that comes along is told that it is not worth spending anything on advertising it because no one went to see the last UK film that came out and so the same thing happens. Catch 22. Now, no one can afford to take the risk.

"When *Small Time Obsession* was released there was advertising on Shooting People, coverage on London Tonight, CNN and in the Evening Standard. Were you aware of it? I hope so but probably not. It gets lost. I say all this just to underline what you are up against and it's not pretty. It's competition and, most of the time, it is not fair but that's the reality and you have to know what you, and the distributors, are up against. Only when you know the truth can you do anything about it because, I believe that, having said all this, it is possible to beat the system. Make a great film and do great marketing.

"Unfortunately, that is what everyone is trying to do and there is no formula. All you can do is get stuck in. I tried and never thought I would get this far. But we have to work together. If everyone who reads Shooting People had gone to see my film when it opened, it would have blown the cinemas away. They weren't expecting anyone to come. As it is, I got a second week because it did so well. That is the first step. Make someone some money and they will come back for more." *JM*

BEN HOPKINS NINE LIVES OF TOMAS KATZ

Ultra Low - £400,000 - 16mm / Super 16mm / DV / Beta

Ben Hopkins trod the path dreamt of by many – a graduation film from film school touring 30 festivals worldwide, scooping 14 awards and leading to a near £3m picture deal from British Screen. His debut feature Simon Magus with Ian Holm was critically acclaimed, yet landed on scarce few screens. His cult follow up, The Nine Lives of Tomas Katz, was shot on a ninth of that budget and was described by the press as the mutant love child of Monty Python and Fritz Lang. The black and white multi-format film didn't secure UK distribution and Hopkins distributed the film himself.

"*Simon Magus* cost £3m and was very carefully planned, very particular and very ornate. *Tomas Katz* was very cheap - shot in three weeks on a small budget - really knocked together. Shooting on such a tight budget was very enjoyable actually. As soon as you are over a certain level of funding, insurance companies and financiers have a much stronger element of control over you and more of a vested interest in what you are doing. It becomes important to make it look like money has been spent on it. Magus, like my short films, is very intricate and quite elegantly made and I got fed up with that so I thought I'd do something that looked like I'd just knocked it out for next to nothing. I shot Katz on 16mm, DV, High 8, Super16mm and Beta Cam.

"One often feels that without much money you should concentrate on social realism and not light it properly with shit wallpaper. It's nonsense of course, you can be really imaginative with little money. *Eraserhead* is a fine example of how to create a entirely different universe with no money, that's inspiring. I'm just not very interested in daily life to be honest. I live in daily life and I don't need reminding of it every time I pay my money for a ticket, I'd much prefer to pay my money and be taken to another world!

"I don't think we have any imaginative, creative and interesting distributors and I wonder why they bother spending good money on a product that is quite clearly shite. It's so stupid and a terrible waste of money. If you think of what could have happened to the celluloid that made up the 200 odd prints of *Maybe Baby*, why? What if the apocalypse happens tomorrow, all that's left is 200 prints of *Maybe Baby* in a warehouse somewhere.

"You can make a masterpiece on a DV camera with a couple of unknown actors in a room and you can make a total piece of shit with $120m and all the help in the world. There's a magic thing in filmmaking, a sort of alchemical process where something is either working or it's not and it's very difficult to get into that realm - there's no formula to that. It either works or it doesn't." *TF/NW*

ELEMENTAL FILMS   SOLID AIR

Micro to Low - One Life Stand cc £50,000 - DV, Solid Air cc £1m - HD

Elemental Films, run by the husband and wife team of writer/director May Miles Thomas and producer Owen Thomas, are passionate advocates of digital cinema. They completed in 2000 one of the UK's first DV features, the multi-award-winning One Life Stand, shot on a micro-budget with a prosumer DV camera. The Glasgow-based company's follow-up feature is Solid Air, shot on HDCAM in late 2002 with full backing from Momentum Pictures, Scottish Screen and the Glasgow Film Fund. Elemental, judged by BT Vision 100 as one of the UK's most 'visionary' companies, is an excellent example of a producer that has stayed true to its values while progressing from acclaimed first micro-budget feature, through to properly financed follow-up.

THE CALLING CARD

"From the get-go, *One Life Stand* (2000) was conceived of and produced as a demo movie. We certainly never intended it as a commercial prospect, more a way to demonstrate May's abilities as a writer and director, who, despite her broadcast and music video experience, found it virtually impossible to break into movies. Essentially the film was a self-financed calling card. Only after the fact it attracted attention, partly because no-one else in the UK had made a digital feature and partly because it was deemed a critical and popular success.

"There's a line in *One Life Stand* which goes, 'Hindsight, my fat and lazy friend'. Looking back, we realise we didn't finish our thinking when we set out to make the movie - whether it would be screened at festivals, whether anyone would review it, let alone win any awards. A pick-up was beyond our wildest dreams. What we did know was that as a micro budget project - a low five figure sum - we were very much the underdogs. The advantage of that position is the degree of creative freedom that afforded us as filmmakers. We never sought any funding, either development or production, a decision which effectively freed us from top-down compromise.

"Limited as it is, *One Life Stand* was pretty much the film we set out to make and it's interesting to reflect now that here was a film with no 'developed' screenplay, shot on a camcorder on a tiny budget which was one of the best reviewed British films of 2000, winning eight awards, including four BAFTA New Talent Awards and the BIFA for Achievement in Production. What we learned, we would never have learned had we been funded - how to approach festivals, how to promote the film, how to do many of the jobs that otherwise would have been delegated. But the most important lesson we learned was that in order to keep making films, and equally important, to reach an audience, is an engagement with the industry first and foremost. Lottery funding is seen as requisite in UK film production, as is access to tax breaks, but neither can actually put your film on the screen. You have to attract the industry. And that's exactly what we did with our forthcoming film, *Solid Air.*"

"We were interested in talking to Momentum Pictures because they seemed one of the more interesting distribution outfits in the UK, and although they handle few British films, their choices were more adventurous than others. What attracted them was the script, pure and simple. Owen approached Momentum with a second draft script and a budget. While they liked the script, they didn't like the budget, which although modest, (GBP1.5million) didn't make sense for the kind of commitment they were willing to come in for. Once we revised the budget, they decided to offer us a minimum guarantee (MG), a rarity in the industry, especially for this type of film."

PUBLIC MONEY

"There's several ways to look at public funding. As a company we've been candid about the failings of 'soft' Lottery funding and the way it has created a climate of dependence and in some cases, a sense of entitlement that simply doesn't exist in the US. We extend that criticism to the lack of risk-taking by public funders because we feel that the one of the declared intentions of bodies such as the Film Council and Scottish Screen - to support and promote new and emerging talent - is disingenuous. Our position has been informed by what we know is the majority experience of any filmmaker trying to attract funding - inevitably demand outstrips supply.

"In trying to develop *Solid Air*, we felt justifiably aggrieved by Scottish Screen. In recognition of her achievement with *One Life Stand*, May had become the first-ever recipient of the Scottish Screen Outstanding Achievement Award, with the financial reward going towards the development of a future project. We contacted Scottish Screen with the proposal that the future project would be *Solid Air*. So it was ironic that when we made an application for project development (with a second draft and after substantial outlay for High Definition camera tests), we were told that we wouldn't receive the amount requested. After protracted discussions, we decided to withdraw the application, which meant the project never received development funding. The fact that development funding comes at a premium (50% on top of the investment), meant our decision was in part pragmatic. On a low budget project such as ours, it doesn't advantage the producer to rack up development costs, which only points out a major failing of public development funding - it works - but only if you don't produce the film.

"After much soul-searching, in 2002, we bit the bullet and decided to make an application for Lottery Production funding at Scottish Screen, reasoning that if we didn't succeed the sooner we knew, the better. Their independent panel unanimously backed the *Solid Air* project, at third draft, for the amount requested."

THE BROADCASTER

"In UK filmmaking, it's generally advantageous to have a broadcaster on board. Shortly after *Solid Air* was awarded Lottery Production funding, we got the dream phone call from BBC Films, asking if we would be interested in their involvement. Gratifying as it seemed, we decided that we would ask for substantially less than other projects, but enough to make the budget a little more comfortable. A deal was done, but never closed, during which time we had little contact with the numerous people at BBC Films charged with overseeing the project, which we, perhaps wrongly, interpreted as a vote of confidence.

"Unfortunately it didn't work out. Five weeks into prep, it was clear we shared different agendas. A combination of bad timing, onerous terms and a creeping suspicion that BBC Films was more interested in making a cheap TV drama than a theatrical feature film forced us to conclude that their demands outweighed their relatively small investment. We took an extremely tough decision, made at a crucial time in the production; in order to protect the project we declined their offer. As a small company with little clout, we realised that to proceed on the BBC's terms would have resulted in an unsatisfactory outcome for the film. Had the level of investment been higher, we may have considered a compromise, but the fact it was so low made our decision all the easier."

PRODUCTION

"The budget will turn out to be just about £1million, but inevitably lots of figures will be bandied about if the film is visible. What matters is that for a film with a cast of 70 and 350+ extras and over 40 locations this is an absurd sum, roughly one quarter of the UK average. Yet it has so far been accomplished on time and budget with industry rates paid across the board. It begs enormous questions about what everyone else is doing, let alone the findings of the Relph Report and its compromised conclusions.

"Going from a five to a seven figure sum, one would assume that filmmaking gets easier. That said, *Solid Air* is an ambitious project, already pitched at a lower than ideal budget. But over the last few years, we've tested and refined the digital filmmaking process. From the outset we had committed to shoot on tape - in this case on HD24P, having worked out the advantages, everything from the size of the crew, the shooting ratio, the ease of post production and the high standards achievable at comparatively lower cost than on 35mm.

"The biggest change was the numbers of cast and crew involved. On *One Life Stand* we had no camera crew, no grips, no sparks. In 'Solid Air' we widened the loop, giving breaks to people with no feature experience, but who were experienced in other areas - TV, shorts, documentaries."

"The benefits of HD over 35mm aren't easily quantifiable, but there are pluses, especially on a low budget. What we've found over the last few years is that few productions positively choose digital over film. Perhaps that's why the whole digital issue in the UK has been relegated to the low budget ghetto, reinforcing the perception that film will always be superior as an acquisition format. Yet most films made today undergo a digital stage - whether in editing, in grading, or FX work. Many end up as 2K anyway.

"The direct savings are, as is well known, not great - stock, processing, telecine and so on. It is the savings that come from imaginative working that really count. In addition there can be real advantages in enhanced production values, which assist the film in the market and raise it out of the low-budget aesthetic ghetto. For example, *Solid Air* will be finished to 35mm Cinemascope ratio, but had we shot on film, we couldn't have shot Scope on location. We would have required bigger lights, with a genny permanently on site, all leading to significantly more manpower. On film, we would have had a lower shooting ratio, because of stock costs and inevitably we would have lost time due to mag changes every three-four minutes, instead of having the option to continuously shoot for up to forty minutes. May would have been unable to run whole scenes as she - and the actors - prefer. On *One Life Stand* we found that by running whole scenes, rather than cut in camera, the standard of performance was enhanced.

"Working directly in the HD domain leads straight into digital post-production, contributing greatly to the quality of the finished image, moving the film closer to the mainstream and acceptable to the industry."

THE INDUSTRY

"Crudely, there are two ways of getting a film made, but remember that nothing comes for free. One can attempt to produce a project that satisfies all established criteria, targeting the mid-ground of taste and pursuing a typical budget - all of which demands compromise. Alternatively one can be distinctive, look for less money, but retain one's editorial and creative freedom and a higher bite of recoupment. The trade-off is either psychological or physical exhaustion. Take your pick.

"Some might say that a co-production deal with a larger, more established production company can help to move the project along, by providing access to the money. It's a reasonable option to consider, but be prepared to give away rights to your project and control of the budget and production. People don't steal scripts, they steal cash. At best, you'll get the film made - at worst, you'll get robbed blind.

"By all means apply to the public funders - but again be prepared for compromise. Under certain existing schemes, you may be forced to have a completion bond. You may also be subjected to unwarranted cast and edit approvals and other concessions. Similarly with broadcasters, always be aware of the terms, and if you're making a film aimed at theatrical release, be sure that your film isn't killed at birth by being transmitted before release. A TX will tear up prospects for international sales.

"While it's always possible to make a film on digital with very little resources, we found that unless you're visible, your film will be completely overlooked. In our case, the advantage of making a micro-budget film was to gain attention and a degree of credibility which we hoped would help to get a more ambitious project made. Making a no-budget movie worked for us to a certain extent - but we did it at a time when no-one else did. It seems there's a resistance to the no-budget DV movie now - ask any film festival director, who has to trawl through hundreds of submissions. Ask yourself why the EIFF is now charging 90 quid just to consider your film for screening.

"We have an almost maniacal belief in what we do and the people we choose to do it with. We love making films, just as we believe that the audience in the UK deserves more intelligent, original and challenging pictures. This may sound idealistic, but so far we've never been motivated by money, or by taking the easy option. It also helps if overheads are kept to a minimum. One way to ensure this is to have the courage to make your own decisions, rather than defer to so-called 'executives'. British films can't make money because producers generally have to pre-sell the world to raise budgets, which erodes the prospect of profit participation. A lot of money is squandered in unnecessary offices, staff and facilities. If you're not in production, you're in hock, requiring the producer to chase his or her tail, giving away chunks of properties just to stay in business. As business models go, it's a non-starter because you'll always have to revisit the Lottery or source expensive money on a project-to-project basis, rather than attempt to generate real profit and reinvest in your future projects." *NW*

www.elementalfilms.co.uk

GAVIN EMERSON

RATCATCHER

Top-end low - £1.8m - 35mm

A screening at the NFTS got Lynne Ramsay noticed by Gavin Emerson who over three years worked with her to make the short film Gasman, winner of the Special Jury Prize at Cannes, and then the award winning follow-up feature Ratcatcher.

"I met Lynne Ramsay at the graduation screenings at the NFTS in 1996 and saw *Small Deaths*. She graduated as a cinematographer and, I think for more political reasons, the school just wasn't pushing the film at all and it wasn't being sent to any festivals. She did it as part of the cinematography course but ended up directing it. I saw her film and thought it was absolutely astounding and revealed a unique talent. I went up to her afterwards and asked her if she wanted to work with me and gave her a small amount of money for a treatment for what turned out to be *Ratcatcher*. Really it was a three-year process and we were very lucky to be given the opportunity to work with a £1.8 million budget but at the time we didn't have a clue what we were doing.

"You have to go through the short process, you have to make mistakes so, at the very least, they give you the opportunity to fuck up and learn from it in order to make a feature. The more short films the better but when you think you've got something, build on it and think about future projects like feature length scripts or acquiring the rights for something. I say this because the chances are, once the short is finished you'll be in a really good position to go to someone with a feature script and to ask them what they think.

"*Ratcatcher* was about building on the existing relationship we had with the BBC in that we were commissioned to make the short *Gasman* for Tartan Shorts. It was off the back of that that we managed to get the BBC to put the money into Ratcatcher. It was quite fortunate that Andrea Calderwood, who was head of BBC Scotland, moved over to Pathé and was already interested in the project. Also it was all about building awareness, attending film festivals and societies and so on. There was a key player called Jim Wilson who was at Fox Searchlight at the time and is now at Channel 4, he'd seen the shorts when we met up at Edinburgh and after *Gasman* played we just got chatting. We ended up sending him the script despite the confidentiality agreement with the Beeb and Pathé and he was really enthusiastic about it and started showing it around Fox Searchlight who'd probably never have noticed otherwise. But he was great at raising that awareness, saying to Searchlight that the BBC and Pathé had greenlit it, which they hadn't at that point. By getting involved in it he acted as the catalyst for Pathé to agree to finally commit to it. So my role really was the PR, you know, getting out there as a producer and raising awareness for the film.

"I was pretty naive to be honest. What I really believed in was Lynne's talent and the talents of the group of people around her and I knew that if we planned it carefully and were judicious about it, we'd end up making a feature. I learnt that the key issue about making a feature is that politics plays a huge part. I had to get constant approval from three executives, not just the basic costs and crewing but on everything. They were all supportive but I had to constantly communicate to them that they were all being treated equally well. I didn't handle that too well but I've since realised that that is a principle element of producing, whether it should be like that is debatable but that was the reality. The other great thing I learnt from *Ratcatcher* is that it was always so possible. If you've got a good idea or a good short film planned properly it is so, so possible to get a feature made." *Clifford Thurlow*

Script & Project Development

A major aim of the Film Council is improving the quality of British scripts through the £5m-a-year Development Fund (see chapter 3), which provides the script development money for writers to continue working on improving their script and bringing in additional support where needed. Project development funds provide the resources to help a producer with a market-ready script get a budget drawn up by a line producer; build a talent package with a casting director and produce the materials needed to attract investment in the film. Development is not only a process to improve the standard of the script, but it also proves to potential backers that the project has been worked on and assessed by more people than the core creative team

Filmmakers in this book who've successfully used development finance include; Fresh Paint Pictures, New Found Land Films (page 151); Wanton Muse, Media II (page 212); Tim Clague, Jerwood Prize (page 187).

Scheme	Max Investment	Organisation	Page
25 Words or Less, the Development Fund at the Film Council	£10,000	The Film Council	101
Developing talent and innovation		South West Screen	132
Development	£25,000	EMMI	123
Development and assistance towards the production and distribution of low budget films	£10,000	Em Media	121
Development and distribution of low budget films	£10,000	Screen Yorkshire	136
Development Finance	£10,000	Screen East	118
Development Fund		The Film Council	100
Development of film and moving image projects	£20,000	North West Vision	126
Development of screenwriting talent and content innovation	£5,000	Em Media	121
Featurelab Tender		Screen East	118
First Development		First Film Foundation	186
Individual Screen Writers Awards	£5,000	Arts Council of Wales	162
New Writer Integration	£5,000	Glasgow Film Office	155
Production Development	£20,000	Screen West Midlands	133
Production development across all screen-based moving image media, in all categories	£20,000	North West Vision	126
Project Development Funding	£75,000	Scottish Screen	148
Script Development	£25,000	SGRIN	160
Script Development	£20,000	NIFTC	165
Script Development	£5,000	North West Vision	126
Script development and screenwriting talent	£10,000	Screen Yorkshire	136
Script Development Funding	£25,000	Scottish Screen	148
Single Fiction Project Development	E50,000	MEDIA Plus	209
Slate of Project Development	E125,000	MEDIA Plus	209

ALEX USBORNE
DEVELOPING LARGE

Low - £1.6m - 35mm

Alex Usborne, producer of the Acid House, spent a year developing Justin Edgar's Large and managed to secure finance much quicker than most as a result.

"The previous film I produced was *The Acid House*, and that won best new British film at the Birmingham Film Festival. The winning best short film was called *Dirty Phone Calls*, which was directed by Justin Edgar. Anyway we met up that night, and shared a few drinks. The next day when I got back to work, Justin had sent me his script, the first draft for *Large*. A little letter arrived with it, saying 'Dear Alex, this is a story about a character called Jason who has to prove himself responsible in order to inherit his rock star father's millions'. So I just sat down right away and read the script and thought well I've got a script here that's got the core of something really funny and a director who can make me laugh, let's give it a go.

"I signed up the project, and we began a really long process of working on the script. We worked about a year and worked on it without showing anybody as a policy. Each project has it's own way of developing - with this one it was clear to work in little steps and examine each draft to kind of look at one problem, one mechanical aspect of the engine as it were, and try and fix that, then stop, look at it and then go 'is this bit of the engine working' and go and tinker with that. That worked fine because they were very young, and I wasn't in a position to be able to pay a lot of money for each new draft. So we did ten drafts before anyone even saw it, which was a huge amount of work but it was really fun to do because we were all working with gags. We had this challenge that with every draft we'd do we'd try and get one brilliant joke in. So after about 10 drafts I was like, we'd better start, people are going to get this or they aren't.

"Justin has his own troupe of actors called the 104 Players who he'd worked with and developed in his short films. So I thought, well if we can kind of do something that's not a read-through, not a full performance but something that gives a sense of the flavour and the energy of the piece and invite people up to it, that would be great. But then I thought fuck, there's a really serious downside here: you can do this and it'll fall completely flat. But I thought, well we'll do it anyway, we've got nothing to lose. We really spent a long time: we spent two weeks rehearsing the actors, working with the actors. We invited Robin Gutch up from Film Four and a few other financiers and we put it on. And it was great, and I think that's when Robin thought 'yes there is something here'. But out of that workshop me and Justin went 'we really need to work on the scripts, some things are working, some things are not working'. And we did another two drafts, and then we did a big mail out. And it did get a good reaction. First there was Lions Gate who we met with, and then Film Consortium came on strong, came on really strong! It was Colin Vaines at first who was really keen, and then Chris Auty flipped out about it. In fact Chris said 'my teenage children have read it, and they said they loved it', and I realised it could really work, and Robin had stuck around as well. I think it was quite interesting for him, because he was sat there thinking what am I going to do at Film Four Lab, should I be doing really serious pieces? And he must have read *Large* and gone 'Comedy, entertainment, fun, hell! I'm going to do that', It was about October, November 1999 that the money was getting locked in – we got £800,000 from Film Four, £600,000 from the Film Consortium and £200,000 from the Yorkshire Media Production Agency. It was quite a quick process really - a year and a half - developing to shooting. The film was premiered in Cannes in 2000, got to number 12 in the UK video charts and with strong international sales has just about broken even." *NW*

Shorts

The arrival during the dotcom years of well financed websites hungry for content led to a big rise in production and exposure for the format. While many web ventures have since closed down or left town, such as Atom Film which left London in 2001, shorts still have many outlets beyond showreel fodder with the potential for sales to international TV, airlines and occasionally DVD compilations and pre-feature theatrical screenings.

Short budgets in the UK vary enormously from the virtually no budget (where the director uses their own production and post equipment) to rare examples of over £100,000, such as Warp Films/Chris Morris's BAFTA-winning *My Wrongs 8245-8249 and 117* (see interview with head of Warp Films, Mark Herbert on page 92). The possible range is broken down as follows:

Micro-budget - £500 and under
Ultra low - £5,000 and under
Low - £15,000 and under
Mid budget - over £15,000, average £35,000

Short filmmakers profiled in this book include Janey de Nordwall (page 17, over) Jacqueline Swanson, who raised much of the budget for *Checkout Girl* short in product placement and sponsorship on page 77; Irvine Allen who made Cannes Palme D'Or winner *Daddy's Girl* on page 152; Darren Ward on page 204, whose three shorts have been released on DVD internationally.

Scheme	Maximum Investment	Organisation	Page
4 Minute Wonders scheme - Wales	£5,000	4 minute Wonders	158
4 Minute Wonders scheme - Scotland	£5,000	4 minute Wonders	164
48 Hours	in kind support	Edinburgh Mediabase	155
ALT-W scheme	£2,500	ALT-W	153
Box Room	in kind support	Edinburgh Mediabase	155
Cinema Extreme		The Film Council with Film Four Lab	113
Cineworks scheme	£15,000	Cineworks	153
Comedy Shorts		First Film Foundation	186
Completion awards for short films and EPK's	£5,000	North West Vision	126
Croydon Media Awards	£1,500	Croydon Council	138
D.M. Davies Awards	£5,000	International Film Festival of Wales	164
Digicult		Digicult	154
Digital Shorts	£8,000	The Film Council / RIFE	114
Digital Visions	£10,000	SGRIN	162
Enfield Film Fund	£2,000	London Borough of Enfield	138
First Cut	£1,000	Screen South	129
First Cut	£1,000	Screen West Midlands	133
First Light Pilot Awards	£5,000	Hi8tus / Film Council	188

First Light Studio Awards	£36,000	Hi8tus / Film Council	188
Free For All		Screen South	129
Hitchcock Production Fund	£5,000	Waltham Forest Council	139
Innovation in short film and television production across a range of genres and contexts	£10,000	Em Media	120
Jerwood First Film		First Film Foundation	186
New Director/Producer Integration	£7,500	Glasgow Film Office	155
New Voices		Screen East	118
Newham Film Fund	£5,000	London Borough of Newham	139
One to One		Screen South	129
Production Finance	£20,000	Screen East	118
Production of short narrative films	£10,000	North West Vision	126
Sci-Fi Shorts		First Film Foundation	186
Screen Gems		SGRIN	162
Short film development, production and distribution	£10,000	Screen Yorkshire	136
Short Film Production	£36,000	SGRIN	161
Short Film Production Funding		Scottish Screen	148
Short Film Production Schemes		EMMI	123
South West Scotland Screen Commission production fund	£5,000	South West Scotland Screen Commission	158
Studio Film Completion Fund		First Film Foundation	186
Take One Production Award, in kind support only	in kind support	City Eye Media Centre	141
Take Two - Dance for Screen	£8,000	Lighthouse with South East Dance	143
Take Two production Award, in kind support only	in kind support	City Eye Media Centre	141
Taped Up		Screen South	129
Tartan Shorts, a total budget of £65,000	£65,000	Scottish Screen with BBC Scotland	150
Tartan Smalls, a total budget of £40,000	£40,000	Scottish Screen with CBBC Scotland	150
The Ignition Network	in kind support	The Ignition Network	142
Tower Hamlets and Hackney Film and Video Fund	£4,000	Tower Hamlets Film Office	139
Virgin Shorts	£1,000	North West Vision	126
Wandsworth Film & Video Awards	£5,000	London Borough of Wandsworth	140
Westminster Film, Video and Moving Image Awards	£1,250	City of Westminster Arts Council	138

JANEY DE NORDWALL   SILVER FILMS

Janey de Nordwall founded Silver Film in 1996, and in 2000 decided to focus the company solely on film production. She approached the North West Business Angel Network – Techinvest – and sold a percentage of her company to raise capital to part-finance two shorts – About a Girl and Jump - and a relocation to London. About A Girl was a runaway success for her and director Brian Percival, nabbing the BAFTA for Best short in 2002 and winning first prize in Turner Classic Movies short film award.

"Few people really understand business angels. Back in 2000 I did my first presentation to 70 angels in the same room. They were not investing in the films, they were investing in the company – I pitched doing a slate of three short films as a research and development process to build awareness of Silver Films in the industry and build relationships with creative talent, ahead of producing features.

"I also saw making shorts as the route to learning about producing films. I already knew how to produce, production manage and build a budget and so forth from my time doing promos, but realised very quickly how different film is to commercials. I wanted to see if I could pick up on a script that I believed in and take it forward. When I sent the *About A Girl* script to people in the industry, they all said the same thing 'you don't want to make that, it'll do you no good, you want to make a comedy'. I had to sit back and think am I right, are they wrong, and after a while I decided 'this is what I believe in and want to move forward with'. What I had wanted to learn as a producer was how to trust my instinct, and the success of *About A Girl* proved to me, and the industry, that I could.

"My angels are advisors as well as investors, they offer help with the business, planning, legal issues and so forth - we have monthly board meetings – they're there for the long haul, and may not get a return on investment in the next five or six years. At the end of my presentation to the business angel network I said, 'this is long term, high risk, but potentially high return' and three guys came along and said lets go for it. One in Manchester, one in London and one in Chicago. They all reinvested for more money, and I'm currently looking to a fourth investor with a bigger lump for development on the feature slate.

"If you can get a slate of films together it allows the investors choice on what they want to put their money into. They may dislike foreign films for example so its nice to have a range of films on your slate, there's also slate funding out there through the Film Council and other organisations that appreciate the slate over the individual film. It adds to the longevity of production companies and of the industry. It lets people hedge their bets! Out of five films maybe one will be OK. I had three shorts slated and made just two of them: *About a Girl*, which cost £35,000 and *Jump*, which cost £55,000. My first year at Silver Films, which included moving from Manchester to London, was funded by £100,000 of investment – a mixture of money from selling equity in the company to the angels, matched by the same amount from North West Vision, my own money, sponsorship and product placement cash.

"The sponsorship and product placement came from my contacts in the gaming industry. Sponsorship was from 3DO, who were making a new PR marketing campaign about how gaming crosses over so many mediums, ie that gamers are interested in sport, fashion and film. The campaign was that they are supporters of new talent in the industry, they sponsored someone in music, fashion and film and gave us £10,000 in return for a logo at the end of the Jump and use of us as marketing on the website and so forth. And they gave £2,000 for the premiere at Planet Hollywood. For product placement, we sold ad space to games that were coming out around the time of the film's premiere so we had Final Fantasy 9 on a t-shirt in a bus for £1,000.

"*About A Girl* was winning awards at the same time as Yousaf Ali Khan's *Skin Deep*, which got 3rd in TCM, was a BAFTA nominee and Kodak award winner. Yousaf and myself looked at working on a feature project together, and decided to test the relationship by making a short film– *Talking With Angels*, made in Salford with much of the 80 cast and crew sourced from locals. It cost about £50,000 just to shoot and the funding on it is very different to the other two shorts: we got money from the LFVDA, from North West Vision, and some cash from Fox SearchLab which finances shorts. SearchLab is the little sister of Fox Searchlight, with whom we have a first look deal. I began discussions with them after *About A Girl* was the only British short to be accepted into Sundance. I then met up with them in LA whist I was on the Inside Pictures course. They were great and said do it in your own timescale, we want to work with you, they didn't want to read the script, they just trusted my instinct. We got funding also from B3 Projects who give money for ethnic minority work and are going to get involved in the distribution and marketing. We've also, unusually, got regional government cash, because we are making a big difference to the Salford community by using locals. There's money from Salford Council, Salford University, the Regeneration and Employment Agencies and the Cornerstone Community centre. Mike Knowles who runs the Northern Film Network, is my co-producer on this and helped set that up as he's based in Manchester still.

"I'm getting my feature slate together. While it's very important to have a slate I only want to work on films that I believe in. I just go for things that turn me on – my films tend to be very social issue films, very personal, that have a message, that have social awareness – but not depressing regional drabness.

"You get used to having that feeling of hitting walls. You're kind of living on the edge all the time, and there are these big highs and then these incredible lows when you don't want to have anything to do with this industry. I do get really down, in fact recently I was about to write the email saying I was about to quit the industry and go sit on a beach and plat my hair – when you hit that sort of point you need to take some time out and think about what you're doing and what you want to achieve. The highs and lows are going to be a constant thing and you have to ask yourself, what do you want out of this? Is it kudos, is it awards, is it money? I want to achieve an emotion from an audience and that kind of makes it a lot easier than being motivated by money or fame." *NW/TF*

Company Development

A large number of government and local authority grants are available to new and established companies. Some of these are regionally focussed, designed to attract companies to an area, while others are to improve skills, access and use of technology, and overall sustainability. In addition most of the regional screen agencies have funding available to help foster solid and sustainable media companies within their region.

Company development	Max Investment	Organisation	Page
Arts Connection		East England Arts	145
Capacity Building and Development Fund	£50,000	Arts Council of Wales	162
Company Development	£20,000	Screen East	118
Company Development Programme	£70,000	Scottish Screen	147
Creative Advantage Fund		West Midlands Arts	145
Creative Development	£15,000	Scottish Arts Council	159
Creativity Unit	£50,000	DCAL, Northern Ireland	167
Cultural Business Venture		North East Arts	146
Developing the film, television and digital content sector		South West Screen	132
Development Grants	£500	The Prince's Trust	174
Development of Companies	£25,000	Northern Film & Media	125
Development of local partnerships for media businesses		Em Media	120
Development of People	£10,000	Northern Film & Media	125
Development of viable film and media businesses	£10,000	Screen South	129
Enterprise Grant Scheme	£500,000	Regional Govt.Offices with the DTI	172
Europe Grants		The Prince's Trust	174
Organisational and capacity development projects		Em Media	120
Organisational development and capacity building		Screen Yorkshire	136
Product Commercialisation		Glasgow Film Office	155
Professional development of individuals	£20,000	North West Vision	126
Professional Development: Creative Wales Awards	£25,000	Arts Council of Wales	162
Regional Selective Assistance		Regional Govt.Offices / DTI	173
Regional Venture Capital Fund		Regional Fund Managers & DTI	72
Research, feasibility and company development studies		Em Media	120
Research, feasibility, and company development studies		Screen Yorkshire	136
Schemes which encourage networking, collaboration and partnerships		Screen Yorkshire	136
Sector Development	£20,000	Screen West Midlands	133
Sector specific support for companies or organisations	£20,000	North West Vision	126
Small Firms Loan Guarantee Scheme (SFLGS)		Small Business Service at the DTI	173
Small Scale Capital Awards	£5,000	Screen East	118
Training	£20,000	North West Vision	126

Documentary Funding

Documentary Filmmakers Group

by Andy Glynne, Director, Documentary Filmmakers Group

The recent proliferation of cable, satellite channels and internet streaming in conjunction with the commissioning of an increasing number of documentaries for mainstream television, is very exciting for documentary makers as they have more potential opportunities to show their work to a wider audience. This, combined with much more affordable digital technology, means that more and more people are starting to consider documentary filmmaking as a career.

However, despite this surge of interest in documentary filmmaking, there is still a big 'bottleneck' out there, and there are far more people wanting to make documentaries than there are opportunities for funding. Even though it is relatively easy today to make your own documentary film (with a mini DV camera, and non-linear editing software on your home computer), it still remains difficult and complicated to actually find funding.

Television

When most people think of funding their documentary, they think of getting a commission from a broadcaster. There are three main ways to obtain funding here: commissioned directly (as an individual) by a broadcaster, obtaining funding from a broadcaster through a production company, and trying to sell your finished product directly to the broadcasters (known as Acquisitions)

THROUGH PRODUCTION COMPANIES

This involves basically sending an idea that you have to a production company (for production companies that specialise in documentaries have a look in the PACT handbook, www.pact.co.uk). They will then look at your proposal and, if they like it, will possibly develop it a bit before submitting it to a broadcaster. Be careful here though, because you need to establish what role you are going to have on the film, if it gets commissioned. Often (though not always), first time directors, may not be given the opportunity to direct, even if it is your idea that gets commissioned. In some instances this is fair, as you may have little experience in knowing all that is involved in directing, say, a half-hour piece for Channel 4. In these circumstances you may be offered the role of Assistant Producer (AP) or Researcher. The important thing here is that you talk about all these options to the production company before you give them your proposal.

GETTING COMMISSIONED AS AN INDIVIDUAL

This mainly occurs for specific schemes operated by the broadcasters, including:

> **Independent Film and Video (IFV),** Channel 4. IFV offer a range of opportunities for new directors, including the popular ALT-TV slot. For full information about this initiative, go to www.4producers.co.uk

> **Metroland** – Carlton Television. See page 185

ACQUISITIONS

Sometimes it is possible to sell your finished product directly to the broadcasters, although this is not ideal for two reasons. Firstly this is quite hard, as there are not many slots available for the acquisition of new directors' work (Independent Film and Video at Channel Four is probably your best shot; other strands, such as BBC 4's "Storyville" are really only interested in buying well known, costly feature documentaries). Secondly, this is not really a good means of covering your initial costs; most of the time, you will only be paid a fraction of what it cost you to make the film. However, if you have already made the film, and wantto get your name out there, then this is worth a try.

Public Money

The Film Council. The Film Council has indicated that they are going to launch a fund specifically for documentary filmmaking, although no further details were available at publication. The funds listed in Chapter 3 (Development Fund, the New Cinema Fund, and the Premiere Fund) do currently include a provision for documentary, with both Passion Pictures and October Films recipient of Film Council slate funding to produce a number of documentary features.

Regional and local funding. Many of the Regional Screen Agencies and local funds listed in this book provide funding for short fiction and non-fiction work – the listings in the Nations and Regions chapter provide details. In Scotland see Scottish Screen's This is Scotland on page 150 and Bridging the Gap on page 153.

National Lottery funds. The Millennium Commission, Awards for All, the Heritage Lottery Fund, and in some instances, the Arts Council provide funds that in some cases could be used for documentary work. See the Other Sources chapter.

Charities, NGO's and Human Rights Organisations.

People often overlook this area, seeing it as somehow inferior to making a documentary for either television or theatrical release. However, making these types of films can often give you both invaluable experience and an opportunity to make a film in the area that you are really passionate about. There are no hard and fast rules of how you get funding from these organisations. Its best to make direct contact with them, and present them with a proposal. Sometimes, they may want to see an indication that you actually know how to make films. If you have any previous work, then you need to present them with a showreel. If possible, try to shoot a small pilot or teaser (doesn't need to be any longer than a few minutes) just to give them idea of both your competence as a filmmaker and/or the way you have visualised the idea you are trying to sell.

Competitions.

A few international competitions provide funding for documentary film and filmmakers, including Roy W Dean Grants (page 214) and the Sundance Documentary Fund (page 215).

European and International Funding

There is actually a pot of money out there within the EU to fund documentaries. The trick is knowing exactly what European financers are looking for, and how to pitch your project in the right way. This article does not have the space to go into too much detail but as a starting point, the best thing to do is immerse yourself in the world of international co productions and co financing.

Since much European (and indeed international) funding is based on co-financing, in which your project may be financed by two or more production companies, broadcaster, or European Union Funds, you need to ask yourself the following questions before you consider approaching them: does the documentary work as a co production? ie is there really an audience in two territories for your project, or is it too 'nationalistic'?

What about the use of subtitles? Is there a market in the non-native territory for your film?

It is important to note that the process of getting work commissioned in Europe and Internationally can often be very different from in the UK. For a start, in some countries there are no commissioning editors as such, but rather 'Executives' and the process of writing a proposal can be very different (for example, in France a 'proposal' is much more like a treatment, requiring lots more information and sometimes including a script).

Some starting points for international funds:

MEDIA FUNDING.

MEDIA Plus is a 5-year programme of the European Union to strengthen the competitiveness of the European film, TV and new media industries and to increase international circulation of European audiovisual product. For more information see page 209. The UK MEDIA desk (see www.mediadesk.co.uk) will also advise on pan-European co-productions.

THE IDFA.

Try to attend the 'Forum' at International Documentary Festival, Amsterdam (www.idfa.nl) - either as a participant or just an observer. The FORUM is Europe's largest gathering of television commissioning editors and independent documentary producers. Its aim is to stimulate co-financing and co-production of new documentaries by enabling producers to pitch their project concepts to the assembled commissioning editors and other professionals.

HOTDOCS.

Hotdocs (The International Documentary Festival in Canada www.hotdocs.ca) hosts the Toronto Documentary Forum, which has quickly established itself as a highly effective international market for both producers and broadcasters. Over two days, 36 production teams pitch their projects to an international assembly of broadcasters and other documentary financiers. In 2002 over 75 broadcast representatives from Europe, Australia, South Africa, the U.S. and Canada participated in the TDF and 60% of the projects pitched reported success in attracting additional financing.

The Big Picture

Background to the UK Film Industry

It's over 21 years since Colin Welland infamously declared that the British were coming as he collected the Oscar for *Chariots of Fire* in 1982. For a brief moment it looked like he might be right - the following year Britain won 10 Oscars, while Goldcrest was financing international hits such as *Gandhi*, the *Killing Fields* and *The Mission*. But in 1984 the Thatcher government abolished the Eady Levy, which had channelled a share of box office receipts into domestic production, and ended tax breaks for production, and the industry all but collapsed. Much of Britain's leading directing and producing talent migrated to America with great success and Goldcrest, after 24 films, ran out of capital and was sold off. Other than the new-launched British Screen, which supported non-commercial work from the likes of Mike Leigh and Ken Loach, British production came to a near standstill.

Stephen Frears' 1985 *My Beautiful Launderette* signalled a change in direction for the industry, with TV-backed film investment feeding local productions. The Channel 4 film encouraged the broadcaster to increase investment in filmmaking over the late 80s and launched Working Title (see page 88), initially run by Tim Bevan and Sarah Radliffe (who left in 1992 to run her own company) and later Eric Fellner, with whom Bevan runs the company today. Video distributor and producer, Palace Pictures, run by Nik Powell and Stephen Woolley, followed the success in 1985 of Neil Jordon's *Company of Wolves*, with *Mona Lisa* in 1986. The British Film Commission was launched in 1991, and in 1992 Section 42 tax relief was launched offering tax relief on film investment over three years. Palace Picture's 1992 release *The Crying Game* was a massive global success yet the company collapsed and Powell and Wolley set-up Scala Productions. In 1993 newcomers Danny Boyle, writer John Hodge and producer Andrew MacDonald made *Shallow Grave* for Channel 4's film division FilmFour, and provided inspiration to a generation of young British filmmakers. The following year Rank released *Four Weddings and a Funeral*, grossing over £27m at the UK box office and heralding the start of a new wave of popular British filmmaking.

London-based PolyGram Filmed Entertainment (PFE), part of Philips-owned PolyGram, was behind both *Shallow Grave* and *Four Weddings.* During the mid-90s, PFE supported and nurtured British talent; financing, acquiring and distributing Working Title projects such as *Bean*, *Elizabeth* and *Notting Hill*, and dozens more British films such as *Backbeat*, *Trainspotting* and *Lock Stock and Two Smoking Barrels*. In May 1998, however, PolyGram was sold for £6.5bn to Canadian drinks and media conglomerate Seagram who were mainly interested in merging the group's music library with Universal Music. A sale for the film division was not secured after a bid from EMI was pulled at the last minute, and it became merged into the Universal empire as Universal International Pictures, with its pre-1996 film library sold to MGM. After the merger of Seagram with Vivendi in 2000, PFE's former activities continued almost solely through the financing of Working Title via Universal Pictures.

As with the collapse of Goldcrest and Palace Pictures before it, the UK film industry had lost its key driver. Focus now shifted to Channel 4's now independent film production, sales and distribution arm FilmFour, which had begun producing, acquiring and releasing higher budget films; and the Lottery Franchises. In 1997 three franchises - DNA Films, Pathé and The Film Consortium - had successful bid for almost £100m between them over a six year period from the Arts Council to part-finance a slate of feature films with the intention of becoming self-sustaining 'mini-studios' at the end of the franchise period. Labour's election victory of 1997 injected further life into the UK film sector, with the launch of Section 48 tax relief reinstating 100% first year tax write-offs for British film, and new consultation within the industry. A Department of Culture Media and Sport (DCMS) commissioned policy document, A Bigger Picture, steered by former PolyGram International chief Stewart Till, had called for a new public film body and the need for a distributor-led approach to the industry.

In 2000 the Film Council formally took on the functions of a host of national film agencies with the target of directing funds at initiatives that will move the industry forward as a whole, making up for a lack of sector-wide structure and strategy that had dogged the UK in previous years. This comes through investing not just in production, but also training, distribution, exhibition, development and – through industry consultation – new initiatives to address shortfalls as they arise.

DOMESTIC FILMS' MARKET SHARE AND REVENUE 2000-2001

	2000 (%)	2001 (%)	2001 domestic revenues ($m)
Belgium	2.8	3.3	3.7
Denmark	17.5	27.9	21.7
France	28.5	41.5	373.1
Germany	12.5	18.4	162.2
Italy	17.5	19.4	108
Netherlands	5.5	9.4	12.5
Spain	10	17.9	98.4
Sweden	25	23	28.5
UK	**21.2**	**11.7**	**122**
Norway	0	4.8	3.7
Switzerland	4.2	2.7	3.8
Czech Republic	23	30	6.5
Korea	32	46.1	186.8
Japan	31.8	39	642.8
Taiwan	0	1.6	2.4
Australia	7.9	7.8	32.8

Source: Screen Digest

However, despite this injection of new energy and cash, the lottery franchises, sizeable tax breaks and a supportive government, the industry has been in contraction for several years. In 2001, inward investment – foreign productions shooting in the UK – slumped by a massive 57% over 2000, recovering just 16% in 2002 to £265m. Local production of UK films fell in 2002 to 40 from 84 in 1997, with total investment down 9% to £164m. In July 2002 Channel 4 announced the closure of FilmFour, bringing back the divisions film operations in-house, reducing the budget by two thirds, and leaving the UK without a serious integrated financing, production and distribution operation. In September, Granada followed suit, closing its film arm which had been responsible for such successes as *Ghost World*, *House of Mirth* and *Bloody Sunday*.

If the British industry was to be valued on Oscar wins, then perhaps Colin Welland would have been proven right, with the British taking 21% of all statues since 1991. There is no doubt that the UK has the talent, skills and ideas. What it has long lacked, though, is sustainable sources of finance, a coherent infrastructure and a distribution-centric approach to ensure that the only films being made are those which can – and will – be absorbed by the world market.

ALL-TIME TOP 30 FILMS AT UK BOX OFFICE

	Title	Distributor	Released	Gross £m
1	Titanic	20th Century Fox	1998	£68.9
2	Harry Potter and the Philosopher's Stone	Warner Bros	2001	£66.0
3	The Lord of the Rings: Fellowship of the Ring	Entertainment	2001	£62.8
4	The Lord of the Rings: The Two Towers	Entertainment	2002	£ 56.5
5	Harry Potter and the Chamber of Secrets	Warner Bros	2002	£ 53.8
6	The Full Monty	20th Century Fox	1997	£52.2
7	Star Wars Episode I: The Phantom Menace	20th Century Fox	1999	£51.0
8	Jurassic Park	UIP	1993	£47.8
9	Toy Story 2	Buena Vista Int.	2000	£44.3
10	Bridget Jones's Diary	UIP	2001	£42.0
11	Monsters, Inc.	Buena Vista Int.	2002	£37.7
12	Star Wars Episode II: Attack of the Clones	20th Century Fox	2002	£37.4
13	Independence Day	20th Century Fox	1996	£37.1
14	Men in Black	Columbia TriStar	1997	£35.8
15	Die Another Day	20th Century Fox	2002	£ 35.1
16	Gladiator	UIP	2000	£31.2
17	Notting Hill	UIP	1999	£31.0
18	Chicken Run	Pathé	2000	£29.5
19	A Bug's Life	Buena Vista Int.	1999	£29.4
20	Shrek	UIP	2001	£29.0
21	Spider-Man	Columbia TriStar	2002	£28.7
22	The World is Not Enough	UIP	1999	£28.6
23	Four Weddings And A Funeral	Rank	1994	£27.8
24	Ocean's Eleven	Warner Bros	2002	£26.4
25	The Lost World: Jurassic Park	UIP	1997	£25.8
26	The Sixth Sense	Buena Vista Int.	1999	£25.8
27	Austin Powers: The Spy Who Shagged Me	Entertainment	1999	£25.8
28	Cats and Dogs	Warner Bros	2001	£24.0
29	Austin Powers in Goldmember	Entertainment	2002	£23.4
30	Ghost	UIP	1990	£23.3

Source: EDI Nielson

ALL-TIME TOP 10 BRITISH FILMS AT UK BOX OFFICE

		Released	Country	Gross £m
1	Harry Potter and the Philosopher's Stone	2001	US/UK	66.04
2	The Full Monty	1997	US/UK	52.23
3	Harry Potter and the Chamber of Secrets	2002	US/UK	50.80
4	Bridget Jones' Diary	2001	US/UK	42.01
5	Die Another Day	2002	UK/US	33.80
6	Notting Hill	1999	US/UK	31.01
7	Chicken Run	2000	UK/US	29.51
8	The World Is Not Enough	1999	UK/US	28.58
9	Four Weddings and A Funeral	1994	UK	27.76
10	Shakespeare In Love	1999	US/UK	20.81

Source: Nielsen EDI, BFI

The Global Perspective

After the lacklustre global cinema slump of the 80s, cinema admissions during the last decade rose almost uninterrupted year on year across the globe. In the US, box office receipts skyrocketed from $4.8bn in 1991 to $9.5bn in 2002, while UK screen admissions in the same period rose from 100m to 175m. Total global non-US box office revenues rose a massive 20% to $9.6bn in 2002 from 2001, while total non-US admissions were up 7.5% to 7.3 billion in the same period.

As film audiences have flocked in ever-greater numbers to the cinema, film producers have found an increasing number of potential platforms for exploiting their product, with the birth of DVD, video on demand (VoD), and the explosion in pay-TV. In the 1950s ancillary media such as TV were a threat; nowadays, they make up the vast majority of a film's total return.

And yet this increase in the public's appetite for film hides a contraction in film production worldwide. In 2002, US box office takings leapt 13.2% over 2001, yet in the same period the number of films produced fell from 611 to 543 and films released fell from 482 to 467. A similar situation occurred in the UK, where the cinema boom helped by multiplex expansion and an increased dominance of film culture in the mainstream media, has taken place side-by-side with a slump in UK production.

Part of the problem is a dramatic rise in the costs of production, release and marketing, which has made distributors keener to bring fewer more bankable films to market with a greater marketing push per film. In the US, the average combined production budget and studio overheads ('negative' cost) and print and advertising (P&A) expenditure for a studio feature hit $89.2m in 2002, 13.6% up on the year before and 230% up on 1990. Meanwhile the average negative and P&A spend of films from studio 'indie' divisions such as New Line and Miramax, was up 10.2% from 2001 to $45.2m in 2002.

Yet the major issue in the international production slowdown is a fall-out in new sources of film finance, which emerged alongside the 'irrational exuberance' (Alan Greenspan) of the late 90s stock market boom. New funding options that were in the 90s briefly postulated as the saviour of international film finance, such as insurance backed loans, gap financing and many German funds have all since collapsed. In the late 90s dozens of German media companies made an Initial Public Offering (IPO) on the Neuer Markt, using over-ambitious sales estimates to raise significant amounts of money for film investment. Many, such as Helkon and Kinowelt, filed for bankruptcy protection, and the short lived ambitions of the German sector to compete with Hollywood as a major financier, have come to epitomise the heady days of deal-making at the time. With an average drop of 96% in the value of media companies traded on the Markt, the index is to close at the end of 2003.

This collapse of new funding sources has been accompanied with a significant reduction in the prices paid for free and pay-TV rights for feature films for all but the most high profile product as the TV advertising market dried up. Meanwhile distributors and sales agents have grown more cautious about pre-sales, typically favouring slate deals from a smaller pool of established 'safe' producers, reducing the opportunities for producers selling individual projects.

In the excitement of the dotcom boom many decisions were made that the industry came later to regret, from the top of the chain with the mergers of AOL and Time Warner, through to a surge in half-baked Europe-backed high-budget product that was green lit before it was ready. In Variety's 2002 overview of independent financing Alliance Atlantis CEO Peter Sussman says 'we went through a period where even if a film was going on five cylinders you could still do well. Today if you're not going on all eight cylinders, abandon it.' Paul Brooks of Gold Circle Films added 'essentially, the indie world has been financed by crazy money in the last few years, and there's no crazy money out there anymore.'

It would be easy to despair as a producer but this fallout has occurred alongside a big increase in global box office receipts and the emergence of countless new 'soft finance' sources (ie public funds and tax incentives). Furthermore, any industry contraction works to flush out the management whose profligacy led to the boom and bust in the first place, so while independent producers have rarely been as tightly squeezed, those that survive the downturn should be well placed to feed a constantly increasing consumer appetite for films.

CINEMA ADMISSIONS AND BOX OFFICE IN SELECTED MARKETS 2001-2002

	Admissions			Box Office		
	2001 (m)	2002 (m)	change (%)	2001 ($m)	2002 ($m)	change (%)
Denmark	12	13	8.2	82	92	16.5
France	186	185	-0.4	959	966	13.6
Germany	178	164	-7.9	933	908	19.7
Italy	110	119	7.6	590	662	4.9
Spain	144	137	-5.0	573	581	13.0
Sweden	18	18	-0.3	132	135	12.1
UK	156	176	12.8	969	1,134	12.6
Ireland	16	17	8.6	77	86	8.2
USA	1,487	1,625	9.3	8,413	9,506	9.8
Australia	93	94	1.5	1,494	1,554	17.8
Japan	163	161	-1.5	1,598	1,572	17.1

Source: Screen Digest

Cutting Budgets - The Relph Report

With a reduction in available funds for fully financed feature film production, the British industry has finally begun to look at ways to reduce the cost of shooting in the UK. The Film Council commissioned Simon Relph, film producer and chairman of BAFTA to produce a major study into the financing structures and options for low-budget UK films, with an eye to helping bring down average budgets through a series of proposals. The Relph Report, published at the end of 2002 and described by Alan Parker as 'the best industry report I've ever read', is mainly targeted at films currently costing between £2 and £4 million, though it studied 26 'low budget' British films ranging from £76,000 to £7 million.

The study (downloadable via www.filmcouncil.org.uk) compared the UK environment with the US and mainland European market, and concluded that Britain was one of the more expensive places in the world to shoot. In the US 'enthusiasm for the work is as important as pay and conditions' allowing the US indies to pay low wages in return for greater potential at the back-end, while mainland Europe typically employs smaller crews over longer periods with shorter hours. Ultimately, Relph concludes, the UK will need to follow one of these two models – big crews on lower wages and intense shooting schedule, or much smaller crews over shorter hours and a longer schedule.

The report blames many of the UK's current problems with the film finance mini-boom at the end of the 90s: 'lottery money, tax breaks, bank finance and insurance deals coincided, making it easier to fund films and establishing a new and higher going rate. Now that production funding is less freely available, it is hard for the industry to return to the lower cost ways of working'. Central to the report is an ambition to bring the average cost of 'low budget films' down from £2.5m to £1.5m, largely through greater employee flexibility with the creation of an equivalent to the PACT/Equity low budget film agreement, for crew.

Summary of Relph's Points

DEVELOPMENT & PRE-PRODUCTION

- Cheaper films begin with writing to budget. The producer should have a realistic idea of the potential value of the film and with the director encourage the writer to work to that budget.

- Development is a vital stage, but the upfront cost of the script and options should be kept to a minimum until there is a clear idea of the size of the project and the investment it can attract.

- Long films cost more and can be harder to sell. Footage that ends up being cut in post production because the film is too long is a waste of money that should have been spent on the rest of the film.

- Maximum preparation time saves money. Ideally producers would confirm financing at least three months before the start of shooting to give enough time to creatively maximise the budget with the director and production manager. Too often money is confirmed – or even slashed - at the 11th hour.

- The director and producer must work hand-in-hand. Too many directors see the relationship as a battle where they must try and get away with as much as they can. In a good working relationship the director will be aware of budget limitations and search for creative alternatives. Storyboards, rehearsals and shot lists lengthen the lower-cost pre-production process and save time during the far more expensive shoot.

- Schedule in pick-ups. It can be cheaper to schedule pick-up days after the shoot rather than have a long shoot that tries to cover for every eventuality.

PRODUCTION

- Cut crew numbers. The smaller the crew, the longer you can afford to shoot, and hence the smaller crew you need.

- The line producer is the most important factor in controlling the final cost of the film. Small production departments are possible where other departments take on a greater share of administration, while the line producer or production manager needs to have a hearty appetite for finding ways to produce the same effect for less money.

- Seasoned cinematographers can cause problems, in having greater expectations of equipment, crew size and speed of working. As the camera department's costs can be highly unpredictable, it's important that the DP is working closely with the production department to bring the film in on budget.

- Top line acting talent can be attracted to the right project by offering, rather than a deferred fee or profit share, a gross position, ie a share of all film revenues from the first receipt.

- Crew can take the place of Film Artists Association (FAA) stand-ins, while large crowds of background artists can be gathered cheaply by offering prizes rather than paying each extra.

- DV and Super16mm offer advantages not just in cheaper kit and stock, but also in making the production quicker, allowing for smaller crews and less lighting.

- If shooting on 35mm, money can be saved by only developing and telecining the rushes, ie not printing until the film is cut.

- Finding a location where good quality sound can be recorded makes a huge difference to post-production costs, as can employing a sound recordist who will also mix and edit the film's sound in post.

- Studio sets are increasingly dressed to shoot in all directions, even when only one or two walls may end in the final cut. Better planning and more decisions on shots up front allow the art department to save resources in shooting. Working with what is found on the location rather than imposing a design can save costs and time massively.

- Basing locations close to each other and the production base can save massively on both time and transport costs. Reduce the number of drivers - electricians drive their own equipment vehicles, yet props, construction and camera departments very rarely do.

- Location caterers working from a van charge between £11 and £15 a day per person – getting a cook and providing equipment and ingredients is far more cost effective, although not all locations allow for this.

- Delivery costs have risen dramatically in recent years and tend to be the same for low budget films as higher budgeted work. Some sales agents have been persuaded to accept some of these costs as a distribution expense. Digital post production provides some savings in that the digital master replaces the interpositive and DVD/video copies can be easily run off that.

full report available at www.ukfilmcouncil.org.uk/filmindustry/?p=relphreport

Presenting to Investors

If you're looking to raise private finance you need to be able to present a coherent business plan. 'But the script is the business plan' many filmmakers argue. While the script is the basic vital asset in financing and packaging a successful film, any investor is going to want to see that you understand the market and that the numbers for your film can add-up. Most individual private investors capable of providing money for your film will have made their fortune in industries where a business plan and long-term, financial strategy are vital for success. A good pitch and the promise of getting 'that guy from *East is East*' may grab their attention in the short term, but will never allow them to take your project seriously as an investment vehicle.

At the most basic level a business plan needs to convince the potential investor that your film, or slate of films, can comfortably make a return on the investment and provide a profit a certain number of years down the line. Making this argument convincing requires you to prove that the creative team possess the skills and experience, the management team possess the know-how and contacts, and, most importantly, that the market displays the demand.

To present a convincing argument you need to be very honest about your films' strengths and weaknesses in relation to similar films that have successfully come to market. In turn, how does your company's creative and production skills match the film and its likely adueince. Your project may be a moving personal story of the toils of childhood in a Scottish village in the 70s, and you could certainly point to *Ratcatcher's* success. But had NFTS graduate Lynne Ramsay not already established herself as an art-house auteur with two Cannes nominations and one Special Jury Prize for her short films, then raising £1.8m to make a film destined for the festival circuit rather than multiplexes would have been near impossible.

Indeed if you are not planning to produce directly commercial features, it may well be worth factoring in the production of a series of shorts to gain an international festival reputation as part of the business plan. Janey de Nordwall, (see page xxx) producer of BAFTA and TCM-winning short *About A Girl* part-financed her first three shorts by selling an equity stake in her company to individuals found through a business angel network. She pitched making shorts as 'research and development' expenditure, allowing her to form creative relationships, introduce herself to the industry and master the art of producing for a world cinema audience.

If you are looking to produce more straightforward commercial films you will need to illustrate how similar films have succeeded and why your film is similar to those. Many filmmakers believe that their idea is commercial because 'it contains all the elements – sex, action, comedy' or because it is comparable to a breakout critical hit such as *Pi* or *Blair Witch Project*. Steve Mackler of Bedford Entertainment points out "you can't take the anomaly and make that the rule, that just doesn't work. Everyone all of a sudden goes out and makes Blair Witch, there were probably 20 Blair Witch knock-offs that did nothing."

You will need to indicate that – at the least – you have talked with suitable distributors and sales agents about your project and feel confident that it will meet the criteria for the sorts of films they are looking to acquire. The process allows you to form a relationship with a distributor early, and get an assurance that you are not planning to produce something completely unsuited to the market's appetite or that the way in which you wish to shoot will only hinder your success. If you plan to shoot in black and white, the success of *Schindler's List* should not form the basis of your argument, especially with two recent strong B&W independent British features, *One Life Stand* and *Nine Lives of Tomas Katz* failing to secure a UK distributor. Likewise if you plan to shoot on DV, the success of 28 Days Later is not enough to prove that your film will be released theatrically. A majority of sales agents and distributors refuse to look at DV-based projects, no doubt partly because of the vast number of them out there, but largely because they know it will be harder to sell.

The business plan should illustrate that you have done this research and are confident that the budget of your film, your company overheads and the costs of selling it once complete, are less than its realistic potential value at market. This may mean rethinking the films budget, or deciding to target straight-to-video, or TV sales instead.

Writing the business plan

There are various models of business plan for film investment, which will vary dependent on the type of funding being sought and the projects on offer. Ideally you should work through your business plan with a lawyer or accountant, though if you can't afford this, the business support contacts in chapter 7 may provide some help. Louise Levison, who wrote the plan for the *Blair Witch Project* has written a good, albeit US-focussed book, Filmmakers & Financing, Business Plans for Independents (Focal Press, 2001).

A typical plan may include:

Executive summary. Write this section last as it should summarise the rest of the plan in a clear and concise manner. You should also state the amount of investment your are looking for, and, if you wish, indicate the nature of your proposal and the amount of equity you are offering.

Company background. This should outline why the company has been formed, what its objectives are, and how it is placed to achieve those objectives, as well as describing the legal nature of the company and how long it has been running. You need also to provide details of your management team, illustrating the skills, experience and contacts of the core team. If each member of the team lacks substantial experience it is worth trying to find other partners with experience, or at least form an advisory board of your best contacts to illustrate that your inexperience is compensated by the involvement of people who know what they are doing.

The Film(s). As well as outlining the project(s) you are seeking finance for and their budget, this is your opportunity to convince the investor that you have a hot property. If you own an option on a book, have the confirmed interest of a named actor or director, have crew attached with well-known credits, have got the support of your regional film agency, or a foreign distributor - state this here. Testimonials from seasoned producers who have already read the script will help, as will a sensibly costed budget illustrating how the film is being made cheaply without sacrificing quality.

The industry. You should provide an overview of how the film industry operates, as many investors will not completely understand, and provide market data to illustrate its workings. The BFI Handbook provides useful figures for the UK industry, the MPAA provides in-depth analysis of the US (www.mpaa.org). Describe each of the different exploitation opportunities – theatrical, video/DVD-rental & retail, pay-per-view, pay-TV, free-TV.

The market. Here you should describe why there is a market for your films. What films similar to yours have been released successfully and why is your film similar to those. What similar films have failed, and what are doing to ensure this won't happen to yours? How do you intend to bring your products to market, and in such a competitive environment, stand out? How will you find a distributor and what would your distribution strategy be?

Financing and forecasts. You should list your planned sources of finance to fund start-up and production, and produce with an industry accountant or lawyer the meaty part that any investor will be looking most closely at; your projections, cashflow forecasts and assumptions. List the budget and returns – across all platforms - of successful films similar to yours. Use these numbers as the basis for sales forecasts for your film(s) which should be broken down by territory /region and platform. Use this, combined with the film's budgets to make a quarter-by-quarter cash-flow statement for the first three or five years of operation. The key is to show that the numbers balance and that the investor could make an X% profit over Y years, based on a number of assumptions which you should state.

If you can't get a sales agent to provide sales estimates to support your forecasts, then you should at least provide a table of worldwide returns of similar films across platforms (theatrical, video/DVD, TV-sales) and territories. A lot of this data is available online through sites such as www.showbizdata.com, www.variety.com, www.bfi.org.uk, and journals such as Screen International, Screen Finance and Screen Digest. However, be careful with quoting box office data – a film that grosses £100m does not equate to revenues of £100m for the producer: in the UK the exhibitor typically takes off 50% and a further 17.5% goes on VAT, while prints and advertising costs, and the distributors royalty share come off before the producer sees a penny.

JOHN WATERS   REAL GUERILLA CINEMA

"They say write what you know, I knew 60's terrorism really well and radical terrorism and cults - I still know a lot about that - I read all about them - I have a giant library on them and I know the movie-business and I put them together to make Cecil B Demented.

"My father lent me the money to make Mondo Trasho and I paid him back. He lent me the money to make Multiple Maniacs, I paid him back and then he lent me the money to make Pink Flamingos and then I started to pay him back and then he said you're set up in business, don't pay me back and don't ask again. I had very loving parents, even though every one of the movies I made were completely against everything that they believed in, and no one said they were good for ten years. Cecil B Demented's parents do not give him any money, they force him to work in a movie-theatre, which would drive anybody crazy. Then even after his big moment when he's known all over the country - it's his Oscar equivalent, when he's going to kill himself at a drive-in movie as he gets the last shot for his movie, they humiliate him by standing out in front of the press and the national guard, and say whatever made you think you could direct?

"Think how exciting it would be if movie going was really political. In Film Direct they had a joke as an article saying that readers should attack the offices of Premiere Magazine, only some did and their lawyers, like flipped up and had to put a retraction in. I love that idea of Screen on the Green forming a pact with other cinemas and just starting to whack the multiplexes - if you had wars here - if people lost their lives through their taste in film. If reviewers attacked other reviewers; if there was complete war because of movie-taste." Tony Pomfret

HARRY HICKS   SELLING TO AN INVESTOR

"Let's assume the producer is going to meet the investor, rather than just sending something through the post. I would have thought the investor would only have the meeting if he or she liked the script, which they will have read in advance. It is paramount that the script is well developed and polished with a good story and commercial potential.

"The producer should lead the meeting, especially if the investor is not fluent in film investment. During the presentation, the producer should give a very clear idea of the tone of the film, the genre, it's place in the market, and how the producer sees the marketability of the film. After all, investors are going to be interested in what sort of return they are going to be getting. We all know in film that is a very difficult thing to predict, but the investor would need some idea.

"What are the ambitions of the producer? For the director? For the top cast? What is the budget? I would suggest the producer turn up with a detailed budget from a good line producer, so the investor can take it away and have a look at it if they want to. Certainly the investor won't be impressed if no thought has been given to the budget. The producer should also be clear on their own role. Are they exec producing, or producing? The investor needs to understand who they are speaking to.

"It would impress the investor if the whole funding package had been sorted out. What I mean by this is whether the producer has given thought to pre-sales and sources of soft money. Have they been given a commitment from a Sale & Leaseback organisation with an offer of say 12%, 13%, or 14%? Has the producer got a commitment from a production partnership to finance 25% or 30% of the budget through soft money? Has the producer thought about regional funding? In short, has the producer culled the rest of the budget together and does the investor know precisely what gap he or she is being asked to fill?

"The more back-up documents the producer can show the better: the script, a print out of the budget, letters of intent from the main cast, and from a good director, the director's filmography. The director doesn't have to be well known, but thought should have gone into it. I have to say that if a producer comes to me with a glossy package (I'm not an investor, but I know people who are) that in itself does not impress me. I would be more interested in the guts behind it.

"The investor would want to know what sort of rights they would be getting, what sort of return, where they would stand in the pecking order, when the film is going to be finished, when they come out of the deal, and whether there is a recoupment corridor. The investor will also want to know what investment scheme is available to them, for example the Enterprise Investment Scheme, or Section 48. The producer should prepare all this in advance with an accountant and lawyer and maybe bring one of them along to the meeting depending on the financial and legal ability of the producer. The producer could also ask the director into the meeting.

"Some general advice for new producers would be to try not to over cook the budget. It should be kept as low as possible, allowing for creative quality. The other thing is to keep an eye on what is more likely to sell in the market place. People can get carried away with a really good script which is unlikely to sell, which will at the end of the day be a harder sell for the producer." *CH*

Harry Hicks is head of film & TV at WJB Chiltern

Harry Hicks   Stephen D. McMello

WJB Chiltern Expand Media Services

Central to WJB Chiltern's active film penetration is their acquiring 66% of First Up Film Limited ("firstupfilm") an executive production company run by Harry Hicks, Steve McMellon and creative director and 33% shareholder Matthew Campling.

WJB Chiltern's stake in firstupfilm will enable the media and entertainment division to offer a fully-serviced production company facility, to benefit producers, writers (as firstupfilm will offer script development assistance on projects it takes on) and the industry generally. The unit is also developing a similar arrangement for music production.

Armed with lengthy specialist knowledge of the film sector, Hicks is widely recognised in the industry for his skills in structuring finance for films, for instance having been closely involved with Baker Street Media Finance from its outset in 1999. McMellon's area of expertise is media copyright law and its taxation and rights exploitation. He works very closely with music publishers on the provision of music for film and TV. Campling has extensive creative experience in assessing and developing scripts, and has one of his own screenplays currently in development by September Films.

Our activity will include:

- Partnership financing models
- Other financing models for producers and to assist production
- Executive production – particularly via firstupfilm
- Co-production sourcing and introductions to prospective partners
- Scripts, review, creative input and development
- British Qualifying Film audit
- Business management and production accounting
- Music supervision, identification and negotiation with relevant parties
- UK and international tax planning in relation to exploitation of content

Cobblers: the art of film financing

It's no secret to film producers that funding films from commercial sources is currently a lot more difficult than it was a few years ago due to the general economic downturn and especially the drop in advertising revenue to broadcasters. The upshot of this is that producers are looking more and more to finance their films with the help of soft money by entering into co-production with producers in the likes of Canada, Luxembourg, Australia and Germany (to name a few).

The UK is a popular co-production territory due to the current generous section 48 tax relief and the resulting (currently 15%!) net benefit available from sale and leaseback deals. The 25-30% funding from section 48 production partnerships is also attractive to producers (both UK and overseas). Indeed accessing UK tax money (whether that be sale and leaseback or production funding or both) and overseas soft money can provide 50% or more of a film's budget.

Co-productions, of course, are not total panacea. It is vitally important to work with co-producing partners who can be respected, trusted and relied on to deliver. Co-producing can also result in significant extra costs to a production which should be weighed against the advantage of any soft money. Obvious extra costs are the legal costs in structuring the co-pros; less obvious are the costs of the tax advisers who will often need to be called upon to ensure that financing structures do not prejudice the tax position of investors in certain co-producing territories (and most notably the UK). There can also be higher crew costs because of shortage of supply due to the influx of productions taking advantage of soft money.

Simply keeping cost down is a very obvious way of getting a film made and most independent producers will know the pain of having to slash their own fee – or even to take all of this fee as a deferral. There are other, less painful, ways of cutting budgets, however, such as shooting on DV and upgrading at post stage. It would be surprising if this practice did not grow over the next few years.

Let's not forget sponsorship or product placement as potentially funding part of the budget; always worth considering of course, and last but not least there are the (few remaining) banks providing gap finance. But we're back to where we started from: the need for pre-sales and substantial sales estimates before the banks will lend.

So nothing is really new! But one point financiers repeatedly make is that they are more inclined to consider projects where the financing structure has been given serious thought – and that is something that we at WJB Chiltern are experts at.

Main contacts:

Harry Hicks
Head of Film and TV,
Direct +44 (0) 207 153 2232
Email hicksh@wjbchiltern.com

Matthew Campling – for firstupfilm –
Head of Script Development,
Direct +44 (0) 207 153 2234
Email camplingm@wjbchiltern.com

Steve McMellon – Head of Media Rights,
Direct +44 (0) 207 2231
Email Mcmellons@wjbchiltern.com

Negotiating

Sooner or later you will come to the point of negotiation, be it with financier, buyer, or even a key creative whose talents you wish to employ to help package the film. Negotiations are the make-or-break point of any deal, and are one of the most intense and nerve-wracking parts of financing, particularly for a first-timer. Experienced producer, lecturer and writer on media business affairs, Dorothy Viljoen, offers some good advice in handling them:

Preparation. Find out as much about the financier beforehand and the style they are likely to adopt. "If they are known to be tough negotiators work out ways in which they might have the satisfaction of winning, without actually doing so; for example, by asking for a far higher fee than you expect to receive in order that they can be seen to bear you down."

Establish deal parameters in advance. You should identify for each of control of rights, production fee and profit share: the maximum you can ask for, the target value that you would hope for, and the minimum value that you are prepared to accept. Knowing this in advance helps you to approach the negotiation in the secure position of knowing the parameters of what you would accept and what you would ideally like. "With these goalposts and lines firmly in place you can then play around with the various balls the other side may lob into the field."

Don't go to the meeting alone. Bringing in a lawyer too early in the deal-making process can appear heavy handed, instead go with a colleague who can "take notes, confirm impressions or recollections and generally give moral support."

Dress to impress. Typically it is a lawyer or accountant that negotiates contracts who by nature of their training are often "instinctively unwilling to grant monies/rights/ownership to someone wearing jeans, t-shirts and trainers and carrying papers in a carrier bag."

Start with your dream deal and work down. If the other party opens negotiations, remember that they will most probably be employing the same tactic, "stay calm, don't accept the first thing that's offered (even if it exceeds your wildest dreams): you can almost certainly do better."

Keep your nerve. If your asking price isn't being met "offer to drop certain terms which are not so important to you before you start negotiating down on the key provisions." Make sure you don't agree to parts of the deal or terms that you don't understand, and avoid being pressed into agreeing terms on the spot. "It is very rare for there to be such urgency about a deal that it has to be settled there and then, and great caution should be taken in dealing with anyone who insists on an immediate decision."

Follow-up. Keep notes on all that is said and agreed and follow-up each meeting with an email or fax outlining what has been established and what remains to be resolved. If you realise that terms agreed are less favourable than you first thought don't try and renegotiate the deal, "put it down to experience: don't keep going back and trying to tinker with a deal once it has been set. It looks unprofessional and can damage chances for more successful dealings in the future."

Quoted from the Art of the Deal (PACT, 2002) – strongly recommended for the shelves of any serious film producer (order via www.pact.co.uk).

Seven tips

Film is an industry with thousands of people with viable projects fighting to get in, and a relatively small and close-knit group of people acting as gatekeeper. It's easy for frustration to boil over at what can feel like an impenetrable old boys club, but more often than not it is just about getting noticed in a way that doesn't present yourself as a potential risk. If you're trying to raise a substantial amount of money for your first feature then you need to be in it for the long haul, present yourself seriously, and take the knockbacks as part of the training. Of course you would rather be making films than filling in forms, networking and making presentations but proving that you can jump through hoops is what the market is looking for to feel confident you won't be a risky green light.

To help navigate the film finance circus and in the honoured tradition of self-help books, we've put together seven tips based on the advice of those who've been there already.

1   Build the right team

"I was both the producer and the director, a situation I don't ever want to be in again. The conflicts between the artistic imperatives of the director and the financial and practical considerations of the producer are bad enough when they are fought between different people but when that battle is raging constantly in your own head, it's enough to drive you stark raving mad." *Owen Carey Jones – Baby Blues (£30,000 feature)*

There are two drivers to a movie – the creative vision that makes a film good and the entrepreneurial energy that gets the film made. While some filmmakers successfully combine both producer and director roles this is generally the exception. At one extreme the film gets made and is sold, but suffers artistically, or the film is a creative success; at the other, the film is never sold, runs out of money or is not finished. Building the right creative team is the prime factor behind success in raising finance, production and eventual sales. The situation is made more difficult by a shortage of good producers in proportion to writers/ directors, which has led some, such as Guerrilla Filmmaker Handbook authors Chris Jones and Genevieve Jolliffe, to partner and take it in turns to produce each other's movies. Also remember that these relationships take time to build up and that if someone seems too good to be true, they probably are.

"I don't mean to be cynical, but when it comes to any kind of business, you can't really trust anyone, so check them out and try them out. The minute someone lets you down or doesn't keep a promise then be very wary. If it happens again, drop them immediately." *Piotr Szkopiak, director, Small Time Obsession*

2   Know your audience

"People think they can make anything and it will find an audience. This is not the case. You have to be really honest about your film. Go to the video store and hire five successful films like yours and ask yourself how does yours stack up? Too many new filmmakers are so wrapped up in the excitement and glamour they forget about the end purpose of a film." *David Nicholas Wilkinson, Guerrilla Films*

The 'if I build it they will come' philosophy is a way of putting off facing the unpleasant realities of the film business until the end of post-production, when the filmmaker hopes that their skill and imagination will be sufficient to attract a magical distributor and sales agent who will sign up their film and whisk them away to a studio to start work on their next project. This never happens. The rare low-budget success stories were still made with a focus on who would want to see that film at the end of the process. Robert Rodriguez knew that there would, at the least, be a video audience for his $7,000 *El Mariachi* especially if he got a few 'money' shots to put into a trailer. *The Blair Witch Project* raised finance with a solid business plan that identified who would go and see the film once produced, backed up with a well-planned debut at Cannes.

Once you know who your audience is, (clubbers, couples on dates, genre-hungry film-geeks, Guardian-readers), you can look at the films competing for that audience's attention and see what your project has to offer that will make it stand out. Find out as much as you can about the audience, and make sure that your film is better than anything else they are currently being offered. This also gives you an idea of how much your film could expect to make, which in turn allows you to figure out how much money you can spend making it.

"If you know there are millions of teenagers out there desperate to see your film then go online, do your research and get your statistics. So many independent filmmakers have the passion but not the interpretation that convinces those with the money that there is some commercial, and I don't mean formulaic, but financially sound reason to make it and that you are trying to reach a certain audience." *Amanda Posey, producer Fever Pitch*

3   Embrace development

"Don't rush development, and don't abandon the script the moment it looks like your funding has fallen into place. It can always be made better" **Working Title executive**

Before showing the script for *Four Weddings and a Funeral* to anyone, Richard Curits wrote five drafts working closely with his script editor and wife Emma Freud. Then came further rewrites for his producer, for Working Title, for the director, and more for budget cuts, subsequent budget cuts, responses after the first read-through – a total of 17 re-writes in all. And this from a screenwriter who had already proved his skills in writing some of the most successful British TV comedy of the last 20 years. As Curtis says in the introduction to the screenplay "don't resent the rewrites – the awful painful truth is that the script probably did get a bit better each time."

The development process is a mixture of reworking a film until it's at the best possible place creatively and from an audience's perspective; and making sure that the main people involved with the project – financiers, producer, director and even key cast if a named actor is on board – are happy enough with the script to put their name, time and money behind it. It has been said that a successful screenwriter is not only one with a good script, but one who is able to rewrite and stay on board the project at every step of the development process.

"It's really important early on to invest in a good script editor, it gives you someone who understands where you are coming from but who can keep you on track. Have your work read aloud, see if it works before an audience. Be as honest as you can to yourself about your script's weaknesses" *Farah Abushwesha, Rocliffe Writers Forum*

4   Network carefully

"I think another common mistake people make is to tire the contacts they make or approach people the wrong way - they think they have to pitch to everyone all the time. I think that when making contacts you need to be as natural as possible, not harassing them with phone calls." *Pikka Brassey, Wanton Muse.*

The nature of the British film means that the gatekeepers – be they financiers, festival chiefs, journalists or successful producers – are in constant demand. Try to remember that you are only one of many people attempting to get as much as you can out of them. Few successful people in the industry are purely altruistic, so always consider what a contact is getting in return from you. Networking is too often seen as the process of convincing everyone in a room that you are great, when in fact making friends with a few people at a party can set-up useful long-term relationships. It is not the quantity of contacts, but the quality of the relationships. And once you've got a bursting contact book, think before using it – there's only so much you can ask for before needing to give something in return.

"Let the work speak for itself; don't try too hard to convince anybody that it's any good (it can easily sound like desperation). I've gone to a lot of festivals now and seen how other filmmakers operate. Some cruise the jury, some even buy them presents. I like to keep out their way until after the adjudication. Best strategy is be yourself and meet as many people as you can." *Irvine Allen, director Daddy's Girl (winner short Palme D'Or 2001)*

5 See the bigger picture

"Filmmakers may make wonderful films, but know nothing about distribution, so they can shoot themselves in the foot, quite unintentionally. You have to approach the market very carefully to get as much out of it as you can" *David Nicholas Wilkinson, Guerrilla Films*

While developing and promoting your project it is very easy – almost inevitable – to be caught up only in the part of the industry relating to where you are, be it development or fundraising. Taking a step back to address the bigger picture can help in understanding why you may not be moving forward with your project as you would hope.

The production executive who isn't returning your calls is beholden to their management and must field dozens of potential projects at any one time. Their management is in turn dependent on the company's backers, and the company as a whole is investing vast sums of money in product that they must be able to sell on the international market to survive. The distributors and sales agents they sell to in turn need to acquire a certain number of hits to assure their survival or at least their management survival. The studios and corporations that own these distributors are accountable to their shareholders. At every step of the way the success of your project is dependent on an awful lot of people believing that backing you won't risk them their job.

That's the bottom line and while it can feel like you're a Kafkaesque cog at the bottom of a giant machine, film is a $60bn a year industry and until you are a proven safe bet with a commercial or critical hit under your belt it's not going to be any other way. You may have the best script in the world, but as far as the gatekeepers are concerned you're just as much a risk as anyone else until you've proven otherwise.

"The key issue about making a feature is that politics plays a huge part. I had to get constant approval from three executives, not just the basic costs and crewing but on everything. They were all supportive but I had to constantly communicate to them that they were all being treated equally well. I didn't handle that too well but I've since realised that that is a principle element of producing, whether it should be like that is debatable but that was the reality." *Gavin Emerson, producer Ratcatcher*

6 Have a long term plan

"Prepare yourselves for a long process. When we started out everyone said it would take several years to get this film made and we thought, oh yes, but we'll do it in six months. Now it's been, what, three years?" *Philippa Goslett, writer Little Ashes/Wanton Muse*

Ambition and drive tends to come hand-in-hand with wanting success fast, which is usually followed by despair when success doesn't come. Filmmakers and producers with a long term game-plan are better equipped to cope with the constant let-downs of trying to get their project made than those expecting overnight recognition. How many short films do you realistically need to make to both get noticed, and equip yourself with the skills to make a feature? How long are you prepared to push your feature project forward for and how many compromises will you make on the way? Each new project that doesn't get finance or a release, can be a useful training experience if you are honest enough about the mistakes you made on the way.

"The approach to a short film should be the single off the album, the full album is the rest of your fucking life." *Peter Mullan, actor/director*

7   Stay Focussed

"It's one of the most frustrating, fucking irritating and problematic jobs around - especially working in Britain at this time. And one is constantly dispirited and crushed by the system in trying to get your film forward and struggling for the available funds. But there's always that possibility you will get to make your film. And once you're actually there standing in a field and the cameras are turning over and the actors are just doing what they're doing, there's nothing more exciting in the world and then it's all worth it." *Ben Hopkins, director, Simon Magus/the Nine Lives of Tomas Katz*

Even in America, which employs half a million people in the film business, wanting to become a filmmaker has never been a sensible career path. In the UK, which is currently producing less than 50 properly financed local features a year, it's even more uncertain. So it is worth knowing what you want to achieve from the start.

"You're kind of living on the edge all the time, and there are these big highs and then these incredible lows when you don't want to have anything to do with this industry. The highs and lows are going to be a constant thing and you have to ask yourself, what do you want out of this? Is it kudos, is it awards, is it money? I want to achieve an emotion from an audience and that kind of makes it a lot easier than being motivated by money or fame." *Janey de Nordwall, Silver Films, producer About a Girl, Jump (shorts)*

If the process of making films and getting a strong positive reaction from an audience is pleasure enough, you are probably much better equipped to face the wilderness years of the development, fundraising and rejection circuit, than those whose understanding of success is a an oak panelled Wardour Street office and a cabinet of Oscars. As you keep hitting walls it is easy to lose faith and blame your woes on the Film Council, distributors or even Shooting People, bemoaning endlessly the state of British film. But if you enter the industry with your eyes open and a clear focus on what you want to achieve it is harder to get knocked off course.

"Experience teaches you that there are no external forces capable of preventing you achieving what you've set your mind to. I've come up against some pretty intransigent forces in my time, but the only true obstacles are internal ones like self-doubt and pessimism. Once you've conquered these, the outside world is a relative pushover." *Omid Nooshin, director, Panic (short)*

Chapter 2
FINANCE & INVESTMENT

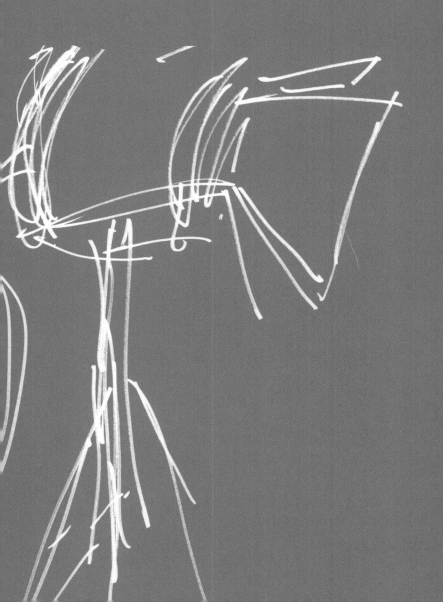

Finance Options

By Adam P Davies with Caroline Hancock

Tax incentives

Tax incentives are designed by a government to boost the local economy by attracting investment into a sector, such as the film industry. For producers, this is becoming an increasingly important source of film finance as other forms such as pre-sales and large "gap" loans become harder to obtain. Broadly speaking, there are two kinds of tax incentives for the film industry; tax credits or offsets, and tax allowances.

Tax credits/offsets

These encourage investment in a particular country by foreign producers, who receive a form of rebate on amounts spent in that country. In making the film, the producer will spend money locally on resources, infrastructure, locations and personnel, which can qualify him/her to receive a tax refund from the relevant governmental authority. Sometimes credits are limited to certain types of expenditure (such as a repayment of income tax spent in relation to the employment of local personnel), and sometimes they relate to the entire local spend. Canada, Australia, Iceland and Malta are countries that offer this type of incentive, more details are given in the International chapter. These are direct rebates on money actually spent out of the budget by the producer, rather than a tax incentive aimed specifically at the investors in the project.

Tax Allowances

Unlike the rebates referred to above, tax allowances apply specifically to the amounts "invested" in films by financiers, rather than the amounts "spent" by the producers in making the film. In essence, the financiers can write off some or all of their investment against other taxable income (see below for detail). Producers and film financiers in countries offering this investment incentive (including the UK) can often benefit from so-called production "equity" funds, which utilise the tax allowances when they invest in a qualifying film.

To qualify in the UK, the film must be classed by the Department of Culture, Media and Sport as a "British Film" under Schedule 1 of the Films Act 1985. Briefly, the Films Act provides that, to qualify as a British Film, at least 70% of the cost of production must be spent in the UK. For these purposes, the cost of production does not include financing costs, overhead expenditures, underlying rights acquisition costs and certain labour costs. In fact, there is a specific additional requirement relating to the production's labour costs, in that a minimum percentage of such costs must be spent on EU, EEA or Commonwealth nationals (referred to here as "qualifying" nationals). This minimum percentage of the labour costs to be spent on qualifying nationals is the lesser of 70% after deducting the labour cost of one non-qualifying national (such as a leading US director), or 75% after deducting the labour costs of two non-qualifying nationals, one of whom must be an actor.

Note that an official UK co-production complying with a relevant treaty will also automatically qualify as a British Film, and therefore be entitled to utilise the UK's tax incentives. For more information on official co-productions see the International chapter.

SECTION 42

The investors in a production fund formed for the purposes of investing in UK qualifying films can benefit from one of two tax allowances, set out in section 42 and section 48 of the Films Act 1985 (as amended). Section 42 allows income tax relief for investment in a qualifying film. Under section 42, income tax relief is made available to the producer or acquirer of a film at 33.3% per annum over a three-year period, by which time the entire budget can be written off by the investor(s) if the film is 100% financed in this way.

The introduction of section 42 stimulated a lot of activity by clearing banks, leasing companies, specially formed partnerships and high-net-worth individuals who access relief to mitigate their corporation or income tax liability, particularly through "sale & leaseback" transactions (see later).

SECTION 48

In July 1997 the UK Chancellor introduced section 48 of the Finance (No.2) Act 1997 ("section 48") which enhanced the incentives offered under section 42 by increasing the relief permitted on films costing under £15 million to 100% in the first year. This means that the fully-financing investor is entitled to a tax rebate during the year of production of 100% of the film's production costs.

"COMPLETION" BY JULY 2005

The legislation has been extended twice since its original implementation, and is currently due to expire in July 2005. It is important to note that a film cannot be certified (and therefore will not qualify for tax relief) until it is "completed", which effectively means in a state where it is capable of being distributed or exhibited, even if not technically "delivered" in accordance with relevant contracts. Accordingly, under current legislation, only films completed by July 2005 will qualify for the relief. As mentioned above, the film must also qualify as a British Film if the investors are to be eligible to access the tax allowances.

"DOUBLE-DIPPING"

There is a potential issue where a film that used section 42 (or 48) finance in its production, then gets sold through a sale & leaseback scheme (see next page). This is known as "double-dipping", as two sets of investors could obtain up to 100% tax relief on the same film. Worse still, a film could potentially be sold and resold

several times with each new purchaser claiming a tax break on its acquisition costs. Regulations and amendments to the legislation are being introduced to prevent this type of abuse of the system, although they should not prevent the use of section 48 for the purposes of obtaining relief once each for both production expenditure and acquisition expenditure (usually in the form of sale & leaseback) in respect of the same film.

Production Funds

A number of funds utilising these tax breaks have been put together through which investors can pool their money and share the risk with other investors. These usually involve the formation of a partnership between the investors, and these partnerships will sometimes invest in more than one film in order to reduce the risk further. The legislative structure even allows for the investors to "borrow" a large amount (up to about 75%) of their investment from participating banks, and to claim tax relief on the whole lot (ie. not just their actual "out-of-pocket" expenses). Where investors put in differing amounts into a fund, the rebate provided will be split according to their share of the investment. Investors with high earnings who belong to the high tax bracket will benefit most from this kind of tax allowance. The percentage of the budget provided by these funds varies wildly (from 10% to 100% on occasion) according to the objects and format of the fund itself, the film's budget, the contribution (if any) of other financiers, the right to income streams (if required), and so on. The commercial sustainability of certain production funds, which have a "revolving" investment system, are very dependent on the success of the earlier investments made by them. Their ability to continue over the medium-term will become apparent in the next couple of years as the profitability (or otherwise) of the first wave of pictures financed by these funds becomes more evident.

As an alternative approach, a couple of very recent entrants to the fund market aim to use traditional accounting practices, rather than sections 42 and 48, in order to provide a tax-efficient scheme to their investors. These funding schemes (with names such as "Fast Track" from Ingenius and "First Choice" from Grosvenor Park) have been constructed following receipt of much professional advice but, again, only time will tell as to how successful they are and, perhaps more importantly, how the Inland Revenue (or, for that matter, the legislative arm of the Government) reacts to them. However, they are likely to be very popular at least in the short term. Contact details for companies specialising in tax-based and investor financing are listed at the end of the section.

THE EFFECT OF THE 2002 BUDGET

In his 2002 Budget, the UK Chancellor removed television production from the scope of these tax incentives. The amount of tax-break money being raised overall has not yet seemed to decline, and so the number of financiers looking for films (rather than television) in which to invest has increased. Since there is currently more investor capacity than there is content, film-financing companies are offering attractive financing packages for the producer. However, investing in film is considered more risky than television, and investors will be looking for strong projects, which usually means films with names, reputation and experience attached.

Sale and Leaseback

·Sale and Leaseback has been in operation in the UK in various industries since at least the 1980's, and it works in conjunction with the legislation on tax incentives. The schemes offer comparatively risk-free benefits to both the producer and the investor, as the benefits do not necessarily depend on the film's success in the market place.

"Vanilla" Sale & Leasebacks

Nowadays there are companies who will offer "sale & leaseback money" up front, ie. in the form of production funding. However, traditionally, the transaction took place only when the film was "completed", as it is only then when the tax breaks kick in. We will look at how this works first, and then look at the newer "products" available to the producer in today's market. Set out below is how the "traditional" or "vanilla" sale & leaseback works (in somewhat over-simplified language).

Say a producer makes a British Film for £10m and wishes to enter into a sale & leaseback transaction. When he has completed his film and obtained the relevant "British qualifying" certificate from the DCMS, a sale & leaseback partnership will be identified to purchase the film. The partnership will be made up of investors who wish to avail themselves of the tax breaks referred to above (together with a "managing partner" who is part of the administrative structure). As the film has already been "completed", and certified as British qualifying, the partnership (effectively being the investors) can legitimately write off their investment (ie. the purchase price) for tax purposes, reducing their income tax bill by 40% of the amount invested. Note that much of this will actually have been borrowed from a bank. So, in this example, the partnership would typically pay the producer £10m for the film (saving the individual investors a total of £4m in tax liability), as this is the amount it cost to make, and the Inland Revenue will accept that this is an appropriate price.

However, on its own, this simple sale transaction would leave the partnership with a film it does not know how to exploit, and the producer with £10m (most of which would have to go back to pay the original investors) but no film. The partnerships, acknowledging that the producer is probably better placed to exploit the film, immediately leases the film back to the producer in return for periodical lease payments. The producer gets all the rights s/he needs to exploit the film for a period (usually) of about 15 years, much in the same way as if s/he were leasing a building. It is generally considered that most of the income from the film is likely to be received within this 15 year period following completion, after which the film usually reverts back to the partnership (who will ultimately own it as part of its "library"). The lease payments will be fairly substantial, and the partnership will therefore insist that most of the £10m it paid to the producer for the film goes straight into a separate secured bank account, from which the lease payments will be made. Using simple numbers, one could say that about £8m (including the interest earned on it) will probably be enough to pay the lease payments for the 15 year term, £0.5m will be required for the various transaction fees (especially legals), and the remaining £1.5m (equal to about 15% of the budget) can go straight into the producer's pocket.

The receipts from the lease payments are themselves taxable in the hands of the partnership, so effectively the investors obtain an interest-free loan from the Government, and may be able to set off these receipts in future years against other losses and/or allowances they may have at that time. Where the partnership has also taken a profit participation (which some of them do), the investors will additionally end up with a "share" in the motion picture.

Discounted Sale & Leaseback

It was felt by many producers that, as much as 15% of the budget might be a well-earned present after they have finished the picture, in fact they would rather have some money up front in order to help finance it in the first place, production funding being extremely difficult to obtain. So, many sale & leaseback facilitators now offer to "discount" the amount available and, through a bank (often the one involved in the transaction itself), provide it to the producer in time for production, albeit on certain conditions. Naturally, the partnerships will be concerned because they will be providing money up front without the benefit of DCMS certification (and therefore without the guarantee of being able to access the tax write-off). The investors will, of course, not be able to write off their investment until after the film is "completed". Accordingly, there is usually a "completion bond" company brought on board who, amongst other things, will make sure that the producers make the picture strictly in accordance with the criteria required for the film to qualify as a British Film. The bond company (who will usually also look after the interests of any financiers involved in pre-buying rights in the picture - see below) will also make sure that the picture is delivered on time so that the investors can utilise the tax-break within the anticipated financial year. The amount of the budget currently available in this way is upwards of 10%, depending on the partnership used, the bank and its "discount" rate, the amount that would otherwise have been available had the money been provided after completion, the profit participation taken (if any), the time of year of the transaction (it all gets very competitive each Spring as the financial year begins to close), and so on.

Other Incentives

As the market for films to invest in has become much tighter, sale and leaseback facilitators have been offering producers more and more incentives to use their product(s). Some have offered much more than the standard 10% or 12% in return for both the sale & leaseback transaction and the UK (including Republic of Ireland) rights, by way of effective pre-sale – see below. Often close to 20% (although more typically usually 16% to 18%) of a budget can be obtained in this way from those companies that offer this type of deal.

More popular at the moment are transactions known as "Super-sale-and-leasebacks". Here, the partnership will offer a large proportion of the budget in return for the sale and leaseback transaction and an equity stake in the project. If, say, 35% is offered, this would effectively be seen as approximately 15% representing the sale and leaseback transaction itself, and 20% representing a pure equity investment. In this regard, the producer would have to give a percentage of the "back end" (profit) to the investors, probably between 12% and 20% in the above example.

Companies that deal with tax-based and investor financing:

Baker Tily
2 Bloomsbury Street
London, WC1B 3ST
Tel: 020 7413 5100
Fax: 020 7413 5101
Web: www.bakertily.co.uk

Ernst & Young
London (North)
Rolls House, 7 Rolls Buildings
Fetter Lane
London, EC4A 1NH
Tel: 020 7951 2000
Fax: 020 7951 4001
Web: www.ey.com

Future Film Group
25 Noel Street
London , W1F 8GX
Tel 020 7434 6600
Fax: 020 7434 6633
Web: www.futurefilmgroup.com

Grosvenor Park
53-54 Grosvenor Street
London, W1K 3HU
Tel: 020 7529 2500
Fax: 020 7529 2511
Web: www.grosvenorpark.com

Ingenious Media
100 Pall Mall
London, SW1Y 5NQ
Tel: 020 7024 3600
Fax: 020 7024 3601
Email: enquiries@ingeniousmedia.co.uk

Invicta Capital
33 St James Square
London, SW1Y 4JS
Tel: 020 7661 9376
Fax: 020 7661 9892

Matrix Group
Gossard House
7/8 Savile Row
London, W1S 3PE
Tel: 020 7292 0800
Fax: 020 7292 0801
Web: www.matrix-securities.com

Park Caledonia
Glasgow Office
4 Park Gardens
Glasgow, G3 7YE
Tel: 0141 332 9100
Fax: 0141 332 5641
Web: www.parkcaledonia.biz

London office
1 Printers yard
90a The Broadway
Wimbledon
London, SW19 1RD
Tel: 020 8543 8882
Fax: 020 8543 3007
Web: www.parkcaledonia.biz

ScottsAtlantic
The Communications Building
48 Leicester Square
London, WC2H 7DB
Tel: 020 7004 7060
Fax: 020 70047050
Web: www.scottsatlantic.com
Email: info@scottsatlantic.com

Gap Financing

This is a form of loan issued by a bank to provide finance for a shortfall between other finance raised, and the amount needed to make the film. Generally, banks lend against the projected "sales estimates" relating to the unsold territories, as provided by a reputable sales agent. These figures represent the amount that the sales agent reasonably thinks the film will sell for in the market place, once completed, taking into account key elements of the film such as budget, cast, director, producer and genre. They are prepared on a territory-by-territory (and often format-by-format) basis, showing a likely "best case" and "worst case" price attainable. The bank will only lend if it is satisfied by the reputation of the (established) sales agent, and if the sales agent is actually "attached to" (ie. committed to sell) the project. It will want to see a clear "margin" indicating that the loan can be repaid. This margin will often be 200% or 300% of the gap to be provided. In other words, if a £10m picture has £8m of finance already secured, the producer will need to fill the gap of £2m (ie. 20%). A gap-financing bank will require that the "worst case" sales estimates for all territories that have not already been sold (and often also excluding North America) are at least £4m to £6m (being 200% to 300% of the gap required). This will provide the bank with some comfort, as its loan will be re-paid out of these sales (when made). The large margin allows for full repayment even if the film sales ultimately only make half (or a third) of the revenue anticipated by the sales agent.

The bank will insist on being the first to be paid back out of income received from exploitation of the film. Sometimes it will allow for other financiers (usually just government bodies and "deferments") to take a small "corridor" and recoup *parri passu* (on an equal footing).

Traditionally, gap finance was fairly easy to come by, and banks were prepared to put up about 20% of the budget in this way. Later, particularly in the late 1990s, a number of insurance companies wishing to expand their exposure to high-risk markets offered to "insure" the gap loans on individual films. This additional security (the risk of the film not meeting its sales expectations now being moved to some extent from the bank to the insurance company) allowed the banks dramatically to increase the size of the gap loans, sometimes up to 50% - but more usually 30% to 40% - of the budget. Naturally, many films did not meet even their "worst case" targets, and numerous insurance companies were "called in" by the banks to cough up the difference when gap loans were left unpaid. Mass-litigation ensued (most of which is still on-going) as insurance companies claimed that they were misled as to the risks of the projects, either by the banks or the producers (or both). Accordingly, insurance-backed gap financing has all but disappeared (although not necessarily for TV projects), and banks are now reluctant even to put up the 20% which was common before the insurance companies' heightened involvement.

However, gap finance is often the only way for a producer to meet the full budget costs of a film. Generally, it would not really be his/her chosen form of finance, due to the high cost of the loan. These costs will include a gap "fee", an arrangement fee, a loan fee and a high interest rate (due to the risk factor) to be paid on the loan. One advantage of gap financing is that the lender will not hold an equity share in the film so, once repaid, it will receive no share in the revenue.

Gap Financing Contacts:

Royal Bank of Scotland
Mayfair Corporate Business Centre
65 Piccadilly
London W1A 2PP
Tel: 0207 290 46 49
Web: www.rbs.co.uk

Barclays Bank Media Banking Centre
27 Soho Square
London, W1A 4WA
Tel: 020 7445 5773
Fax: 020 7445 5802
Email: geoff.l.salmon@barclayscorporate.com

LHO Group
41 Grove Street
New Canaan
Connecticut
USA, 06840
Tel: +203 966-4449
Fax: +203 972-7253
Web: www.lhogroup.com

Benfield Imperial Entertainment Finance
55 Bishopsgate
London EC2N 3BD
Tel: 0207 578 7037

DZ Bank
London Branch
10 Aldersgate Street
London, EC1A 4XX
Tel: 020 7776 6000
Fax: 020 7776 6100
Email: london@dzbank.de
Web: www.dzbank.de

Completion Bonds

A completion bond (or "guarantee") is a form of insurance taken out by a producer in order to guarantee that the completion of the film occurs without it running over budget or (equally importantly) schedule. Financiers will normally require a producer to take out a completion bond to help secure their investment; a film is worthless if it is unfinished due to running out of funding, or if delays result in losing cast or a particularly desired exploitation opportunity. Should it be impossible to finish the film on time and on budget, the completion bond company will, under the guarantee, be required to repay all financiers who are party to the completion bond agreement their entire investment to date. Naturally, no bond company will want to do this unless absolutely necessary, and so the guarantee will include rights of "take-over" so that the bond company can step in to manage the production if it feels that targets are being missed. The bond company will periodically visit the set, and producers have to send daily and weekly reports to the bond company, setting out over-costs and over-runs to-date, and so on. Where problems look imminent, the bond company will offer advice, and in extreme circumstances, will remove and/or replace the director, producer, or other key elements in order to get the film finished. In such circumstances, the bond company will not necessarily be interested in the artistic quality of the film; its concern will be getting it finished on time and in accordance with the various technical delivery requirements.

A producer will usually approach a completion bond company with a script, schedule and budget approved by the financiers and (where relevant) the distributors. The company will examine these documents, and may require further documentation to satisfy itself that the film can realistically be completed within the proposed budget, and that key elements such as personnel, insurance and locations are properly dealt with.

The financiers will have to guarantee their contributions to the budget, and the bond company will require that a contingency equal to 10% of the budget is specified as a line item and set aside to cover budget overruns. The fee for the completion guarantor will also be agreed as a line item, and is often expressed as a percentage of the budget (usually in the region of about 5% or 6%). If the guarantee is not "called upon" (ie. the bond company is not required to pay up any money), there will often be a rebate equal to approximately 50% of the bond fee.

It is important for a producer to establish whether or not the completion guarantor is actually able to pay up if called upon. The bond company itself will often take out an insurance policy to cover itself in the event of being required to pay large sums back to the investors, and the producers should inquire about this, as well as the bond company's track record.

Completion Bond company contacts:

Film Finances Ltd
14/15 Conduit Street
London, W1S 2XJ
Tel: 020 7629 6557
Fax: 020 7491 7530
Web: www.ffi.com

IFG Group PLC
IFG House
Booterstown Hall
Booterstown
Co. Dublin
Tel: +353 1 275 2800
Fax: +353 1 275 2801
Email: securemail@ifg.ie
Web: www.ifggroup.com

International Film Guarantors
25 Maddox St
London, W1S 2QT
Tel: 020 7493 4686
Fax: 020 7493 4696
Email: ukinfo@ifgbonds.com
Web: www.ifgbonds.com

Owen Thomas (Elemental films) on Completion Bonds for low budget

"The great untold story of completion bonds is that bond companies don't like low budgets and generally dissuade producers who approach them. We didn't choose not to have a bond, it was more a case of the bond companies telling us they don't encourage a bond at a certain budget level. Having a bond alters the way a film gets made; the majority of our crew would never have been acceptable to a bond company, who prefer tried-and-tested talent. Our working methods would have been challenged all along the line. It would not have been the case that we needed to find the 40k to pay the bond, we would have had to find an additional one million to meet their requirements. We'd have been killed before we started.

"This way we have an accomplished production which has given significant opportunities for new talent to assert itself and should provide an examplar of how to conduct film making as a fiscally sound business - profit will arrive far sooner than for comparable films made on typical budgets. What better way is there to move forward than to earn on one's own film?

"From a producer's perspective, it doesn't make sense to bond a low budget picture. The cost of a bond is a big chunk of the budget, money that's better spent on the screen. We were fortunate in that our financiers accepted that 'Solid Air' would be unbonded and given that we fulfilled their requirements - that the shoot would be adequately crewed, that the schedule was achievable on the budget, they were satisfied to proceed without one."

Sale and Leaseback

In recent years sale and leaseback deals have become a common, and often integral, element of the funding of feature film productions. The popularity of such deals arises from the special tax treatment afforded to the film industry by the 1992 and 1997 Finance Acts.

The scheme in summary:

The master negative of a completed "British" film is sold by the producer, usually at production cost, to a UK lessor, often a specialist film investment partnership.

The film is leased back to the producer over a period of typically 15 years. The producer can then continue to exploit the film over the period of the lease but during the period of the lease must pay lease rentals to the lessor. In order to guarantee that the producer will meet these rentals as they fall due then sufficient of the sales proceeds received by the producer must be placed on deposit with a guaranteeing bank which will release the rental payments as they fall due. The bank will charge a fee for this service, typically around 0.5% of the amount deposited.

The tax benefits:

Strictly speaking the benefits of sale and leaseback do not constitute an actual tax saving. The acquirer of the film will still pay the same amount of tax as before, however they will pay this tax later than they would normally and therefore benefit from the use of cash which they would otherwise have had to pay over to the Inland Revenue. The benefit of such a tax deferral can be quantified in monetary terms and the acquirer will be willing to share this with the producer. The producer's share is given to him by a reduction in the amount of the lease rentals payable, which will be calculated such that, discounted over the period of the lease, they total less than the sale price. The difference represents the "net benefit" to the producer.

The amount of the net benefit is dependent on various factors including the state of the sale and leaseback market, the production cost of the film and the timing of the deal but currently some deals are producing net benefits of up to 13% of the cost of the film.

To qualify for the tax benefits the maker or acquirer of a film will need to obtain a Certificate of British Nature of a Film from the DCMS. A certificate will only be issued where a film is completed, and where the maker or acquirer of the film has submitted an application for certification accompanied by an accountants' report prepared by a firm of Chartered or Certified Accountants.

Does the film need to make money?

Whilst it is obviously desirable that a film is successful, curiously enough for this purpose it is not actually important. The producer has entered into a binding contract to pay the lease rentals, which will still be payable regardless of the success or otherwise of the film, however the proceeds placed on deposit with the guaranteeing bank should be sufficient to generate the income necessary to meet the rentals as they fall due (and he will already have had his net benefit). The acquirer of the film is similarly guaranteed to receive his rentals. These will amount to less than the amount paid for the film but the tax deferral benefits should more than compensate for this.

What guarantees that the lease payments will be made?

The system of bank guarantees ensure that this will happen. The funds placed on deposit are calculated such that, with interest, they will cover the lease payments to be made in the future

The current tax legislation:

The current tax benefits have been in place since 1997 and the most recent extension of the legislation covers film expenditure incurred up to and including 2 July 2005. There has been pressure on the Government to justify the special tax treatment afforded to the film industry and what have been seen as abuses of the system have in recent times been clamped down, notably the restriction of the benefits to feature films rather than television productions, and restrictions with regard to the amounts and nature of deferred fees which can be included in the allowable production cost.

What is a "British" film?

The definition of a "British" film is one that qualifies as such under the Films Act 1985. A film can qualify in either of two ways:

- ### Under Schedule 1 to the Act
  The criteria for qualifying under Schedule 1 relate mainly to the proportion of the cost of the film spent in the UK and the proportion of the labour costs of the film paid to "qualifying" individuals.

- ### As a co-production
  An increasingly common route to qualifying as a "British" film is as a co-production, under the terms of one of the UK's official co-production treaties. These apply to films made by two or more co-producers, usually consisting of one UK co-producer and one or more co-producers from countries with which the UK has a treaty. This is particularly useful where films do not meet the schedule 1 criteria. The criteria for qualification as a co-production relate to ensuring that each of the co-producers meets minimum levels of creative input and financial contribution. The regulations also contain provision for both creative input and financial contribution from third party non-treaty countries. Where a co-producer is from a European country with which the UK does not have an official co-production treaty, or where there are three or more co-producers from different countries, then qualification can be achieved under the European Convention on Cinematographic Co-production.

The massive increase in the number of co-productions achieving British Film Status in the last couple of years is expected to cause the UK government to significantly increase the required amount of the UK contribution necessary to obtain that status, thereby making it more difficult for some productions to be organised in this way. Producers should be careful to bear this in mind when considering the co-production route.

Any producer who wishes to take advantage of the tax benefits of sale and leaseback should, at the earliest possible opportunity, seek the advice of suitable firms of accountants and lawyers in order to identify and avoid potential problems

---

Willott Kingston Smith specialise in providing financial, fundraising, accountancy and tax solutions to companies from the creative industries. To discuss how to make the most of your company's creativity, contact Geraint Howells or John Mills.

Willott Kingston Smith

A Kingston Smith specialist business

Willott Kingston Smith, Quadrant House, Air St, 80-82 Regent St, London W1B 5RP

Tel: 020 7304 4646 / Fax: 020 7304 4647
ghowells@kingstonsmith.co.uk / jmills@kingstonsmith.co.uk / www.kingstonsmith.co.uk/wks

Pre-Sales and Advance on Rights

A common way for a producer to raise finance for a production is through selling off the exploitation rights to a film in certain territories before the film is actually made (known as "pre-selling"). This is where a distributor who approves certain elements, including the script, cast, budget and shooting schedule, agrees in advance to purchase all the rights necessary to exploit the film in his local territory. The price he agrees to pay is known as a "minimum guarantee" (or "MG"), and is payable once the film is made and – most importantly – delivered on time and in accordance with the approved elements. Often, the distributor will agree to acquire the rights to exploit the film in all formats, keeping for itself any income thereby derived. It will probably sub-license to other distributors in the territory the rights in those formats in which it does not specialise (eg. TV, video and/or DVD). Other than the MG, the producer will therefore not expect to see any future income from any territory(ies) which are pre-sold, and this will affect the likely profitability of the film. Accordingly, any other investors in the picture will have to consent to the rights being sold off in this way.

In most cases, these promises to pay the MG will be used to raise finance elsewhere from a bank. The bank will only lend against the buying distributor's promise to pay the MG if it has a good relationship with the distributor and believes that it is likely still to be solvent at the time of delivery of the film. The bank then lends the producer a discounted amount of money up front, and collects from the distributor upon delivery of the film by the producer.

A bank entering into this kind of deal will often insist on the producer taking out a completion bond to ensure that the film is finished on time and on budget (so as

to prevent the distributor from trying to avoid payment). Further, the distributor's own bank may be required to issue a letter of credit on behalf of the distributor, guaranteeing that the payment can (and will) be made, as long as the producer meets the delivery requirements.

The advantage to the distributor of agreeing to buy a film before it is completed is that it may get a good price; the rights to a "finished" film will usually cost more as the distributor will be able to "see" what s/he is getting. For the producer, it is a way of getting a large proportion of the production funds together, although of course s/he is unlikely to see any further income from any territory (or format in any territory) that has been pre-sold. It is not healthy to do too many pre-sales, as it will limit future income, and therefore reduce the return on investment for the other financiers.

One point to note is that a pre-sale to a TV network might have an effect on a future sale made to a theatrical distributor. A TV pre-sale made without an appropriate "hold-back" window could affect the timing of a potential release in the cinemas (and therefore reduce the attraction of the film to a theatrical buyer). The theatrical distributor will also lose the opportunity to sub-license the picture for TV in its territory, so its offer price to the producer will be lower. However, a sale to one buyer might increase the status of the film, and thereby help to secure a sale to another buyer.

This form of financing often works for established producers with a good reputation and a good project, but increasingly buyers are less keen to enter into this kind of deal (or to pay the traditional prices), due to the very real risk of not being able to achieve the estimated box office figures. Naturally, this has had a negative impact on established production companies. Today, an established producer with a good script, cast and production team might expect to raise maybe 20% to 60% of the film's budget this way, compared with upwards of 70% a couple of years ago.

Some other points to note are that a film without a major distribution deal (pre-sale) in place is likely to be a less attractive proposition for other potential financiers, including public funding bodies. This is because the existence of pre-sales is often considered a "signal" that at least some distributors in the market believe the project to be commercial. Additionally, an inexperienced producer might benefit more from the market experience and guidance of a distributor who is already on-board while the film is being made, rather than afterwards, when the film might be turned down for reasons that could easily have been addressed during production, had the producer known.

Acquisitions and Negative Pick-ups

An "acquisition" (or "straight sale") is a rights purchase made by a distributor on the strength of the finished film. This is common practice for established and non-established filmmakers, but is especially important where the producer has a minimal reputation and is unable to raise an advance from a distributor. The advantage of this kind of sale is that it is based on an existing film which the distributor will (usually!) watch before buying (often at a market screening), so the producer and distributor both know exactly what they are selling and buying, thereby hopefully preventing any unwelcome surprises. Naturally, as the film is completed at the time of purchase, the sums received from a straight sale do not help in the financing of the movie.

There is, however, a "middle-ground" between straight and pre-sales, where a distributor is persuaded to sign a letter of intent rather than an enforceable contract. This letter acknowledges an intention to buy the film for an agreed price once it has been completed and delivered. As with a normal pre-sale, the letter will indicate certain conditions that the producer and the finished film must meet in order for the distributor to proceed with the acquisition. Although possessing a letter of intent would be better than approaching a potential investor without any distribution deal at all, it is by no means actual proof of a sale, and in itself would probably not persuade financiers looking for a reasonably secure investment. At the very least, a letter of intent would establish a relationship with a distributor and might be a useful guide as to what they are looking for.

A "negative pick-up" is an acquisition of all the rights to all territories; in other words effectively picking up all rights to exploit the entire negative of the film.

The Value of Merchandising and Ancillary Rights

Intangible assets are becoming increasingly more valuable and form a huge part of the entertainment, content and sport industries. The global Entertainment and Media market grew by 1.5 % in 2001 and has been reported by PWC to exceed U.S. $1 trillion. It is further predicted to rise to U.S. $1.4 trillion by 2006.

The European consumer spent U.S. $15 billion on film and entertainment in 2001. Box office receipts are reported to be healthy and with the massive explosion of the DVD market during recent times together with the arrival of video-on-demand it is not surprising that a 38 % increase has been predicted by 2006.

In the movie business the income which can be generated from the exploitation of ancillary rights, particularly merchandising and product placement, should not be overlooked. Such rights should be heavily protected and guarded to ensure maximum revenue is captured and not diminished by infringement.

George Lucas is said to have earned U.S. $1 billion from the merchandising and sequel rights to the Star Wars films. Lucas pre-empted the value of such rights at a time when their true importance had yet to be determined by reserving the merchandising and sequel rights in return for a smaller share of the pie. The financial return effectively enabled him to have complete creative control over the next 3 movies – a rare treat for any film maker!

The makers of the Harry Potter films spotted the value early on and applied for registered trade mark protection for some of the key brands and character names before the first film was released, with merchandise including wizard coins and "Bertie Bott's Every Flavor Beans" hitting the shops in anticipation.

The value can also be seen in other sectors: for example, Nintendo sold more than 65 million Pokemon games worldwide and revived sales of the GameBoy in the process. The total merchandising revenue for Pokemon reached U.S. $14 billion worldwide in 2001.

So as a film maker, how do you make the most of these rights?

Merchandising rights are effectively made up of registered and unregistered intellectual property rights — copyright, trade marks and design rights or a combination. The exploitation, protection and enforcement of such intellectual property rights is key to unlocking the value, whether by creating a unique brand for your film or using the brands of others.

Essentially in real terms we are talking about the use and exploitation of the names and images of celebrities, fictional characters and even brands together with certain copyright works used in relation to particular goods or services. However, it has long been recognised under English law that the use of a name, image or brand to promote particular goods and/or services is difficult to protect. Therefore, a clear and well advised strategy is needed to ensure success and maximum reward.

Staying Ahead

This is not a comprehensive guide but the following are some tips when looking at ancillary rights:

- When discussing or disclosing your ideas make sure it is done under an obligation of confidentiality. Use a non-disclosure agreement or confidentiality agreement where possible;
- Film makers take careful steps to protect the copyright in a screenplay, but it is equally important to protect the copyright in other ideas, for example characters. Wherever possible, put your ideas into material form to attract copyright and use the © [name] and [date]. Also keep and date all drawings and notes;
- Obtain and adhere to a full rights clearance checklist before investing time and money in any particular idea;
- Obtain searches on any name or brand;
- Register the brand and the characters (possibly including their outline shapes) as trade marks and get appropriate domain names;
- Obtain effective assignments and a waiver of moral rights from the creative talent covering copyright and any design right, including the right to sue for infringement;
- License these valuable rights where possible rather than assigning them;
- Consider new media rights and format rights. Interactive rights and the rights over certain formats have increasing value and are readily sought after. Don't underestimate the link between the film and the computer games sector; and
- When negotiating an agreement closely review the revenue stream and the definitions relating to any royalty payment.

Most importantly, it is essential to know and understand the value of these intellectual property rights and how to exploit them to your advantage. Remember the two most important elements to any agreement – the money and the rights. Dorsey & Whitney's Creative Industries Group can assist in film makers realising their true potential in such a competitive market.

If you want further advice and information, contact Dorsey & Whitney's Creative Industries Group:

London – Victoria Lockley   +44 20 7588 0800   (lockley.victoria@dorseylaw.com)

New York – Helene Freeman   001 212 415 9200   (freeman.helene@dorseylaw.com)

Distributors & Sales Agents

UK Theatrical

Arrow Film Distributors
18 Watford Road
Radlett, WD7 8LE
Tel: 01923 858306
Fax: 01923 859673
Email: info@arrowfilms.co.uk
Web: www.arrowfilms.co.uk

Artifical Eye Film Company
14 King Street
London, WC2E 8HR
Tel: 020 7240 5353
Fax: 020 7240 5242
Web: www.artificial-eye.com

bfi Collections
21 Stephen Street
London, W1T 1LN
Tel: 020 7957 8905
Fax: 020 7580 5830
Email: bookings@bfi.org.uk
Web: www.bfi.org.uk/collections

Blue Dolphin Film & Video
40 Langham Street
London, W1N 5RG
Tel: 020 7255 2494
Fax: 020 7580 7670
Email: info@bluedolphinfilms.com
Web: www.bluedolphinfilms.com

Buena Vista International (UK)
3 Queen Caroline Street
London, W6 9PE
Tel: 020 8222 1000
Fax: 020 8222 2795
Web: www.bvmovies.com

Colombia TriStar Films (UK)
Europe House, 25 Golden Square
London, W1R 6LU
Tel: 020 7533 1111
Fax: 020 7533 1105
Web: www.columbiatristar.co.uk

Entertainment Film Distributors
Eagle House, 108-110 Jermyn Street
London, SW1Y 6HB
Tel: 020 7930 7744
Fax: 020 7930 9399

Guerilla Films
35 Thornbury Road
Isleworth, TW7 4LQ
Tel: 020 8758 1716
Fax: 020 8758 9364
Web: www.guerilla-films.com

Helkon SK Film Distribution
Ariel House, 74a Charlotte Street
London, W1T 4QT
Tel: 020 7299 8800
Fax: 020 7299 8801
Web: www.helkon-sk.com

ICA Projects
12 Carlton House Terrace
London, SW1Y 5AH
Tel: 020 7766 1416
Fax: 020 7930 9686
Email: projects@ica.org.uk

Icon Film Distributors
The Quadrangle, Fourth Floor, 180 Wardour Street
London, W1V 3AA
Tel: 020 7494 8100
Fax: 020 7494 8151
Web: www.icon-online.com

Metro Tartan Distribution
Atlantic House. 5 Wardour Street
London, W1D 6PB
Tel: 020 7494 1400
Fax: 020 7439 1922
Web: www.tartanvideo.com

Metrodome Distribution
110 Park Street
London, W1K 6NX
Tel: 020 7408 2121
Fax: 020 7409 1935
Web: www.metrodomegroup.com

Momentum Pictures
Second Floor, 184-192 Drummond Street
London, NW1 3HP
Tel: 020 7388 1100
Fax: 020 7383 0404
Web: www.momentumpictures.co.uk

Optimum Releasing
9 Rathbone Place
London, W1T 1HW
T: 020 7637 5403
F: 020 7637 5408
Email: info@optimumreleasing.com
Web: www.optimumreleasing.com

Pathé Distribution
Kent House, 14-17 Market Place
Great Titchfield Street
London, W1W 8AR
Tel: 020 7323 5151
Fax: 020 7631 3568
Web: www.pathe.co.uk

Twentieth Century Fox Film Co
20th Century House, 31-32 Soho Square
London, W1V 6AP
Tel: 020 7437 7766
Fax: 020 7434 2170
Website: www.fox.co.uk/

United International Pictures (UIP)
12 Golden Square
London , W1A 2JL
Tel: 020 7534 5200
Fax: 020 7534 5201/5202
Web: www.uip.co.uk

UGC Films
Power Road Studios
Power Road
London, W4 5PY
Tel: 020 8987 1503
Fax: 020 8987 1501
Email: info@ugcfilms.co.uk

Warner Brothers
98 Theobolds Road
London, WC1X 8WB
Tel: 020 7984 5000
Fax: 020 7984 5211
Web: www.warnerbros.co.uk

DAVID NICHOLAS WILKINSON   **THE DISTRIBUTOR**

Guerilla Films was founded in 1994 to distribute independent British features to the UK market. David Nicholas Wilkinson, founder and director of the company has worked in the industry for 33 years as actor, producer and distributor and has a unrivalled perspective over the UK independent scene.

"I have been quoted as saying this before, but I feel the point should be made here: filmmaking is like sex – every new generation thinks they have discovered it and that previous generations could not do it right or enjoyed it as much – their generation knows how to do it. The idiot filmmaker will not take advice. They will work with equally inexperienced partners, technicians and actors because their egos cannot take being seen as not knowing very much. They are convinced they know best. The clever filmmaker will surround themselves with as many experienced people as possible. Those others' experience will greatly help the filmmaker, which in turn will lead to a better film and thus a better outcome for the filmmaker."

UK THEATRICAL

"The problem with new filmmakers is that - quite naturally - they all think their film is the best thing since sliced bread. Unfortunately this gives them a false sense of security. They think that they are going to get more than it cost them to make the film from their first sale alone. This rarely happens. Most low budget British films do not even recoup their print & advertising costs from the cinema AND video rental, sell-though and DVD, let alone pay back any of the film's investment.

"If you take a film like *Gangster No1* - NOT in my view a low budget film - FilmFour ran an excellent PR and advertising campaign. It grossed £325,763 which sounds a lot. However it was released on 112 prints which gives it just £2,909 per screen. You then need to deduct 17.5% VAT. Of what's left the exhibitor will take 75% (in some cases if the film played to near capacity it may have had as much as a 50% return but those cinemas will not be in the majority). The net return per print of this film is therefore approximately £6-900 per print. The cost of the print alone will be £5-600. On top of that is the cost of advertising, the PR campaign, shipping each print back and forth to cinemas plus numerous other costs, not forgetting the distributors fee for their staff, and overheads.

"The most successful low/no budget British film I have seen in the 20 years since I saw Bill Forsythe's £6,000 *That Sinking Feeling* was Christopher Nolan's *Following*. I have never known a low/no budget film get such glowing reviews, in fact few high budget films receive such praise, yet it only grossed £36,000.

"Self-distribution in the UK is an option. It's what I did. It took me about three-to-four years to learn it properly and make all the contacts and set up the key accounts. The first three films I did suffered from my lack of experience. It is a new business and it is a long learning curve. It's only worth it if you intend to distribute more films. Not just your own, but other people's. The big problem I had when I started distributing just my own films was that everyone - and I mean everyone - thought that I was having to do this because no one else would take the film, therefore it must be really bad."

SALES

"By the time producers realise that not everyone is chasing their film, one, two or three years have gone by. I know of at least ten British films where the producers turned down offers, believing that something better will come along. I made offers on a number of these myself. Then, after not hearing from these people for a few years, they have come back to me. Much as I would like to take them on, I often no longer have the time or money. They seem to think I have been doing nothing in the meantime just waiting for their film to return.

"Filmmakers may make wonderful films, but know nothing about distribution, so they can shoot themselves in the foot, quite unintentionally. You have to approach the market very carefully to get as much out of it as you can. For example, after I had taken director Piotr Szkopiak on with *Small Time Obsession* I discovered he had once made an approach direct to Channel 4, this was some time before I met him. They had turned his film down at that time and that means I have to work so much harder to get them interested at a second approach. The problem is that when a broadcaster turns a film down, they have a record on their computer of that film being turned down. It acts just like a blacklisting. We are talking perception here. It was turned down, therefore it must be no good. It is hard to break through the resistance being on the rejects list creates. It is no use just sending the broadcaster a tape and hoping to sell your film to them. I like to get them excited about the film, so I get a nice piece in The Guardian and a couple of other nationals, to get the pot boiling. Then I can go to them with some publicity extracts that get them hooked. Get them interested, then we can talk business.

"Going back to Piotr's film, I nearly had to accept a lower price for it from Channel 4 than I would normally have accepted for such a good film. Although they were interested in the film second time round, they were also influenced by their own earlier rejection. That helps bring the price down, when really, you as distributor are trying to get as much for the film as you can. And don't forget, that was a film where I was trying to get back a return on my own investment that had taken the film from final edit to delivery. In the end The Studio Channel bought the film for $25,000, not a lot but it was the best offer around.

"I have over 40 films. I have only paid an advance for one of them. In many cases the producers have given me the P&A costs for the cinema release. A UK release greatly enhances the film's value overseas. Therefore it helps for me to come in early so that I can make the P&A part of the investment in the film. This is what happened with *Small Time Obsession*. The brutal truth is that if I had not released the film in the UK, it would not have had a top sales agent selling the film. Nothing to do with the film. It is very hard for a sales agent to sell a UK film if it has not been released in UK cinemas. Because I was releasing the film I had interest from six Sales Agents and Piotr finally went with J&M.

"The important thing to remember with Sales Agents who do not invest in your film is that all they have to achieve is a few sales around the world and they have recovered their costs and made a profit. Therefore after a while they will move on and they have little to lose if your film sits on a shelf. You lose money. Another fact of life. Choose them carefully. You can replace them but whoever takes on your film is selling shop-soiled goods, they know this, the distributors around the world know this but the poor old producer never realises this. If it has been sold by someone else first, your films is devalued. Every year older your film is, the less valuable it is. There are some exceptions to this rule but not many. Most filmmakers think their film is like fine wine maturing with age. Sadly most films are more like fish.

"Because most countries do not make most of their own films or TV programming unlike here then they acquire more. *The Brylcreem Boys,* which I distribute in the UK, had sold to 58 countries before I took it here. Within the EU, British films are the most popular of all the member states. Ironically it frequently happens that a British film can sell in every EU member state except the UK.

"If you think we have it bad, think about the Turks, or South Africans. The basic problem is that there are far too many films made every year; more than the world market can absorb. Because the American film producing industry has built up a global distribution system, they have become effective at persuading other nations to view their films. Ours is an industry where normal rules do not apply. If you tailor a good suit, people will buy it. Go into any video store and see what people rent. Some really bad films do far, far better than some brilliant ones. I hated *Hollow Man* yet my video store will do better with that than with *In The Mood For Love*.

LEFT ON THE SHELF

"In May 2002, the distinguished journal Screen Finance published details of the UK films produced in the year 2000. It showed that at compilation 58% of films were still without any form of UK distribution. Although this is the highest recorded figure of unreleased films in that publication, reports in previous years show figures of between 30-45%.

"Over the years, those films on the shelf will decrease as many go straight to video/DVD or be sold to television; and indeed a significant number in any one year will never be seen in any form whatsoever in the UK. The biggest single mistake of many UK producers, and it is an extremely common one, is the assumption that their film will automatically find distribution in the UK. Whilst many will secure a satisfactory release in all areas, a large percentage will struggle to secure anything at all; and those that do will either have a 1-2 print release in obscure cinemas or go straight to video.

This is a hard fact that so many people think they can ignore – like death, they think it will never happen to them. I started with sex and now I am finishing with death. That's the film business." *CH/NW/JM*

UK Video Distributors

Abbey Home Media
435-437 Edgware Road,
London, W2 1TH
Tel: 020 7563 3910
Web: www.abbeyhomemedia.com

BBC Worldwide
Woodlands, 80 Wood Lane,
London, W12 0TT
Tel: 020 8433 2000
Web: www.bbc.co.uk

BMG UK & Ireland
Bedford House,
69/79 Fulham High Street,
London, SW6 3JW
Tel: 020 7384 7500
Web: www.bmg.com

Buena Vista Home Entertainment
25 Golden Square,
London, W1F 9LU
Tel: 020 7533 1200
Web: www.cthe.co.uk

Carlton Visual Entertainment
5th Floor, 35-38 Portman Square,
London, W1H 0NU
Tel: 020 7486 6688
Web: www.carltonvisual.com

Columbia Tristar Home Entertainment
Sony Pictures Europe House,
25 Golden Square,
London, W1F 9LU
Tel: 020 7533 1200
Web: www.cthe.co.uk

DD Video (Leisureview)
11 Churchill Court,
58 Station Road,
North Harrow,
Middx, HA2 7SA
Tel: 020 8863 8819

Entertainment UK
243 Blyth Road,
Hayes,
Middx, UB3 1DN
Tel: 020 8848 7511
Web: www.entuk.com

Eureka Video (Bensonworld)
Unit 9, Ironbridge Close,
Great Central Way,
London, NW10 0UF
Tel: 020 8451 0600
Web: www.eurekavideo.co.uk

Fremantle Media
1 Stephen Street,
London W1T 1AL
Tel: 020 7691 6000
Web: www.fremantlemedia.com

Hit Entertainment
5th Floor, Maple House,
141-150 Tottenham Court Road,
London, W1T 7NF
Tel: 020 7554 2500
Web: www.hitentertainment.com

Lace International
Lace House,
39-40 The Old Steine,
Brighton, BN1 1NH
Tel: 01273 202220
Web: www.lacegroup.com

Manga Entertainmanet
8 Kensington Park Road,
London, W11 3BU
Tel: 020 7229 3000
Web: www.manga.com

Metrodome Distribution
(see theatrical distributors)

Metro Tartan Video
(see theatrical distributors)

MGM Home Entertainment
5 Kew Road,
Richmond, TW9 2PR
Tel: 020 8939 9300
Web: www.mgmuk.com

Momentum Pictures
(see theatrical distributors)

Mosaic Entertainment
19-24 Manasty Road,
Orton Southgate,
Peterborough, PE2 6UP
Tel: 01733 363010
Web: www.mosaic-entertainment.co.uk

Paramount Home Entertainment
UIP House,
45 Beadon Rd,
Hammersmith,
London, W6 0EG
Tel: 020 8741 9333
Web: www.paramount.com

Pathé Distribution
(see theatrical distributors)

Sanctury Visual Entertainment
45-53 Sinclair Rd,
London, W14 0NS
Tel: 020 7602 6351
Web: www.sanctuarygroup.com

Telstar Video Entertainment
Prospect Studios,
Barnes High Street,
London SW13 9LE
Tel: 020 8878 7888
Web: www.telstar.co.uk

Twentieth Century Fox Home Entertainment
(see theatrical distributors)

Universal Pictures Video
1 Sussex Place,
Hammersmith,
London, W6 9XS
Tel: 020 8910 5000
Web: www.universalstudios.com

Video Collection International
76 Dean Street,
London, W1D 3SQ
Tel: 020 7396 8888
Web: www.vciplc.co.uk

Warner Home video
(see theatrical distributors)

STEVE MACKLER — THE VIDEO DISTRIBUTOR

Bedford Entertainment has been distributing independent features since 1980, primarily to the US video market. It has handled over 294 titles in connection with its partner MTI Video. Steve Mackler, president of Bedford Entertainment, has been working in the film industry in production and distribution for many years and is connected to the horror magazine, Fangoria.

Do you deal with films of a certain budget?

Anything. If I go to try and sell a movie, if I go to video and I go to a large chain, I never discuss budget, because if a picture is made for $15,000 can I ask for $200,000? They would try to knock me down on price. I only really care how it can be commercialized.

Is theatrical potentially very lucrative?

Potentially of course, it's very lucrative, but it's also very expensive to get involved. Interms of my normal everyday living I normally consider video. And I think most people in independent distribution do. I know the people who actually write the scripts want it to be seen on the screen, but every time I confront producers or directors, by saying sure, I'll put up $50,000 for theatrical, but every dime you lose out of it, has to come out of your pocket because I am cross-collateralizing my recoupment. So if I am going to put up $50,000, I say "I am going to recoup $50,000 from your share Mr Producer in video" all of a sudden it doesn't seem so great anymore. It's great if I put up the money, but if they put up the money, it's not so great.

Do you think the different media expect different things from a film?

Well, absolutely. Theatrical's really, really hard. It's a matter of expectations. If I make $40,000 on a film from video, that's OK. I don't think anyone would want to go to theatrical to make $40,000. If they thought that's what they were going to make, they probably wouldn't do it, because it's a 6 to 10 month process. Everyone has another reason for going into theatrical, either because it's a vanity thing, they want to be quoted, to get reviews, they think they can make a killing, they think it will boost video sales. There's four or five different reasons why one goes into theatrical or does not go into theatrical.

Does the format make a big difference? Digital, Super16mm, 35mm, for example?

It depends on whom you're dealing with. I think we are in a between and betwixt period where the notion of going into digital certainly is acceptable with some places and is not acceptable with others. That seems to be changing and it could take years to change. High Def has its impact. There's a lot of people who will say the film look is much more preferable. It's evolving. It's a hard thing. And it depends where it is being distributed. If it's being distributed on video, and it's an independent film, a small film, that market is far more forgiving for something shot on digital, than if you're going into theatrical for any meaningful distribution. Blair Witch not withstanding, because you can't take the anomaly and make that the rule, that just doesn't work. Everyone all of a sudden goes out and makes Blair Witch, there were probably 20 Blair Witch knock-offs that did nothing.

What stage do you like to see a film at?

The thing I always tell filmmakers is don't show anyone your film until you're ready to have it finally shown. They are never going to look at it twice. Most people say they will. They say, "I know how to look at a rough cut", and I show them the rough-cut and they say, "boy, this is really rough". So assume that you have one shot, put your best foot forward, and show exactly the project that it took you two years to put to bed. Having said that, there are reasons why you shouldn't. Number one you've run out of money. Number two you're racing to meet a deadline for a certain market that you want to hit, and the only way to make that deadline is to show someone something beforehand. So there are certain valid reasons, but you better be smart about what you have, and to whom you're showing it.

Would you say there are any common mistakes made by filmmakers that might put you off a film?

The smartest thing, the underlining word: business. I am not interested in personal films. There are other reasons for making them and business is not one of them. I'm always talking business. I always say to independent filmmakers, before you go ahead with a project, talk to distributors. You don't have to make deals with them, but talk to them. They may save you a lot of work and aggravation by saying don't do it. Take your money and put it into something better. Talking to a distributor gives you an idea of what the market place is like.

Anyone can go and make a film, The real difficulty is once the picture gets into the market place and you're not getting your money back, investors are not getting their money back, and all that goes down the drain, mainly because you didn't ask beforehand. So that's the number one thing for filmmakers to think about – to find out what the market place will take. Incidentally, none of this means the word trash. If I can paraphrase the Eisenstein experiment, ten people can take the same paragraph, or synopsis, and make the same film, and you'll run the level from real trash to really significant, because, it's a matter of how much brains each one has and aesthetic taste. So it doesn't matter that it is low budget or horror; there are some wonderful horror films that are done, really intelligent films that are done. *CH* **bedfordentertain@netscape.net / web: www.mtivideo.com**

JOHANNES ROBERTS **DIAGNOSIS/HELLBREEDER**

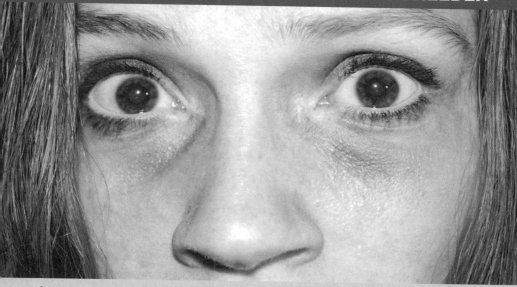

Johannes Roberts and James Eaves together wrote, produced and directed two micro-budget Super16mm horror features: Diagnosis in 2001 (US title Sanitarium) which is due for release in the UK in 2003 and Hellbreeder in 2003. Johannes, who has just completed his first feature film as sole director, Darkhunters (above), describes the lessons they learnt in producing films with a focus on realistic sales.

"James and I had made several short films together at University and decided before university finished to make a film by getting out graduate loans. The basic message of university was 'you will never get a job in the film industry' – so we thought the only way to do what we wanted to do was to do it ourselves. The fact that we knew we could get enough money to film it meant we knew we would film it, but I don't think we really considered this when writing the script!

"We had both followed the same three-year course but it was very theoretical and before we made *Diagnosis* the only time we had used film was in a five-minute black and white short. The longest film we had made was our graduation piece, which was twenty minutes long and shot on SVHS. We certainly knew nothing about producing and distribution as these were totally ignored on the course. We knew nothing of the straight to video industry until our first year in Cannes. I wished we had known and thought more about distribution before writing and filming – it is very important; anyone can make a film, the challenge is getting it released. We just learned as we went along (which probably explains how *Diagnosis* looks!).

"Once *Diagnosis* was made, we went out to Cannes and that turned out to be the best thing we did. Although the first year was hideous it really taught us what people look for and how things sell at the lower end (or any end) of the industry. Initially we had trouble selling the film, partly because it wasn't a very good film, but it also had very little of the elements that sales agents in Cannes were looking for, i.e. a simple but strong story that can easily cross international borders, gore, nudity and violence. These are all visual things that are the same in any language! It is not as easy to do as it might sound – making a film takes a long time so you have to make a film you are passionate about – killing teenagers in a wood might sell but who wants to spend a year of their life making it?

"We decided to re-cut the film and the trailer, which had a positive impact in attracting a sales agent. I guess we finally made a film that made sense and also had some kind of a name (Uri Geller) that people could at least recognise worldwide. But definitely the biggest draw was a trailer that was really very good. I think at the end of the day the people that have bought the film have bought it pretty much on the trailer. It sells the film very well by 1. Telling a mini story in itself – a very tricky but very important thing to do in a trailer – people need a narrative even in a trailer, even if it isn't really the narrative of the film – it has to reflect the film in two minutes instead of ninety. 2. It promised blood, monsters, intrigue and scares. If the film was as good as the trailer we would be a lot more wealthy than we are now!

"We also had to re-cut our next film, *Alice*, after trying unsuccessfully to sell the original version. That was interesting for me because I thought we were sitting on a goldmine – it had gore, nudity and a killer clown as well as a respected named actor with Dominique Pinon. But we violated a really important principle of straight to video – we didn't adhere to genre rules – we were pitching a horror that wasn't a horror and people didn't like it. So we took out all the quirky artistic bits of the film and re-cut it in a linear fashion and retitled it with a horror title, *Hellbreeder*. It is very important to realise that art house films, although tending to be lower budget than Hollywood films are always made with a larger budget than straight-to-video films. Art house films are always made with enough money to go theatrical, whereas straight to video films are just that. No one wants to watch a straight to video art house film – there is no market since they depend on reviews etc – hence you make a straight to video film, you need to follow certain rules as people are renting your title on genre. Mess with these rules at your peril!

"It is important to realise that films like *Clerks* & *The Blair Witch Project* are a tiny fraction of the industry. If you make a film for pennies you have to think that its distribution is going to reflect that – otherwise everybody would make films for nothing. So you need to think – right I'm making a film for almost nothing hence what I am aiming for is the video market – ok what can I do to appeal to this market? For instance USA, Japan and Germany are the three big markets so getting a telly star from Eastenders isn't going help sell there. Horror is big in all three territories – Japan especially like their creature horror. So you start to tailor your film this way.

"I have learned to approach filmmaking in much more commercial terms. A large proportion of my budgets now go on sfx and 'named' cast. The biggest lesson to learn is also to think internationally. The UK market at my level will never bring in the money we need. We started with straight to video films because the money we can raise limits the project – the more experienced we get with profitable films the more we can raise – no one wants to give a nobody millions of pounds. UK financing seems slow and impossible to get so rather than wait around forever trying to get the lottery to fund my 2 million pound masterpiece that will be a financial disaster because I have never filmed before, I prefer to film quickly, cheaply and learn my trade and the industry in which I ply it. My advice to new filmmakers: Cannes is a great place to start – it is truly eye opening." *CH*

UK Sales Agents

Alibi Films International
35 Long Acre
London, WC2E 9JT
Tel: 020 7845 0400
Fax: 020 7836 6919
Email: info@alibifilms.co.uk
Web: www.alibifilms.co.uk

Capitol Films
23 Queensdale Place
London, W11 4SQ
Tel: 020 7471 6000
Fax: 020 7471 6012
Email: films@capitolfilms.com
Web: www.capitolfilms.com

Cori Film Distributors
19 Albemarle St
London, W1S 4HL
Tel: 020 7493 7920
Fax: 020 7493 8088

Jane Balfour Films Ltd
Burghley House
35 Fortress Rd
London, NW5 1AQ
Tel: 020 7267 5392
Fax: 020 7267 4241
Email: jbf@janebalfourfilms.co.uk

Film Sales International Ltd
46 St Dionis Rd
London, SW6 4TT
Tel: 020 7731 1711

IAC Film
Greencoat House, 15 Francis Street
London, SW1P 1DH
Tel: 020 7592 1620
Fax: 020 7592 1627
Email: general@iacholdings.co.uk
Web: www.iacfilm.co.uk

Intermedia
Unit 12 Enterprise House
59 - 65 Upper Ground
London, SE1 9PQ
Tel: 0207 593 1630
Fax: 0207 593 1639
Email: info@intermediafilm.co.uk
Web: www.internationalmedia.co.uk

Myriad Pictures Ltd
Cavendish House
51-55 Mortimer St
London, W1W 8HJ
Tel: 020 7580 9200
Fax: 020 7290 0844
Web: www.myriadpictures.com

Portman Entertainment
Portman Film
21-25 St Anne's Court
London, W1V 3AW
Tel: 020 7494 8024
Fax: 020 7494 8046
Email: sales@portmanfilm.co.uk

Renaissance Films
34/35 Berwick Street
London, W1F 8RP
Tel: 0207 287 5190
Email: info@renaissance-films.com
Web: www.renaissance-films.com

Twinglobe
228-230 Uxbridge Rd
London, W12 7JD
Tel: 020 8743 5528
Fax: 020 8742 9525
Email: twinglobe@aol.com

United Artists Films
10 Stephen Mews
London, W1P 1PP
Tel: 020 7333 8877
Fax: 020 7333 8878

The Works
4th Floor, Parkland House
4 Gt Portland St
London, W1W 8QJ
Tel: 020 7612 1080
Fax: 020 7612 1081

Victor Film Company
Fourth Floor
1 Great Cumberland Place
London, W1H 7AL
Tel: 020 7535 3380
Fax: 020 7535 3383
Email: post@victor-film-co.uk
Web: www.victor-film-co.demon.uk

GARETH JONES   THE SALES AGENT

Winchester Entertainment is a sales agent, representing their own films and other people's; a production company, developing projects in house; and a film financier, assisting producers who have some funding already in place to raise the balance. They have dealt with films such as Heartbreakers (2001), Last Orders (2001) and Shooting Fish (1997). Gareth Jones, head of film production and finance, discusses working with independent producers.

Would you say it's getting more common for sales agents to act as producers?

I think that sales agents can be involved more and more in production as in executive production, which is helping put the finance together, because it's by helping the films be financed that you can have a film you can sell. So sales agents have to become more and more involved in finance.

Do you work with productions of a certain budget minimum?

These days, yes probably. We have done budget ranges from $3m up to $16m dollars.

So low budget or micro budget territory wouldn't be of interest?

No.

Do you think that the level of budget reflects the market that's open to it?

It's difficult for any smaller film to find a release because there are so many films being released. There are seven films being released every week in the UK. The problem with the micro budget films is that the quality tends to not be as good as a 35mm or super 16mm blown up. And because of the limited resources, the film itself won't have had so many elements such as cast and a well known director, etc. there's just not the money to spend. So it's quite hard. Very rarely do DV films make it on to cinema.

Do you work with new and emerging producers?

We do get involved with helping new producers. We are not a charity. I have been involved on a number of films with newish directors and producers such as Lock Stock and Withnail and I; a number of films where the producer is new and the director is maybe a first time director. We tend to be driven by the material itself: the script; and does the director have the potential to make a good movie? Can we make money out of this guy or this woman by selling the film? We're not really supporting somebody just because they are new, we are supporting somebody who's new and who has a good project.

And how would you say a producer would approach you with a project?

First of all we won't even look at a project unless it's got at least 40% of the money attached. So a producer has to show that he's got together 40% of the money. If they have that, they can approach us by contacting us but they have to have a script and a director attached and a cogent finance plan.

Would it make it make a difference if it's someone that you've not come across before or not heard of before?

You tend to be more sceptical of them.

So how would someone build up a relationship with you?

It would be first of all by contacting the development team initially. After they have contacted the development team, they do the initial screening of the project to see if it's worth us getting involved with and then you take it from there.

Should new producers talk to distributors and sales agents before they make a film if all the finance is raised?

They definitely should. They should get some gauge of what a sales agent and a distributor thinks of the saleability of the project.

Companies like Winchester Films would be happy to talk to someone?

Yes but we don't want people to come to us with a script and say "will you finance our film?" That's not of interest to us because the process is too far away, it's just going to take too long. So a producer has to come along with some money attached, a director and a good business plan, and because he hasn't produced before he has to show that he's done his homework and found out how he's going to produce his film. The problem is many producers come to you and they haven't got a full plan and they haven't got a way forward and they are really expecting us to put up most of the money, which no sales agent does.

How would people approach you with a finished project?

They can just phone up. A good way to approach us is at the markets: Cannes, Milan or AFM, come to us and present us with a tape of the finished work. I have to say if it's a DV type work we probably wouldn't take it. We have to sell internationally to buyers around the world and it's our experience that those pieces do not sell very well. It's not surprising because the expectation of audiences is a lot higher and people look at those DV type films and it's not their expectation of how a film looks. Also the subject matter of a lot of these smaller films tends to be very contained. It might be of interest to them and their families but they don't appeal to a wider audience. That's why it is important for people embarking on this to talk to sales agents.

Are you able to give an outline of delivery, what a producer must deliver to you for a finished production?

There is a whole list. They have to deliver a print of the film and various other physical materials: video masters. they may have to deliver a trailer, a hundred colour and a hundred black and white stills for the film, an electronic press kit and a physical press kit, a billing block (details of the credits), publicity materials. A large number of physical and documentary items.

Do you have any advice that you could give producers?

They have to look carefully at the subject matter they are making. They have to look to the ultimate sales target – the audience in the cinema. You can make lower budget genre films easier than other more wide-sweeping bigger films. By genre I mean horror, comedy, teen movie, things like that can find a market easier than just straight-forward drama.

They have to work with a director. It might help if they could have someone who is an established producer to act as a godfather; that can be a useful thing to do. They have to put together a finance plan and get an idea of how films can be financed. In the UK there are various forms of soft money you can use, so they could avail themselves of that. So all those things can make a difference.

And when they go to see a sales company, they want to have a clear idea of what they are asking the sales company for. If they have a script in a relatively advanced form they need a director, they need their plan and they need to have an idea of who is going to be in the film. That way we can make an assessment of it quicker, which is in everyone's interests. *CH*

(sales agents continued)

Vine International Pictures
VIP House
Greenacres
New Road Hill
Downe
Orpington, BR6 7JA
Tel: 01689 854 123
Fax: 01689 850990
Web: www.vine-international.co.uk

Winchester Films
19 Heddon Street
London, W1B 4BG
Tel: 020 7851 6500
Email: mail@winchesterent.com
Web: www.winchesterent.com

For short films:

Britshorts Limited
25 Beak Street
London, W1F 9RT
Tel: 020 7734 2277
Fax: 020 7734 2242
Email: contactus@britshorts.com
Web: www.britshorts.com

The Short Film Bureau
74 Newman Street
London, W1T 3EL.
Tel: 020 7636 2400
Fax: 020 7636 8558
Email: info@shortfilmbureau.com
Web: www.shortfilmbureau.com

Other Sources

Venture Capital

Venture capitalists make high-risk investments in growth businesses with a high potential return. They may be willing to invest in projects and business growth that other lenders, such as banks, might turn down due to the high risk and the high sum required. The venture capitalist becomes a shareholder in the company and they will often take on an executive role informing long-term business strategy. Business Angels are venture capitalists that invest in small and medium-sized enterprises (SME's) which can benefit from the Business Angel's knowledge and experience as well as their finance.

Enterprise Investment Scheme

This scheme has been in place since 1994, introduced by the government to replace the Business Expansion Scheme. The aim is to encourage investment in high risk small businesses by offering tax incentives to investors in the form of Income Tax relief and Capital and Gains Tax (CGT) deferral. It works by offering investors shares in an approved fund that invests in eligible small high-risk companies. Investments of up £150,000 a year can be made by each investor.

There are several manipulations of the scheme. Shares can be bought in one or several companies and through an investment in approved or unapproved funds; the difference for the investor is that the approved funds make the tax relief available immediately. Approvals come from the Inland Revenue, with film production being one of the qualifying business activities, though financing a film in this way is not that common with investors nervous about the potential risk. In general the EIS scheme is not as popular as the Venture Capital Trust which works in a similar way, but offers potentially less risk for the investor (see below).

Anyone considering this scheme should seek advice from a professional organisation and read the guidelines set out by the Inland Revenue.

For further information about the Enterprise Investment Scheme and for approvals contact:

Inland Revenue Small Company Enterprise Centre (SCEC)
TIDO
Ty Glas, Llanishen
Cardiff, CF14 5ZG
Tel: 029 2032 7400
Fax: 029 2032 7398
Email: enterprise.centre@ir.gsi.gov.uk
Web: www.inlandrevenue.gov.uk

To be kept up-to-date with legislation affecting the EIS and for access to expert advice:

The Enterprise Investment Scheme Association (EISA)
Tylers Croft,
Hitchen Hatch Lane,
Sevenoaks, TN13 3AY.
Web: www.eisa.org.uk

Venture Capital Trust

Venture capitalists can benefit from tax break schemes through a Venture Capital Trust (VCT), which encourages investment in small high-risk companies. The investor subscribes to shares of an eligible VCT (approved by the Inland Revenue), listed as a company on the stock exchange and run by a Fund Manager who invests in a range of eligible small high risk unquoted companies (who are not themselves listed on a stock exchange). This is similar to the Enterprise Investment Scheme with similar tax reliefs but with the benefit of being spread over a larger number of companies and being listed on the London Stock Exchange, providing higher security for the investor. Anyone considering the VCT should consult an accountant or professional in the field.

For VCT approvals contact:

Inland Revenue Savings, Pensions, Share Schemes (IR(SPSS))
Technical Advice (VCT)
St John's House
Merton Road
Bootle
Merseyside, L69 9BB
Tel: 0151 472 6154
Web: www.inlandrevenue.gov.uk

For further information about the Venture Capital Fund, contact the Inland Revenue Small Company Enterprise Centre (SCEC) (details above).

There are several organisations that support Venture Capital activity, which bring companies and investors together and provide further information. These include:

National Business Angels Network (NBAN)

40-42 Cannon Street
London, EC4N 6JJ
Tel: 020 7329 2929
Fax: 020 739 2626
Email: info@bestmatch.co.uk
Web: www.nationalbusinessangels.com

The NBAN aims to assist the equity market by promoting the growth of venture capital in small to medium sized enterprises. It is a non-profit-making organisation, supported by the Small Business Service at the Department of Trade and Industry and is sponsored by high street banks. The network provides a point of contact between businesses and investors and helps each to find a good match. It does this through various services including local programmes, issuing monthly bulletins detailing investment opportunities, and a matching programme between business and investor.

British Venture Capital Association (BVCA)

3 Clements Inn
London, WC2A 2AZ.
Email bvca@bvca.co.uk
Web: www.bvca.co.uk

The BVCA is a representative body for the UK equity industry. It seeks to assist growth in the industry and to provide information, guides and guidelines to encourage high standards among its members. It also produces guides to investment and private equity that can be downloaded from the web site, including information about the Venture Capital trust and the Enterprise Investment Scheme.

European Private Equity and Venture Capital Association (EVCA)

EVCA Secretariat
Mínervastraat 4
B-1930 Zaventem (Brussels)
Belgium
Tel: +32 2 715 00 20
Fax: +32 2 725 07 04
Email: evca@evca.com
Web: www.evca.com

The EVCA is a non-profit-making representative body for the European equity industry. It supports the industry in a number of ways including providing training, influencing public policy, research, publications, organising annual events and promoting high and consistent standards which it's members must follow.

Regional Venture Capital Funds

North East Fund
Northern Enterprise Limited
3 Earls Court
5th Avenue Business Park
Team Valley
Gateshead, NE11 0HF
Tel: 0191 442 4300
Fax: 0191 442 4301

East Midlands Fund
Catapult Venture Managers Limited
35 Park Row
Nottingham, NG1 6EE
Tel: 0115 988 6025
Fax:0115 988 6075

North West Fund
North West Equity Fund
Antler House
Crouchley Lane
Lymm, WA13 0AN
Tel: 01925 759 246
Fax: 01925 759 792

London Fund
London Fund Managers
90 Long Acre
Covent Garden
London, WC2E 9RZ
Tel: 0207 849 3025
Fax: 0207 849 3026

Yorkshire and Humber Fund
Yorkshire Enterprise
Handsworth House
35a Handsworth Road
Sheffield, S9 4AA
Tel: 0114 280 091
Fax: 0114 280 0923

West Midlands Fund
Midven Ltd
PO Box 66, 33 Bennetts Hill
Birmingham, B2 5RJ
Tel: 0121 616 1133
Fax: 0121 616 2223

South West Fund
South West Ventures Ltd
Argentum
510 Bristol Business Park
Coldharbour Lane
Bristol, BS16 1EJ
Tel: 0117 906341
Fax: 0117 9063646

South East Growth Fund
2nd Floor Orbital House
85-87 Croydon Road
Caterham, CR3 6PD
Tel: 01883 337111
Fax: 01883 337112

The aim of the regional venture capital funds are to encourage small scale risk investment from the private sector into small and medium enterprises in the UK. The initiative has been set up by the Small Business Service with funds from the DTI and the EU European Investment Fund. The SBS has appointed Regional Venture Capital Fund Managers with the support of the Regional Development Agencies.

The priorities are to close the equity gap in the Small and Medium Enterprise (SME) market in each of the regions, to increase the amount of equity-based finance available to SMEs, to provide a venture capital fund in each of the regions allowing small investments to be made in SMEs, and to demonstrate and promote the commercial benefits of investing in SMEs.

Eight regional funds have been established with Fund Managers attached, who are responsible for managing and administering the funds, which become operational in March 2003. The Funds are expected to run for ten years with each investment reaching a maximum of £250,000. Investments that follow on from the initial investment may be made, again with a ceiling of £250,000.

Eligible businesses may apply to the Fund Manager in their region. Businesses must meet the EU's definition of a Small and Medium-sized Enterprise. Investments must last longer than 6 months and no longer than 5 years.

KENNETH D BARKER   KINGDOM

Kenneth D Barker's debut went against the notion that the first feature should be modest and not too ambitious, but with backing from an angel investor Kingdom set out to get good returns from the family market. The film is set in the world's last dragon sanctuary and is a modern urban fairy tale with full-blown CGI dragons.

"I'd left film school and was gagging to make a feature. I figured that once I'd made it, at least I could sell copies at the local car-boot if there was no conventional interest. Most members of the public buy feature films, how many of them will buy a short? All the usual funding agencies said 'nice idea — but bugger off'. Then in a strange twist of fortune, I kept meeting all these talented people who were also looking for a break in films or television. They were model makers, make-up artists and computer graphics geeks. That's when I realised *Kingdom* was achievable on a modest budget.

"A month before we were scheduled to start filming, I had £200 and a Hi8 camera to my name, which was not quite enough. It was only after a very convoluted set of circumstances that I heard about a Business Angel network and they were prepared to listen to me. I had a comprehensive business plan I had prepared. All the Angels I spoke to were initially more interested in me as a person, then me as a manager. They wanted to know if I could be trusted with their money — which is a fair way of assessing a risk. Perhaps more importantly, I was genuinely excited about making *Kingdom* and I'm sure my excitement spilt over during my presentation.

"I set up a company and the angel sits on it as a non-executive director. Day to day operations are handled by myself, but we both co-own *Kingdom* and all its rights.

"My advice to any other film maker looking at the Angel route is — be prepared to give up a lot of the project to get it financed, but ideally you need to retain artistic control. Then be grateful that somebody's interested in backing your wild notion." *JM*

Sponsorship

Sponsorship generally involves a business paying an arts organisation in cash or in kind to promote its services through an agreed art production. In the film industry for example, a drinks company may supply free beverages throughout the production period in return for a screen credit. In some cases a producer may also be able to secure a cash payment from a company in return for a screen credit. Adrian J MacDowall's £3000 BAFTA winning short Who's My Favourite Girl has a sponsor credit list at the end of the film longer than that for the cast and crew.

There really is room to be creative when conceiving a sponsorship deal, which could come from a most unlikely source. In fact, a producer may have a better chance of securing a sponsorship deal with a company not directly related to film, as they are not dependent on film-related contracts to provide their bread and butter. The glamour of the film industry might be a more effective pull to a company that is not trying to make its living within it. Yet the sponsor will require something in return for their donation and this can make it difficult for an inexperienced producer to attract sponsorship. They might not have as much to offer the sponsor as an experienced producer with a strong distribution deal. In this situation it may be more advantageous to think low key and seek small contributions that can help relieve the budget, rather than large contributions that would form a substantial part of the budget. However, there are no rules, and a producer shouldn't be put off negotiating ambitious deals if they feel it is appropriate.

Sponsorship advice

First Light, the initiative that brings production companies and young filmmakers together, have produced the following short guide on approaching sponsorship:

"Businesses tend to sponsor arts activities to develop their corporate image in three ways: their relationship with their own employees, their relationship with other companies, and their relationship with their local community. Sponsorship is generally part of a wider marketing strategy and most companies won't sponsor you simply because you are deserving. You should approach potential sponsors with a sense of what you may be able to offer them, of how your film project will help their profile in the community. Sponsorship can be a time-consuming process, often for relatively small amounts of money, which are 'one-offs', so it may be best to focus your energy on getting to understand public funding, rather than pinning all your hopes on private sources. If you do find a sponsor who has never sponsored the arts before, it may be possible to get matching funds from Arts & Business – an organisation which aims to encourage links between the arts and business."

Arts & Business

Arts & Business Head Office:
Nutmeg House
60 Gainsford Street
Butler's Wharf
London, SE1 2NY
Tel: 020 7378 8143
Fax: 020 7407 7527
Email: head.office@AandB.org.uk
Web: www.aandb.org.uk

Arts & Business Cymru/Wales
16 Museum Place
Cardiff, CF10 3BH
Tel: 029 2030 3023
Fax: 029 2030 3024
Email: cymru@AandB.org.uk

North Wales Office
1 - 2 Chapel Street
Llandudno, L30 2SY
Tel: 01492 574003
Email: lorraine.hopkins@AandB.org.uk

Arts & Business East
67 Regent Street
Cambridge, CB2 1AB
Tel: 01223 321421
Fax: 01223 365536
Email: east@AandB.org.uk

Arts & Business East Midlands
Carlton Studios
Lenton Lane
Nottingham, NG7 2NA
Tel: 0115 964 5648
Fax: 0115 964 5488
Email: nottingham@AandB.org.uk

Arts & Business London
Nutmeg House
60 Gainsford Street, Butler's Wharf
London, SE1 2NY
Tel: 020 7378 8143
Fax: 020 7407 7527
Email: london@AandB.org.uk

Arts & Business Northern
The Sponsors Club for Arts & Business
Cale Cross House
156 Pilgrim Street
Newcastle Upon Tyne, NE1 6SU
Tel: 0191 222 0945
Fax: 0191 230 0689
Email: northern@AandB.org.uk

Arts & Business Northern Ireland
53 Malone Road
Belfast, BT9 6RY
Tel: 028 9066 4736
Fax: 028 9066 4500
Email: northern.ireland@AandB.org.uk

Arts & Business North West
127-129 Portland Buildings
Portland Street
Manchester, M1 4PZ
Tel: 0161 236 2058
Fax: 0161 236 2068
Email: north.west@AandB.org.uk

Arts & Business North West
70 Hope Street
Liverpool, L1 9EB
Tel: 0151-709 8780
Fax: 0151-707 0758
Web: www.arts@business.co.uk

Arts & Business Scotland
6 Randolph Crescent
Edinburgh, EH3 7TH
Tel: 0131 220 2499
Fax: 0131 220 2296
Email: scotland@AandB.org.uk

HI Arts
Suites 4/5, 4th Floor
Ballantyne House
84 Academy Street
Inverness, IV1 1LU
Tel: 01463 720 886
Fax: 01463 720 895
Email: inverness@AandB.org.uk

Arts & Business South East
Brighton Office
4 Frederick Terrace
Frederick Place
Brighton, BN1 1AX
Tel: 01273 738 333
Fax: 01273 738 666
Email: south.east@AandB.org.uk

Eastleigh Office
The Point Dance and Arts Centre
Leigh Road
Eastleigh, SO50 9DE
Tel: 023 8061 9172
Fax: 023 8061 9173
Email: south.east@AandB.org.uk

Arts & Business South West
61 Park Street
Bristol, BS1 5NU
Tel: 0117 929 0522
Fax: 0117 929 1756
Email: south.west@AandB.org.uk

Arts & Business West Midlands
Suite 16-18
21 Bennetts Hill
Birmingham, B2 5QP
Tel: 0121 248 1200
Fax: 0121 248 1202
Email: midlands@AandB.org.uk

Arts & Business Yorkshire
Dean Clough
Halifax, HX3 5AX
Tel: 01422 367 860
Fax: 01422 363 254
Email: yorkshire@AandB.org.uk

Arts and Business is an organisation that brings arts and business together, mainly through the promotion of sponsorship as a medium with benefits for both partners. They also offer workshops, advice and publications on sponsorship and business practice as well as matching business professionals with an arts organisation to assist their business development. Arts & Business works with arts organisations including film, however, the organisation must usually be non-profit-making.

Katherine Muller, Arts Manager from Arts & Business London

"There are a number of issues which face film production companies specifically when looking at business sponsorship: one, are you asking for sponsorship or investment? And two, if you are asking for sponsorship up front it can be very difficult to guarantee the outlet for the work. Supporting film work can be extremely risky, and the benefits can be difficult to guarantee (especially exposure and publicity).

"Arts & Business exists to promote the development of creative partnerships between businesses and the arts. We are an UK wide membership organisation, with over 300 business members and over 1,000 arts members. Arts & Business does not directly sponsor any arts organisation or projects directly; we bring the two sectors together to facilitate better understanding and more creative partnerships.

"We certainly do recognise Film & Video as an art form, and our programmes and services are open to those working with this medium. The more defining criteria is actually whether the organisation is set up or constituted as a business (profit making venture) or a not-for-profit organisation. Arts & Business works primarily with the not-for-profit arts sector. However, it is worth contacting your local Arts & Business office - some of our offices do offer more locally sensitive programmes in collaboration with the local development agency, for example.

"In the past we have worked with the Glasgow Film Theatre, Regus London Film Festival, The Script Factory, Edinburgh International Film Festival, Leeds International Film Festival, Out of Sight (East Midlands), Brief Encounters (Bristol), Tricycle Theatre (Ballygowan Film Festival), Barbican (various film festivals), and a range of other organisations across the UK. As you can see from this list, the companies who fit our criteria most effectively are often film festivals or film projects attached to education work."

Product Placement

Product placement has become a common source of finance for US film production budgets and is increasingly being used by UK producers. It works in a similar way to sponsorship in that a company contributes to the production in cash or in kind in return for promotion on screen. However, product placement specifically refers to advertising of a brand name or logo during the main action, literally placing products in the film, rather than crediting a company at the end. As with sponsorship, it is more likely that an experienced producer working on a strong project will secure a product placement deal, because the advertiser will want to ensure as far as possible that the product will be seen. Critics of this form of film finance question the involvement of advertisers in production and how much creative control they can exert over it, anxious that filmmakers do not abandon artistic integrity to get the deal. A very real problem for a director and editor is keeping the required product placement shots in the final cut if they coincide with scenes that they would otherwise choose to cut out. An important factor when considering a product placement deal is how it might affect a television distribution deal. In the UK, for example, the Independent Television Commission (over page) produces guidelines on broadcasting product placement and advertising within programmes.

JACQUELINE SWANSON   **CHECKOUT GIRL**

Rupert Grave's Checkout Girl, staring Pauline Quirk, is a comedy short set in a supermarket. Producer Jacqueline Swanson spent a year raising almost £25,000 in product placement fees, as well as stocking an entire supermarket with produce.

"We were first scheduled to shoot in December of 1998 on an RAF base leased to the US Airforce. The whole place was in the process of being decommissioned but the base commissary (the supermarket) was still open and they were very happy for us to use it as our set over their three-day weekends. About five weeks before we were scheduled to shoot I got a call saying that the LA press office were unable to let us continue. Films shot on US bases need to promote the US armed forces and it's recruitment. In all fairness everyone at the base felt terrible that we had gone so far down the line without being aware of the protocol but in the military I guess rules are rules and we were, unfortunately in breach of them. No amount of script doctoring was going to make us fit their criteria.

"After having to call everyone to cancel the shoot I hid under my duvet for a week before resurfacing to reconsider our position. I reckoned the budget was going to go up by another £25,000 if we were going to even consider building a supermarket. To my surprise when I consulted the key cast and crew they all wanted to continue with the project and were happy to re-discuss their fees further down the line should it be necessary. It would be inappropriate for me to discuss the actual final fees but let's just say that as filmmakers Rupert and I are totally indebted to everyone who worked on the film from our runners and local extras right up to the HoDs and main cast. In a perverse way the production was so big and had so much support I did not really have the option of giving up, although we often felt that we really had bitten off too much.

"Because of Pauline's schedule her next available slot was going to be December 1999 which gave me just under a year to raise the rest of the budget. We had already received production funding from Southern Arts (Rupert was from Southampton) who also then came through with post production funding. I had a very good friend at Saatchi & Saatchi who had put the script forward to a couple of account directors with some positive but ultimately non-committal feedback. Product placement was a fairly uncharted territory at that point. However, when Sunny Delight was about to launch in the UK they had generous budgets and more scope for taking risks. It was pretty much left to me to structure the deal and suggest a fee. Although it was a significant amount for the production it really was not a big commitment for the agency so the whole process was fairly straightforward. I had suggested a four-tier payment structure; a sum on first day of photography, another on completion of shoot, a third on sale to a UK broadcaster and the final instalment on sale to a US broadcaster or Trans Atlantic in-flight entertainment programme. We also received product placement monies from HP Beans. That was also fairly straightforward. I explained to them how much the set was costing to build and asked them for a portion of the costs up front. They were happy with my proposal in the knowledge that their product was going to 'colour' the film rather than the distinctive colour of their main competitors. " *TF*

Independent Television Commission (ITC)

33 Foley Street
London W1W 7TL
Tel: 0845 601 3608
Fax: 0207 306 7800
Web: www.itc.org.uk

When considering a product placement deal a producer must also consider broadcasting advertising regulations, as contravening them could hamper a television distribution deal. In the UK this is handled by the Independent Television Commission. They produce the ITC Code of Programme Sponsorship, issued in Autumn 2000 and updated regularly. Although most of the document is concerned with television production, the regulations are applicable' to films acquired for television broadcast but the stipulations are a little more flexible. The full regulations can be accessed and downloaded from the ITC web site.

These regulations may be subject to change towards the end of the year when the ITC is due to become part of Ofcom, the new Office of Communications, which will merge five organisations into one regulating body for the communications industry. In addition to the ITC, the entity will incorporate the Broadcasting Standards Commission, Oftel, The Radio Authority, and the Radiocommunications Agency. The transitional web site for Ofcom www.ofcom.org.uk will have further details closer to the time.

Product Placement Companies

EC&M European Communications & Media Ltd
419 N Larchmont, Boulevard #107
Los Angeles, CA 90004, USA
Tel: +001 323 512 8011, or +001 818 679 7011
Fax: +001 323 512 8511
Email: enquiry@propsonfilm.com
Web: www.propsonfilm.com

1st Place Product Props
Bridge House, Three Mills Studios
Three Mill Lane, Bromley-By-Bow
London, E3 3DZ
Tel: 020 8227 1111
Fax: 020 8227 1114
Email: steve@1stplaceprops.com
Web: www.firstplaceprops.com

Hatched Brands
The Garden, 5A Sterndale Rd
London, W14 0HT
Tel: 020 7603 6343
Fax: 020 7603 6343
Email: phatchedbrands@aol.co.uk
Web: www.hatchedbrands.com

Pro.ag.anda Limited
Teddington Studios
Broom Rd, Teddington Lock
Teddington, TW11 9NT
Tel: 020 8614 2261
Fax: 020 8614 2367
Email: props@prop-teddington.com

Rogers & Cowan
Fox Court, 14 Gray's Inn Road
London , WC1X 8WS
Tel: 0870 990 5422
Fax: 0870 990 5465
Web: www.rogersandcowan.com

CLARE PRINGLE   ROGERS & COWAN

Rogers and Cowan is the entertainment public relations division of Weber Shandwick, promoting films and music, organising events, deals with PR for celebrities, and arranging corporate and consumer marketing, including product placement. Account Executive Clare Pringle outlines how they may help UK filmmakers structure a deal.

How long has Rogers & Cowan organised product placement deals for film?

Rogers & Cowan was founded in Hollywood in the 1950's when the industry first started and expanded to the UK in 1989. It is worth pointing out that here in the UK we currently specialise in brand placement (the placement of branded products in TV/film productions as a free loan without any payment to the production company) as opposed to product placement (the inclusion of branded items in a film in return for payment to the production company). However, we are able to organise product placement deals for film should UK clients wish to participate in this capacity.

Do you tend to work with films of a certain budget minimum?

Although we tend not to discriminate against productions with a low budget and have secured placements for clients in a wide variety of film productions with varying budgets, it is obviously more desirable to secure placements in high profile productions that will bring in a high level of exposure of the clients products. Rogers & Cowan focus on the actual placement opportunity e. g. placement of products with lead character's, active ('hero') placements where the products are physically handled and scripted placements.

Can low budget films benefit from product placement deals?

Low budget films can certainly benefit from brand placement - the loan of props for free due to the fact that they are on a low budget and this can therefore reduce costs of props. It is likely that clients reserve their budgets for higher budget films, which will reach larger audiences. It may be desirable for low budget films to try and secure product placement deals to supplement their funding.

Is product placement used much in the UK film Industry?

Product placement is now used substantially in big-budget UK films as production companies need to make their production look as realistic as possible and we do live in an age where we come into contact with hundreds of brands everyday. In *About A Boy*, for example, Audi secured the placement of an Audi TT to be used by Hugh Grant (and maximised the impact of this placement by running a competition with the Daily Telegraph offering readers the chance to win the car driven by Grant). The important thing is that the placement should match both character and plot line. Otherwise, it looks too much like a placed advert and has much less impact.

What advice would you give a UK producer interested in seeking product placement?

Identify the main products that could be featured in the film (that will enhance the reality aspect of the production), approach the agency that represents that client with the script and a proposal that outlines what sort of coverage the product(s) may expect to receive, character information as well as costs etc. Negotiations will then commence so that a placement deal can be reached that takes into account client budget, coverage, cross marketing. All this will depend on how big a presence the film will have in cinemas, and shelf life of videos etc. *CH*

Major UK Film Companies

BBC

BBC Television Centre
Wood Lane
London, W12 7RJ
Tel: 020 8743 8000

BBC Films
1 Mortimer Street
London, W1T 3JA
Tel: 020 7765 0091
Fax: 020 7765 0194

Web:
www.bbc.co.uk
www.bbc.co.uk/talent
www.bbc.co.uk/bbcfilms
www.bbc.co.uk/commissioning
www.bbc.co.uk/writersroom

The BBC began as an independent radio broadcaster in the 1920's, financed from the outset by the licence fee, a means to keep the organisation independent of commercial and political involvement and pressure. In the 1930's television was introduced to the BBC service.

Film producers can approach the BBC with finished features, or they can approach BBC Films with a project in development. There are also various ways that emerging talent can work with the BBC through the production and writing initiatives promoted online in the Writers Room and the Talent site.

BBC Acquisitions

Who do they work with?

The department deals with independent producers, distributors and sales agents, and inevitably they are offered a lot of product, a large proportion from the US.

How do they work with independent producers?

Generally, the acquisitions department will look at finished product, rather than dealing in pre-sales on unfinished films. Unfinished and new projects would usually be deferred to BBC Films.

How should producers approach them?

They do accept unsolicited material and producers should send in a finished film on tape.

What are they looking for?

Steve Jenkins, senior editor of films in feature film acquisitions says, "we would assess their usefulness to us, i.e. would they easily find a slot in our schedules, and if appropriate, make an offer of a certain amount, based on length of licence, number of runs, rights granted, etc."

BBC Films

Headed by David Thompson, BBC Films has been a major producer of UK films, expanding investment since the successes of *Billy Elliot* and *Last Resort* in 2000. BBC backed films released in 2003 include *Heart Of Me* and *I Capture the Castle*; and in 2002, *Anita & Me, Dirty Pretty Things, Iris, Morvern Caller* and *Sweet Sixteen*.

Who do they work with?

They work with new and established producers as co-producers. Over 2003, BBC films have between six and eight co-production slated for production and release. In 2002, they co-produced seven projects.

How do they work with independent producers?

BBC Films suggest that a new producer work with an experienced producer, depending on the scale of the project.

How should producers approach them?

They do accept unsolicited material from writers and producers, and will read everything sent to them, though newer

PAWEL PAWLIKOWSKI   **LAST RESORT**

Pawel Pawlikowski's feature debut, Last Resort, is that rare combination – a critically acclaimed BAFTA winner that made a good profit for its producers. The average British feature film takes around £350,000 at the box office. Pawel managed to shoot his first feature for less than that with a surprising amount of freedom from the BBC.

"We went to the drama department of the BBC and told them that if they gave us a certain amount of money then we'd come back with an interesting film. I'd done a lot of documentaries that had won a lot of awards before so I had kudos. Anyway we went away and came back with a drama but if you want to be successful you need to have an executive who believes in the thing and will push it - whose career depends on it. The guy who commissioned the thing left the Beeb just afterwards and then the guy who replaced him didn't really know what to do with it because it wasn't his baby.

"It was a documentary budget of around £320,000 - a lot more has been spent since, but shooting that low meant that I had complete freedom. It meant we were very sparing with extras and because we didn't have any sort of production design budget we just stripped the locations down and shot in a particular way, that's why it feels like such a weird place. We rented this house for the cast and crew to stay in to save money and so we could be together. Dina Korzun (Tanya) would come to me in the middle of the night saying 'I don't understand this scene, can we just imagine it again'? Her and Paddy Considine (Alfie) became partners and a lot of the scenes were invented the day before or on the day.

"One of the things about this film, taught by bitter experience in the past - I only worked with close friends and people that I liked. It wasn't necessary to have a great track record; I needed very generous people because it was a pretty risky project. We didn't have much of a script so we would re jig certain scenes while we were shooting. If I'd been with normal British professionals it would have been a nightmare. They would have wanted a perfect script and just executed the plan whereas I had a tiny documentary group who all lived in one house and they were all very, very supportive.

"I tried to short-circuit the system. When you make a film here or in any western country it's all about rewrites and script editors, it becomes a collective effort but the more people get involved the more formulaic it becomes. So we just tried to get a small amount of money and make the film without getting other people involved. The funny thing is the way the media works, it's more important to have a media image than to make a good film.

"England - it's a funny country where you are conned into believing that everything is booming, London is moving and the youth culture is fantastic. And yet everyone carries a misery and total despondency with them. It's a society where all the belief systems have disappeared, where families have collapsed and where joie de vivre has vanished. The simple pleasures just aren't there unless it's drugs or music and it's a very abstract environment. You wouldn't believe that if you were in Soho but that is all just window dressing, it's a very grizzly, empty country and I find that interesting. The question is how to tell a story in an environment like this - I think I've found the key to it. The problem with English films, I don't enjoy watching them actually, is that they just deal with sociology. They translate this (indicating the environment) into social problems, people are miserable because they are unemployed and they all embody some particular social type. Very few English directors look at what's underneath the surface of society." *TF*

writers should apply to the New Writing Initiative (see below). A new producer should submit the source material (if the project is based on a pre-existing work), a treatment or outline, a sample of the writer's work, or suggestions for writers and directors. BBC films says, "We are very accessible; our address is not a secret and we often answer our phones; we have a reputation for responding swiftly; it's best to have something to send us to read - cold verbal pitching is often the trickiest way of trying to get an idea across. People often feel that pitching is obligatory because that's what they do in LA, but it's not really a part of the culture here." They receive over 1000 projects per year in different stages of development.

What are they looking for?

BBC Films says, this is "very difficult to answer, but we are always looking for something that feels different (*Dirty Pretty Things*), hugely entertaining (*Tomorrow la Scala*), of national interest or importance (*Out of Control*, *In This World*), or all of the above (*The Gathering Storm*). Oh, and they have to be really good, too."

The New Writing Initiative

The New Writing Initiative is a scheme that welcomes and identifies new writing talent for all fields of BBC activity, including television, radio, and film. New writers are sought out through agents, readings, and contacts with theatres and films schools. They ask writers to inform them about any forthcoming readings, productions or screenings of their work, and they also accept unsolicited scripts (but only by post to the New Writer's Initiative at the BBC Writer's Room, contact details as above). Scripts will be assessed for their quality and suitability and recommended to the relevant BBC department.

A particular scheme, Northern Exposure, running in the North of England funds writers-in-residence schemes, workshops, master classes, and so on, by working with theatres, film groups and arts organisations.

BBC Talent

BBC Talent regularly holds initiatives to find new talent in writing, directing, presenting, acting and so on. The website (www.bbc.co.uk/talent) holds up-to-date information on any schemes that may currently be in operation.

Channel 4

124 Horseferry Road
London, SW1P 2TX
Tel: 020 7396 4444

Web:
www.channel4.com
www.channel4.com/4producers
www.channel4.com/film
www.ideasfactory.com

Channel 4 was launched in 1982 and is funded by commercial revenue. Film producers work primarily with FilmFour and FilmFour Lab, and may approach Channel 4 Acquisitions department with a finished feature. There are many opportunities for filmmakers to work with the broadcaster through FilmFour and Channel 4 production initiatives.

Channel 4 Acquisitions

Who do they work with?

They will accept material from producers, sales agents and distributors.

How do they work with independent producers?

Channel 4 says, "we acquire feature films which have had UK theatrical release, and these can range from studio pictures to independent films."

How should producers approach them?

Producers should send in a cover letter and VHS screening copy of the film in the first instance. However, producers should note that Channel 4 deals "with the person or organisation who holds the UK TV rights;

this generally tends to be a sales agent/ distributor rather than the producer directly. If a producer has a distributor, then that organisation should contact us rather than the producer."

What are they looking for?

They deal with acquiring feature films and live action and narrative fiction short films as long as they are under 25 minutes. On average, 900 films will be acquired and scheduled each year. In particular they "are looking for strong titles which have made an impact at the UK box office and/or are editorially appropriate for the various film slots on Channel 4."

FilmFour

FilmFour was closed as an independent company in 2002 and brought back in house as an internal Channel 4 department headed up by Tessa Ross, ex-head of C4 drama and producer of *Billy Elliot*. She has a budget of £10 million a year to invest in films, typically as a part-financier with third party distribution. Projects are likely to feel closer to the young and contemporary C4 brand and the Channel 4 Films heyday of *Trainspotting* and *My Beautiful Launderette*, than high budget, high risk, international projects such as *Charlotte Gray*.

Through Peter Carlton, Head of FilmFour Lab, FilmFour will continue to commission fresh and edgy low-budget features from the newest and most striking talents working in and with the UK.

FilmFour releases in 2003 included *The Actors, Buffalo Soldiers, The Emporer's New Clothes* and *Bodysong*; and in 2002 *Birthday Girl, Charlotte Gray, Crush, Once Upon A Time In The Midlands* and *The Warrior*.

Releases for 2004 include *Motorcycle Diaries, Touching the Void* and *It's All About Love*

Julliette Howell, Head of Development for Film Four

Who do you work with?

We work primarily with Independent Producers who will have their own relationships with writers and directors which we can support. We welcome fresh ideas from both established and newer producers.

How do you work with independent producers?

We work with producers at all levels. We have a very proactive development approach, and sometimes ideas will come to us at a very early stage and we will work closely with the producer on the development of a project, including the choice of writer/director/on-screen talent. It is also possible for producers to approach us at a much later stage looking for additional co-production funding.

How should producers approach you?

We like projects/ideas to be submitted in hard copy to Tessa Ross, Head of Film Four or myself, Juliette Howell, Head of Development, and prefer not to receive submissions via email. As detailed above this can happen at all stages of development.

What are you looking for?

Primarily British based, contemporary stories which if not these things, must resonate with a modern British audience. All ideas should be bold and distinctive with a strong sense of identity. We aim to work with both established and emerging film makers across a broad range of material which should feel fresh and original, but also have a commercial edge.

ROBIN GUTCH
FILM FOUR LAB

Film Four Lab was one of the survivors when Film Four was scaled back in 2002. Under Robin Gutch's stewardship, the Lab has pioneered digital work with films such as My Brother Tom. Robin left in April 2003 to join Blast! Films and the post is now taken by Peter Carlton

"We set up Film Four Lab as a focus point in the company primarily on filmmakers about to embark on their first feature or those still doing shorts but who we wanted to keep an eye on for the future. So primarily it's a new talent focus for the production division but from a FilmFour point of view it's a great place to build lasting relationships with filmmakers. At the end of the day, talent is the motor of the industry; no talent, no films.

"That's the key motivation but obviously there are other parts to it. One of them being Channel 4's statutory remit to work with new talent, work with people outside London and to be a multicultural outlet. In film terms that's easier to do, within a lower budget, new talent form. The other part is that FilmFour is a part of the film industry and for the industry to progress you have to have a bigger talent base."

LOW BUDGET

"I don't think we'll bring budgets down hugely by fetishising digital technology. It can be part of the answer but we take a slightly different stance in that, in budgeting a film we include the cost of the blow-up.

"I think fundamentally it's about trying to find the depth and the cinematic and emotional scale akin to someone like Ridley Scott without using the big, expensive equipment. It is hard but that's the essence of it and I think there's a danger of jumping to digital because it will bring costs down - it may be a little cheaper but there are other factors.

"Yes, you need to have directors who can work that bit faster and even actors who are prepared to muck in. Of course, budgets can always be brought down if people are prepared to be paid a little less but generally it's about finding good stories that aren't necessarily dependent on huge apparatus.

"An example would be Darren Aronofsky's *Pi*. That would be an ideal film, in terms of size and depth and amazing new talent, for FilmFour Lab. It was also made very cheaply and admittedly, most of the people that worked on it were only going to be paid off the back end. But then 98% of those low budget films are not going to find distribution so, now there are 100's if not 1000's of filmmakers saying to themselves, 'my film hasn't got into Sundance, what am I going to do now?'"

APPLICATIONS

"Ideally, people should attach to a letter some examples of their work and some semblance of their idea. The most common mistake is, 'Dear Robin, I attach the first draft of my script.'

"The reason that's a mistake, even if it's a short, is that you have to take a very close look at why they are doing the short, who's going to manage the money etc. Nobody puts money into a project without a great deal of understanding and knowledge of who it is, for fairly obvious reasons. A lot of people feel, and it's fair enough, that they don't have enough experience and don't want to draw attention to it, so they put nothing down. Of course you then know that you are dealing with someone with no experience. The key objective if you really are outside is just crossing the threshold with somebody, whether it be someone at the BBC or an agent." *TF*

AMANDA POSEY

FEVER PITCH

Amanda Posey started out at Palace Pictures, and oversaw films such as the Crying Game and Interview with a Vampire before becoming Head of Development at Scala. She went on to produce the profitable British feature Fever Pitch with Film Four through her production company Wildgaze.

"*Fever Pitch* opened on about 220 screens, which is a big release, but the very big American movies will open on 350 - 400 screens. FilmFour tested it and that's what gave them the conviction to put a certain amount of money behind it. They spent nearly £1m promoting it and it cost £1.8m to make. You'll never recoup that theatrically but where they made that back was on video because they'd raised the profile so high theatrically. Meanwhile, they were effectively buying themselves a high profile TV broadcast - this was in the days before FilmFour channel - it's just a business, they have to make the pieces of the puzzle fit. That was all without international sales which they did well with too.

"The problem comes with the big percentages that get taken off from commission. It has taken something like £3m in actual income but once you take off the commission that FilmFour International took from selling it abroad, and the advertising and promotional budget then it comes down and it's not officially in profit. In terms of the channel they've paid almost nothing for a television broadcast in comparative terms, so for them it's very successful.

"Very few people on the creative side have the exposure to the marketing and distribution so they don't know what choices have to be made when putting out a trailer or devising a poster or deciding where to place the ad. I was lucky in that I started in Palace Pictures which went under for all sorts of reasons but it was then the biggest independent distributor and producer. You got to see the film from start to finish, so whether it succeeded or failed you learnt lessons throughout. I remember Steve Woolley having huge trouble with *The Crying Game*. No-one wanted to finance that film and he ended up using cash from the Scala cinema and the connected video shop just to live day to day.

"You can't rely on anybody else to tell you how to make your movie or to tell you why your movie is going to be any good. If you expect other people to give you money, it's a lot of money and a lot of time and commitment, you have to convey to them that you know what your audience is even if they don't know. And you have to be able to back it up. If you know there are millions of teenagers out there desperate to see your film then go online, do your research and get your statistics. So many independent filmmakers have the passion but not the interpretation that convinces those with the money that there is some commercial, and I don't mean formulaic, but financially sound reason to make it and that you are trying to reach a certain audience. What's often levelled at British filmmakers is that they don't give a fuck who their audience is and I think that's something that should be focused on." *NW*

Channel 4 Production Schemes

AIR

www.a-i-r.info

The Animator in Residence scheme is an annual joint initiative between Channel 4 and the BFI which has been running for twelve years. The scheme invites animators resident in the UK to submit a proposal comprising a story outline and storyboard drawings for a three minute animated film as well as a VHS showreel to be judged by a panel of professional animators, writers and producers.

Four animators will be selected to work on their proposal for a three month residency in the new animation booth at the London IMAX Cinema with £1600 for materials and £3000 grant. At the end of the residency the animators are asked to present their idea to Channel 4 with a full storyboard, a completed script, an explanation of the soundtrack and how it will be produced, around one minute of animation, film or video which has been produced during the residency and an animatic of the film. Channel 4 will consider each proposal for further development and broadcast.

ANIMATE!

www.animateonline.org

This animation funding scheme has been running since 1990, a joint initiative between Channel 4 and the Arts Council of England, managed by Finetake. There is an annual call for entries with a deadline in March inviting applications from artists, animators, emerging talent, and collaborations between artists of different media. Four to six entries will be chosen to produce an animation film on a budget between £5000 and £30,000 over a period of no longer than 14 months. Animation in this case is given a broad definition encompassing a range of techniques and technologies excluding live-action.

The films must be made in the UK, be no more than six minutes long, with a 16:9 widescreen aspect ratio. Applicants must

be resident in the UK and students may not apply. Entries should be made in the form of a treatment of an animation idea and include a schedule, a budget, a full or sample storyboard, a script, additional artwork, application form and examples of past work. Proposals will be judged for creativity, originality, suitability for a television audience, and the likelihood of achieving the idea within budget and schedule. The applicant's previous work will be assessed for artistic and technical quality.

The completed films will be broadcast up to three times on Channel 4, streamed on the Animate! Web site, may be internationally distributed on DVD and copies deposited to the National Film & Television Archive.

MESH

www.channel4.com/mesh

This is an annual joint initiative between Channel 4 and NESTA to produce computer generated animation and interactive fiction by emerging talent. Each September digital animators resident in the UK are invited to submit a proposal for a three minute digital film by sending in a synopsis, a storyboard of the first few scenes, an idea of the technique to be used, a VHS showreel, a CV a SAE and submission form.

Six proposals will be selected for further development with mentors and masterclasses over five months. At the end of this time four projects will be commissioned to be completed and broadcast in autumn on TV and online.

VIRO

www.channel4.com/viro

Channel 4 launched this joint initiative with the Film Council's New Cinema Fund in 2002. Through the interactive web site, filmmakers are guided through the making of a viral film – short punchy films that use word of mouth email as distribution – and are invited to submit them to the web site. Applicants must email the film, the director's and applicant's details, a short biography, the viral film title and summary, and the applicant's career plans.

Working Title

Oxford House
76 Oxford Street
London, W1B 1BS
Tel: 0207 307 3000
Web: www.workingtitlefilms.com

Working Title is one of the leading European film producers. Co-chaired by Tim Bevan and Eric Fellner, the duo have produced a host of successful British comedies including *Notting Hill*, *Bridget Jones Diary*, *High Fidelity*, *Four Weddings and a Funeral* and *Bean*; as well as Oscar winners *Elizabeth*, *Dead Man Walking* and *Fargo*. In 1999 the outfit closed a five-year $600m output deal with Universal Studios, after it bought up PolyGram whom Working Title had formerly worked with. At the time of the deal Working Title productions had grossed almost $1bn worldwide from less than $200m investment, making the duo one the world's most bankable producer teams. Releases in 2002 included *The Guru*, *40 Days and 40 Nights* and *About A Boy*; in 2003, *Johnny English*, *Love Actually* and *Ned Kelly*; and in 2004, *Thunderbirds* and *Wimbledon*. The company is also committed to producing lower budget films through their division, WT2, which came to attention with *Billy Elliot* in 2000. WT2 releases include *My Little Eye*, *Long Time Dead* and *Ali G In Da House* in 2002, and *The Calcium Kid* in 2003.

Who do they work with?

They work with both new and experienced producers.

How do they work with independent producers?

They will be creatively involved in any project they co-produce, but the level of involvement depends on the circumstances of the individual production.

How should producers approach them?

They will deal with producers directly or through a writer's or director's agent. The project can be at any stage of development at outline, screenplay stage, or close to production. Producers should approach Working Title with an outline, a pitch or a screenplay, depending on the stage of the project. They say that "it's dependent on the nature of the material and the talent involved whether it's something we would get involved in very early on, or whether we would prefer to see a draft first."

What are they looking for?

Working Title films say they are looking for "original material, or a fresh angle. Sometimes the attachment of an exciting new director or a key piece of cast can make a difference". They give this advice for new producers: "focus on UK or European based films. Take time to unearth the exciting emerging writers and directors that bigger production companies may not have come across. Think laterally in terms of sourcing projects. Don't rush development, and don't abandon the script the moment it looks like your funding has fallen into place. It can always be made better."

The Lottery Franchises

In 1997, three film consortia, DNA Films, The Film Consortium and Pathé UK were chosen by the Arts Council from thirty other bids to act as mini-studios with lottery money, with the intention they would produce ninety features between them over six years. DNA Films headed by Duncan Kenworthy and Andrew Macdonald was awarded £29m to make an expected sixteen films. The Film Consortium, made up of independent production companies, Greenpoint, Parrallax, Scala and Skreba, was awarded £33.5m to make an expected thirty nine features. Pathé UK was awarded £33.1m to make an expected 35 films. By mid-2003 DNA had delivered five films, Pathé had delivered fifteen and The Film Consortium sixteen.

Franchise funding expires in 2003 and it is not expected that these contracts will be renewed, although the franchises will continue to develop and produce features with independent producers.

DNA Films

DNA Films
3rd Floor
75/77 Margaret Street
London, SE1 2PP
Tel: 020 7291 8010
Fax: 020 7291 8020
Web: www.dnafilms.com

DNA credits include *28 Days Later, The Parole Officer, Strictly Sinatra* and *Beautiful Creatures*. 2003 releases include Heartlands and *The Final Curtain*.

Who do they work with?

They work with first time and established writers, producers and directors from film television and theatre.

How do they work with independent producers?

The company Producers Andrew Macdonald, Duncan Kenworthy and Allon Reich act as executive producers on the films made with independent producers. DNA can fully finance films with budgets up to $15m.

How should producers approach them?

They will not accept unsolicited material and should be contacted through a literary agent or production company. Production companies should make an initial contact with the project idea, rather than sending in a script.

What are they looking for?

They are looking for British films of any genre. Priority is for high quality writing, contemporary stories with commercial appeal.

The Film Consortium

4th Floor
Portland House
Great Portland Street
London W1W BQJ
Tel: 020 7612 0030
Fax: 020 7612 0031
Web: www.civiliancontent.com

The Film Consortium was created by a consortium of production companies that joined in their bid for the lottery franchise in 1998; Greenpoint Films, Scala Productions, Parallax Films and Skreba films, together with the then Virgin Cinemas Group. Films that have benefited from the franchise include *Hideous Kinky* (1998), *Hold Back the Night* (1999), and *The Lost Son* (1999) with 30% of their budgets financed by the lottery funds. Film Consortium backed films released in 2002 included *24 Hour Party People, Sweet Sixteen, Bend it Like Beckham, Dust* and *The Intended*.

Who do they work with?

New and established producers, writers and directors. Producers must have writers in place.

How do they work with independent producers?

Established producers are expected to have already sourced part of the finance for the film. The Film Consortium will act as executive producer on films where it works with a third party.

How should producers approach them?

They do not accept unsolicited material, and must be approached through a production company or agent. Production companies should make an initial contact with the business plan and the script or treatment.

What are they looking for?

They are looking for British films with strong commercial potential, intended for the cinema and of a high creative standard.

Pathé UK

Kent House
Market Place
London, W1W 8AR
Tel: 020 7462 4400
Web: www.pathe.co.uk

Pathé UK is part of the French production and distribution company Pathé Entertainment. Films to result from that franchise include Loves Labours Lost, Ratcatcher and Deathwatch in 2000; Talk to Her and Resident Evil in 2002; and The Pianist in 2003.

Who do they work with?

Pathé UK is involved in production and distribution in France and the UK, working with emerging and established talent.

How do they work with independent producers?

Their involvement depends on the project and experience of the producers and key talent. They do not accept projects for distribution unless they have been involved in the production process.

How should producers approach them?

They do not accept unsolicited material and must be approached through an agent or a production company.

What are they looking for?

They are looking for projects with strong commercial potential and of high creative standard, intended for international theatrical release. They do not work with low budget productions.

Selected Other Major UK Producers

Aardman Animation

Gas Ferry Road
Bristol, BS1 6UN
Tel: 0117 984 8485
Fax: 0117 984 8486
Web: www.aardman.com

Films include: Wallace & Gromit TBA, Chicken Run 2000, Minotaur and Little Nerkin 1999, Hum Drum 1998, Al Dente 1998, Owzat 1997, Angry Kid 1995

Bardot Films

28 Dover Park Drive
London, SW15 5BG
Tel: 020 8788 5152
Fax: 020 8789 9239
Email: bardotfilms@aol.com
Web: www.moviemgt.com

Films include: God's Spy TBA, A Different Loyalty TBA, Shooting Star TBA, Nautica TBA, Bedazzled 2002, Arabian Nights 2001, GI Jane 1999, White Squall 1998

The Bureau

3rd Floor, 28 Goodge St
London, W1T 2QQ
Tel: 020 7580 8182
Fax: 020 7580 8185
Email: the.bureau@virgin.net
Web: www.thebureau.co.uk

Films include: Despite All Due Respect 2003, Noi Abino 2002, Ten Minutes Older The Cello 2002, The Warrior 2002

Company Pictures

Suffolk House
1-8 Whitfield Place
London, W1T 5JU
Tel: 020 7380 3900
Fax: 020 7380 1166
Email: enquiries@companypictures.co.uk
Web: www.companypictures.co.uk

Films include: Morvern Caller 2002, A Room For Romeo Brass 1999, Titanic Town 1998

Ecosse Films

Brigade House
8 Parsons Green
London, SW6 4TN
Tel: 020 7371 0290
Fax: 020 7736 3436
Email: webmail@ecossefilms.com
Web: www.ecossefilms.com

Films include: Charlotte Gray 2002, Mrs Brown 1997

Eon Productions

138 Picadilly
London, W1Z 9FH
Tel: 020 7493 7953
Fax: 020 7408 1236

Producers of the James Bond franchise

Fragile Films

95-97 Dean St
London, W1N 3XX
Tel: 020 7287 6200
Fax: 020 7287 0069
Email: fragile@fragilefilms.com

Films include: The Importance of Being Earnest 2002, High Heels And Low Lives 2001, Kevin And Perry Go Large 2000, An Ideal Husband 1999, Spiceworld 1998

Gabriel Films

2nd Floor, The Pierce Institute
840 Govan Road
Glasgow, G51 3UU
Tel : 0141 445 5255
Web: www.gabrielfilms.co.uk

Films include: The Bothy 2003, Vicious Circle TBA, The Silence TBA, Wild Country TBA, Passing Places TBA, Afterlife TBA, Legion TBA

Gruber Films

Office No. 2 Sheraton Street
London, W1F 8BH
Tel: 020 8703 669313
Email: richard.holmes@gruberfilms.com
Web: www.gruberfilms.com

Films include: The Abduction Club 2002, Dead Babies 2000, Waking Ned 1999, Shooting Fish 1998, Soft Top Hard Shoulder 1993

Great British Films

3rd Floor, Hanover House
118 Queens Road
Brighton, BN1 3XG
Tel: 01273 324 122
Fax 01273 326 077
Email: info@johnscottco.com
Web: www.greatbritishfilms.com

Films include: Napolean/Bonaparte TBA, Honour Thy Father TBA, Taking Sides TBA, Plots With A View TBA, Babyjuice Express TBA, Married/Unmarried TBA, Anazapta TBA, Mr Inbetween TBA, Bollywood Queen 2002.

Heyday Films

5 Denmark Street
London, WC2H 8LP
Tel: 020 783 6333
Fax: 020 7836 6444
Email: office@heydayfilms.demon.co.uk

Films include: Harry Potter and the Chamber of Secrets 2002, Harry Potter and the Philosopher's Stone 2001

Kuhn and Co Ltd

5a Noel Street
London, W1F 8GE
Tel: 020 7292 3920
Fax: 020 7287 6860

Films include: Sin Eater 2003, Wondrous Oblivion 2003

Impact Pictures

3 Percy Street
London, W1T 1DE
Tel: 020 7636 7716
Fax: 020 7636 7814
Email: production@impactpix.com

Films include: Resident Evil 2002, The Hole 2001, there's Only One Jimmy Grimble 2000, Stiff Upper Lips 1998, Soldier 1998, Event Horizon 1997

The Jim Henson Company

30 Oval Road
Camden
London, NW1 7DE
Tel: 020 7428 4000
Fax: 020 7428 4001
Web: www.henson.com

Films include: Rat 2000, The Adventures of Elmo in Grouchland 1999, Muppets From Space 1999,

Little Bird (UK)

9 Grafton Mews,
London, W1P 5LG
Tel: 020 7380 3980
Fax: 020 7380 3981
Web: www.littlebird.ie

Films include: Bridget Jones' Diary 2000, Invincible 2000, Gangster No.1 2000, Ordinary Decent Criminal 1999, Joyriders 1998, Croupier 1998

MARK HERBERT   WARP FILMS

Faced with late night only broadcasts of the Aphex Twin's Come to Daddy video, music label Warp elected to sell the video direct to Aphex Twin and Warp fans as a video. This was so successful that the strategy was repeated with the follow-up single Windowlicker. To date, the Come to Daddy and Windowlicker videos have accumulated sales of 90,000 units worldwide. Warp Films, headed by Mark Herbert, launched in 2002, producing Chris Morris' first short film, My Wrongs 8245-8249 and 117, which won the BAFTA for Best short in 2003 and looks set to make a good return from DVD sales. Following this the company is developing a feature project with Chris Cunningham, with the ink drying on contracts for a new Shane Meadows film as this book went to print.

"We got *My Wrongs 8245-8249 and 117* into the top ten of both HMV and Virgin, as a standalone DVD with some nice extras on it. By the end of March we'd sold 12,500 units, more than many British features. If you've got something quality enough it shouldn't matter that the film is a short. In all other arts things aren't judged on size: you get great paintings, small or big; albums of 30 and 90 minutes. Why should everything be a short or feature, it should suit whatever the artist wants to do? If its 15 minutes but good enough we think there's a market for it. Obviously Chris Morris and Warp have a fan-base, but both wholesalers and distributors have now seen that DVD is changing the market for shorts slightly – there's the Cinema 16 DVD which has shown there is a market for the right shorts.

"We're at a time with a bit of a revolution happening in the industry, DV cameras are coming right down in price, Final Cut Pro is getting more advanced. The problem has always been distribution – self-produced DVD releases hopefully mean you won't have to get distribution. Apple has an authoring programme so you can do the whole lot in your bedroom: edit and press DVDs.

"We got a NESTA grant to kick-start Warp Films of which we used a portion to make My Wrongs, we should recoup but it won't make a profit. The film cost more than £100,000 – the post production took up the majority of that because of the talking dog. Most films we do will be for far less than that.

"Right now we're working on a Shane Meadows feature, *Skull*, we've stripped it right down – stripped the crew right down. Budgets and particularly crew are too high and big in this country. It's fine for certain films because sometimes we need that, but in most cases why do you need 75 people to make a film? The Europeans and particularly the South Americans have proved you can do it on far less. This should cost less than three-quarters of a million, and will be shot on film. It's being financed by FilmFour, regional funding and private equity." *NW*

Passion Pictures (documentaries)

3rd & 4th Floors
County House
33-34 Rathbone Place
London, W1T 1JN
Tel: 020 7323 9933
Fax: 020 7323 9030
Email: info@passion-pictures.com
Web: www.passion-pictures.com

Films include: Live Forever 2003, Game of Their Lives 2002, Sneaker Freaks 2002, One Day In September 2000

Pipedeam Pictures

3-5 Barrett Street
London, W1U 1AY
Tel: 020 7486 7848
Fax: 020 7486 7748
Email: info@pipedreampictures.com
Web: www.pipedreampictures.com

Films include: Knickers TBA, Smoke on the Water TBA, Glimpse TBA, Crush 2002

Recorded Picture Company

24 Hanway Street
London, W1T 1UH
Tel: 020 7636 2251
Fax: 020 7636 2261
Email: rpc@recordedpitcutre.com
Web: www.recordedpicture.com

Films include: The Dreamers 2003, Young Adam 2003, The Triumph of Love 2001, The Brother 2001, Sexy Beast 2001

Samuelson Productions

13 Manette Street
London, W1D 4AW
Tel: 020 7439 4900
Fax: 020 7439 4901
Email: samuelsonP@aol.com

Films include: The Gathering 2003, Gabriel & Me 2001, Guest House Paradiso 2000, The Commissioner 1999, Arlington Road 1999, Wilde 1998, Tom & Viv 1995

Sarah Radclyffe Productions Ltd

5th Floor
83/84 Berwick Street
London, W1F 8TS
Tel: 020 7437 3128
Fax: 020 7437 3129
Email: mail@srpltd.co.uk

Films include: Love's Brother 2003, Free Jimmy 2003, Enemy at the Gates 2001, There's Only One Jimmy Grimble 2000, The War Zone 1999, Cousin Bette 1998, Les Miserable 1998, Bent 1997, Second Best 1994, Sirens 1994

Slate Films

91 Berwick Street
London, W1F 0NE
Tel: 020 7287 7944
Fax: 020 7287 6304
Web: www.slatefilms.com

Films include: Laurel & Hardy TBA, El Bulto (Working Title) TBA, The boy Next Door TBA, Girls At War TBA, Last King of Scotland TBA, Benny Lynch TBA, Once Upon A Time In the Midlands 2002, Hotel 2001

Spice Factory

81 The Promenade
Peacehaven
Brighton, BN10 8LS
Tel: 01273 585275
Fax: 01273 583304
Email: info@spicefactory.co.uk

Films include: Napoleon TBA, Honour Thy Father TBA, Taking Sides TBA, Bollywood Queen 2002, Dead In The Water 2001, Being Considered 2000, Sabotage 2000, Pilgrim 1999, Killer Tongue 1997

Tiger Aspect Pictures

5 Soho Square
London, W1V 5DF
Tel: 020 7434 0672
Fax: 020 7544 1900
Email: general@tigeraspect.co.uk
Web: www.tigeraspect.co.uk

Films include: Dog Eat Dog 2001, The Martins 2000, Billy Elliot 1999, Kevin & Perry Go Large 1999

Vertigo Films

The Big Room Studios
77 Fortess Road
London, NW5 1AG
Tel: 020 7428 7555
Fax: 020 7485 9713
Email: mail@vertigofilms.com

Films include: Macbeth 2003, Kiss Kiss Bang Bang 2003, South West 9 2001, Human Traffic 1999

Warp Films

Spectrum House
32-34 Gordon House rd
London, NW5 1LP
Tel: 020 7284 8366
Web: www.warprecords.com
Email: info@warpfilms.com
(see above)

Further production company details can be found from the sources below. It is important to note that most production companies do not accept unsolicited material and should be approached via an agent or production company.

The Knowledge

Kays Production Manual

BFI Film & Television Handbook

British Film Commission's Directory of Co-Producers, available to download in PDF form online at www.britfilmcom.co.uk

PACT members directory (see www.pact.co.uk)

NPA members directory (see www.npa.org.uk)

Screen International's quarterly round-up of UK production companies' projects in development

ROY DISNEY   VICE-CHAIR, DISNEY

"The secret of Disney's success? - Great story telling I think. Great stories, great characters, great music - it's a lot of things, music is an amazing part of people's memories of film. When you play 'when you wish upon a star' it conjures up a whole movie for you and The Lion King is like that as well. We have such a tremendous tradition of what was done in the past, (uncle) Walt kinda looks over our shoulder and says 'this is what you have to live up to - be this good, be this good.'

"I like comedy. I like to go into a theatre and sit back and relax, not to have too many heavy social messages crammed down my throat and if so I'd like to be entertained by that too. I'd like to understand that if people have problems that they have funny sides and sad sides, I want a picture with memorable characters in. I find a lot of disaster movies, shoot-em-ups and exploding planet movies don't really work that way for me, I'd rather be entertained by something small and charming than by someone blowing up the world - unless it's funny!

"I found my way into the business by way of nature movies - turned out to be the greatest film school you could have gone to. We'd go out with a 16mm camera and an endless supply of film and literally shoot pictures of animals for months and months throughout the seasons. Many of the movies involved the birth and growing up of different animals, we'd take that back to the studio and they'd have to try to make a story out of it. The craft of story telling was implicit in everything we did." NW

Chapter 3
UK FILM COUNCIL

The UK Film Council

10 Little Portland Street
London W1W 7JG
Tel: 020 7861 7861
Fax: 020 7861 7862
Email: info@ukfilmcouncil.org.uk
Web: www.ukfilmcouncil.org.uk

The UK Film Council is the UK's strategic body for film, responsible for driving public film policy and helping to foster a sustainable industry through investment in production, development, new talent, training, distribution and exhibition.

The Council's broad-reaching remit has positioned it uniquely as the strategic driver of the UK industry. Its income, which varies depending on sales of National Lottery tickets and recoupment from former film investments is expected to be typically in excess of £55m – for the year ended March 2001 its turnover was £99m.

A strategic national film organisation was one of the recommendations of the Stewart Till-steered Film Policy Review Group, set-up shortly after Labour came to power in 1997. Heralding the start of a new close relationship between the UK government and the film industry, the UK Film Council launched in April 2000 as the interface between the public and private sector. It both distributes public money and acts as a research and lobbying body on behalf of the industry, for example successfully persuading the treasury to extend section 48 tax relief at the 2002 budget.

At launch the UK Film Council took over responsibility for the British Film Commission; The Arts Council of England's Lottery Film Department; The British Film Institute's Production Department; British Screen Finance; and The British Film Institute. The Council's founding strategy is outlined in the document 'Towards a Sustainable Film Industry' which was produced in response to 13 key objectives set by the government.

The UK Film Council Strategic Objectives

1 - UK FILM IN THE GLOBAL MARKET

To help the UK film industry compete successfully in the global market and to use film to raise the profile of the UK and UK culture across the world.

2 - DEVELOPMENT AND PRODUCTION

To encourage the making of distinctive UK films by new and established filmmakers and to help to ensure that those films find their audience.

3 - DISTRIBUTION AND EXHIBITION

To ensure audiences throughout the UK have access to the full range of British and international cinema.

4 - TRAINING AND SKILLS

To support appropriate training opportunities across the value chain to help create a world class UK film industry.

5 - LIFE-LONG LEARNING

To support the development of opportunities for all UK citizens to understand and appreciate film through the generation and dissemination of knowledge about film and the film industry.

6 - CINEMA HERITAGE

To support the development of opportunities for access to cinema history and heritage and the use of film history in understanding identity, representation, culture and creativity.

Overview of funds

The Development Fund. Headed by Jenny Borgars, the fund hands out £5m annually to support the development of feature film projects and production company slates.

The New Cinema Fund. Headed by Paul Trijbits, the £5m annual fund invests in new filmmakers, culturally significant British films and work from the regions and ethnic minorities, as well as a short film program and a commitment to digital cinema.

The Premiere Fund. Headed by Robert Jones with a £10m annual budget, the fund aims to invigorate commercial production in the UK by investing in films that stand a good chance of making a profit, and ideally as was the case with Capitol Film's *Gosford Park*, could not have shot in the UK with such support.

Regional Investment Fund For England (RIFE) The UK Film Council distributes over £6m a year of lottery money to the English regions. Each of the Regional Film Agencies in England have the responsibility of managing the lottery funds for their area and administer them through schemes devised in accordance with their regional priorities. See Chapter 4.

First Light. A digital short filmmaking scheme backed with £1m in funding, aimed at helping young people (aged 7-18) to gain experience in filmmaking. See Chapter 5.

Specialised Print and Advertising Fund. This fund supports the cinematic distribution of specialised films, for example those in a foreign language, culturally, socially or politically significant films, classic or restored films and films which are not aimed at a mainstream audience. Companies with experience of distribution are eligible to apply for between £50,000 and £100,000 to assist with promotional material, cinematic prints, advertising, publicity, media costs and research.

Training Fund. The Council supports training for the industry with this £1m annual fund, with particular focus on development, business and marketing. The training bursary covers up to 50% or a maximum of £500 of course costs for individuals seeking training in script development or production skills outside of the UK. UK-based training organisations are supported by the Film Council, including First Film Foundation, Script Factory, Bournemouth University Media School and Arista Development Executive and Project Training. The film companies that are supported through the Film Council lottery funds are asked to contribute 0.5% of their budgets (up to £39,500) to the Skills Investment Fund which is managed by Skillset, a training organisation that works with the UK Film Council.

The Board

As well as UK Film Council chair Sir Alan Parker CBE and Chief Executive Officer John Woodward, the board includes: Stewart Till CBE, Deputy Chairman of the UK Film Council and former International President of PolyGram Filmed Entertainment; Chris Auty , Chief Executive of the Film Consortium Lottery franchise; Tim Bevan, co-chairman and co-founder of Working Title Films; John Hill, Professor of Media Studies at the University of Ulster; James Lee, film consultant; Duncan Kenworthy OBE, producer of Notting Hill and Four Weddings and a Funeral and founder of lottery franchise DNA; Sarah Radclyffe, co-founder Working Title Films and now independent producer; Iain Smith, UK producer whose credits include The Fifth Element and Entrapment; Parminder Vir OBE, film and TV producer and consultant at Carlton TV; Paul Webster, former Chief Executive of FilmFour and Head of Production for Miramax Films in the UK; Nigel Green, joint managing director of Entertainment Film Distributors; Stephen Knibbs, senior vice-president UCI Cinemas; and Anthony Minghella, director and chair of the BFI.

Building A Sustainable Film Industry – Alan Parker's roadmap

In a keynote speech in November 2002, UK Film Council chair Alan Parker CBE outlined his strategy for attaining sustainability for the UK film industry, providing a good indicator of the body's future development and priorities. The following is summarises his key points.

COMPETING INTERNATIONALLY

"We need to abandon forever the 'little England' vision of a UK industry comprised of small British film companies delivering parochial British films. That, I suspect, is what many people think of when they talk of a 'sustainable' British film industry. Well, it's time for a reality check. That 'British' film industry never existed, and in the brutal age of global capitalism, it never will"

Instead, Parker suggests that we recognise and support two British film industries with separate objectives. "We need to stimulate the growth of an industry that embraces the international market. At the same time, we must maintain an environment which supports the production of British films of enduring cultural significance. It's not either/or. It's both. We must stop talking about the British film industry and start considering our film industries."

FUNDING

Parker also restated his criticism of dependency on public funds as a means to building a sustainable industry. "Now is the time, once and for all, to recognise that our industry's obsession with public funding for production is taking us nowhere. This might seem like kicking someone when they're down, but it's not. As crucial as it is for our short term survival, public funding solely for production is not the answer to the industry's larger structural problems. I'm sorry, but it honestly isn't."

"I know it's tough out there right now. I too work at the sharp end of production and I am fully aware that people are suffering in our industry. But we've had seven years of Lottery subsidy and five years of a production-focussed tax break. Neither has delivered the structural changes that we need in order to deliver the consistent performance and growth to prevent a crisis every five years... Let me throw down a challenge to British filmmakers and British talent: if you continue to make films for which the costs far exceed potential revenues then you have to have a very good reason to ask for public money to support you in that effort, or you need to reduce the cost of low-budget films by changing the way you work."

REINVENTION

Parker places the long term success of the film industry on re-invention as a 'film hub' or creative core, from three key areas: distribution, skills and infrastructure.

DISTRIBUTION

"The basic truth of the film industry is that it is a distribution-led business. It has been since Adolph Zukor, William Fox, Carl Laemmle and the rest of the pioneers planted their flags out west. The formula used now by Hollywood majors is exactly the same as it has been for 80 years. The Hollywood studios' mathematics are simple: money spent on production is more than earned back in distribution, profits are taken and the balance is used to help finance the production and distribution of more films."

Parker sees that the UK industry needs to be driven by distributors demanding 'product', as opposed to producers pushing films on the market that do not reflect its requirements.

"That means an industry that is led by distribution. Production led by distribution, not the other way round. Pull, not push. Robust, UK-based distributors and sales agents with a serious appetite for investing in British films and helping to make them a success all around the world. We have to stop defining success by how well British films perform in Milton Keynes. This is a big world – really successful British films like *Notting Hill* can make up to 85% of their revenues outside the U.K." Parker suggested that the Film Council and industry could collectively lobby for a tax break that gives incentives to distributors to invest in and acquire British films. "If we don't focus on strengthening distribution for our films, then soon we might not have a production sector at all."

SKILLS

"The Film Council intends to put together a coherent training strategy for film, organised at the centre, but delivered at colleges and training establishments all around the country." This has already been initiated with the formation of the Film Skills Action Group and the publication by Skillset and the Film Council in March 2003 of a mapping document, Developing UK Film Talent.

Parker also suggests that in the future the Film Council may divert money from production to training. "As existing funding commitments expire, the Film Council is prepared to shift more Lottery money into training. But in return we will also insist that the industry invests seriously in its own future for the first time - by investing in training right across the board - all the way from script development, through production, to post-production, distribution and exhibition.

INFRASTRUCTURE

This covers everything from facilities and service companies, "everything that is needed for a film to get made. Without which, no industry can function"

"The environment in which all of these companies operate is undergoing radical change and we can't pretend that cosy transatlantic assumptions will endure. Around the world, investment is pouring into new film studios from India to South Korea, from Australia to Thailand, and dozens of other Governments are dreaming up new tax incentives seemingly month-by-month in an effort to attract big-budget Hollywood movies. The world is suddenly a much more competitive place. The Hollywood studios are more cost-conscious than ever before. Once we were fearful that US production would stay at home instead of coming to Pinewood or Shepperton or Leavesden. The new reality is even more worrying; they might even go somewhere else altogether…

"Over time, these non-traditional filmmaking countries will build their own film industries as they further develop their skills. But if we form partnerships with them now, we will have a much better chance of supplying services to them – particularly our high-end skills – as their industries mature."

To help foster these partnerships, Parker proposed changing the DCMS criteria for what makes a British film. "We need to revise the definition of a British film, finding ways to recast it to reflect the fact that actual production increasingly will take place in countries with a lower cost base than ours. We must begin to view the world beyond the UK. We need to encourage greater British involvement in international film production, by creating strategic alliances with new territories outside Europe who are already playing host to big-budget productions and are hungry for more, at the same time ensuring that British talent – technicians and craftspeople – work on these films."

download the full speach at www.ukfilmcouncil.org.uk/usr/downloads/BaSFI.pdf

Development Fund

An annual fund of £5m is available to develop feature films for theatrical exhibition by first time directors and experienced practitioners. The aim is to broaden the range of quality screenplays available, to encourage relationships and creative development, and potentially to assist production companies in developing a slate of projects.

Funding will cover all the stages of development of a feature before pre-pre-production, which includes script-related costs, producer's costs, developing a presentation package for potential financiers and relevant training. Sometimes pre-pre-production will be funded, which covers casting, budgeting, location surveys and so on.

On occasion a project from the Premiere Fund or the New Cinema Fund will be referred to the Development Fund if further development is needed and the referral is approved. Conversely, Development Fund films may go on to receive funding from the New Cinema Fund or the Premiere Fund.

Anita and Me by Starfield Productions, received £23,175 from the Development Fund and £665,000 from the New Cinema Fund in 2001. Interestingly this film received the development money between two instalments from the New Cinema Fund, illustrating that change and development is an ongoing process in a film. *This is Not a Love Song* by Footprint Films received £8,282 from the Development Fund before receiving an investment of £288,500 from the New Cinema Fund in three instalments over the period of a year.

Guidelines specific to the development fund

ELIGIBILITY

Individuals and companies are eligible to apply for this scheme.

DETAILS

If a project is referred to the Development Fund by one of the other lottery funds, it will not automatically be granted funding. Individuals may apply for up to £10,000. Companies may apply for over £10,000. The scheme will fund almost the entire budget but some partner funding must be sought by the applicant which may be in kind.

Once the Film Council has recouped the premium payable on any Development Fund investment, it may credit half back to the production company to be used in the development of another approved project. This will count as the producer's contribution.

APPLICATIONS

Applicants may apply at various stages of development as long as a treatment has been developed. Applicants must submit an application form, details of key personnel, synopsis, treatment, screenplay, underlying work, development budget, example of director's work and any provisions for cultural, social or economic diversity priorities.

CONDITIONS

The investment must be repaid to the UK Film Council once the project goes into production plus a premium of 50%. In addition to this up to 5% of the producer's net profits on the project must be paid to the Film Council. If there are no third parties involved, the Film Council and the producer will share the rights equally. The Film Council will consider sharing the copyright with a third party and will aim to ensure the producer retains a share of the copyright. The Film Council must receive an end screen credit.

The applicant will work with the UK Film Council throughout the development, participating in regular reviews and giving the Film Council approvals over decisions at each stage of development, including hiring of other creatives, agreements and financiers.

The development process must be completed by the agreed date.

The UK Film Council may recommend the project to one of the other funds – although the film is free to apply to the other funds whether or not is has been recommended. If the Film Council declines the opportunity to produce the film, the producer is free to seek finance elsewhere as long as the investment and premium are repaid once production begins and the Film Council receives 5% of the producer's net profits. If the project has not been produced five years after the development agreement, all rights will revert to the producer as long as the original investment, the 50% premium and 5% of the producer's net profits are paid to the Film Council if the project goes into production.

What sort of scripts is the Development Fund crying out for?

Jenny Borgars, head of the fund: "Contemporary comedies, not romantic comedies because that's what the British seem to think is comedy, fantastic thrillers and horrors and British disaster movies. It's easy to speak in genres but I'm looking for films that define themselves."

What does it get too much of?

"Period pieces, romantic comedy, social drama because that is what people see gets made."

What is the biggest mistake a filmmaker can make in applying?

"Many think that their project is ready before it is, many haven't really thought out whether their film sits with an audience. I'd like to assure people that they should not be afraid to think ambitiously. If I read a script that I hate, that will rise to the top of the pile faster than one which is just written professionally. If it provokes a reaction on any level then we have to study that reaction and find out a way to harness it in order to sell it. I watched the last ten minutes of *Se7en* the other night and I was immediately hooked and so infuriated when Brad Pitt kills him! I love that because it still provokes the same reaction as the first time."

25 Words or Less

This initiative from the Development Fund aims to encourage the development of new writing talent by producing high quality, high concept, genre-led scripts with commercial appeal. Three times each year there is the opportunity for twelve writers to benefit from this scheme. Each call presents three genres for story ideas to be developed into first draft script stage.

DEADLINES

This scheme is run three times a year.

ELIGIBILITY

Individuals only with a literary agent are eligible to apply.

The scheme selects three genres for each deadline; applications must fall in to one of the genres with the intention of being developed into feature films for cinematic release in the UK and world wide. The film must be able to achieve British Status. The scheme will not accept projects based on pre-existing works, and the project must not be developed to draft script stage (if it is, it may be eligible for the Development Fund). Previous applications to the Development Fund are not eligible.

DETAILS

Each writer will receive £10,000 to write the first draft of a script. They may also receive support form a script editor, which will be paid in addition to the £10,000 paid to the writer. The writer's award will be paid in three stages; when writing begins, when the first draft is received by the UK Film Council and when any revisions have been received by the Film Council.

APPLICATIONS

Applicants must submit an application form, an equal opportunities monitoring form, a pitch line of 25 words or less, an outline of the idea, a 10 page sample scene from the story and contact details for the applicant's literary agent.

CONDITIONS

The UK Film Council will receive the first option to further develop the screenplay and may suggest it be submitted to one of the other lottery funds. Should this option be turned down in writing by the Film Council, the applicant will be able to approach other potential partners. The investment must be repaid if the project goes into production with a third party. The Film Council must receive an end screen credit for its support. Throughout the development period, the writer will work with the Film Council, and participate in regular work reviews. The screenplay must be delivered by the agreed date.

Development Slate Funding

For a year over 2001 and 2002 the Development fund offered slate funding to production companies looking to develop more than one project. These projects are still in development but the scheme is now closed to new entrants. It is possible the scheme may re-open and all details would be published on the Film Council web site.

DEVELOPMENT SLATE AWARDS

Company	Amount	Date Made
Company Pictures	£100,000	12-Mar-02
Little Bird (UK)	£150,000	12-Mar-02
Tall Stories	£100,000	12-Mar-02
Fox Phillips	£160,000	13-Mar-02
Gruber Films	£100,000	24-Jul-02
Passion Pictures	£100,000	21-Aug-02
Kuhn and Co	£250,000	2-Oct-02
Recorded Picture Company	£150,000	8-Oct-02
October Films	£75,000	6-Dec-02
Bend It Films	£115,000	11-Dec-02
Shona Productions	£44,000	11-Dec-02
Gruber Films	£100,000	8-Jan-03
Autonomous	£125,000	5-Mar-03
Channel X Communications	£60,000	5-Mar-03
Company Pictures	£130,000	19-Mar-03
Ecosse Films	£250,000	19-Mar-03
Fragile Films	£200,000	19-Mar-03
Mission Pictures	£250,000	19-Mar-03
Ruby Films	£70,000	19-Mar-03
Tall Stories	£50,000	19-Mar-03
Impact Pictures	£108,500	26-Mar-03

Source: UK Film Council

JENNY BORGARS   DEVELOPMENT FUND

Jenny Borgars runs the Development Fund with an annual budget of £5m to tackle the often bemoaned probelms with British scripts, with increased focus on development central to the Film Council's strategy of building a more sustainable British industry.

"The Film Council has tried to identify some of the main problems afflicting the industry. We found that production funding was being introduced too early, the range of projects developed isn't broad enough in terms of their audiences, the quality of scripts isn't high enough and the management of individual production companies isn't strong enough. We tried across the whole organisation to address these problems.

"The aim is to get a broader base of projects. We want to give those companies at the higher end enough resources to go out and compete for the top projects and then have the human and business resources to hold on to them, to strike a better position for themselves as the films get made.

"For the middle range (this is just a rough three-tier system) established companies that have made a number of films need to consolidate, take a long look at their business and maybe step up a gear.

"Then we are also talking to newer producers, people who are moving over from some other activity, or producers who haven't made a film but have demonstrated a hunger and who have developed relationships with talent that are worth nurturing. We need to help them establish relationships and let them demonstrate their ambition and their talent to find ideas, we can then help develop their business with them. To help them get their first feature made and to grow up to the next level."

DEVELOPMENT

"For some people the best training is to read ten great American scripts that got made. For instance, a young filmmaker is making a very poetic ghost story, a beautiful and personal vision - one of the first things I gave her was a copy of *The Sixth Sense* script. I told her to look at how the writer/director has written the script. It's actually a very enjoyable read, purely by reading you get involved in the story and that is part of the craft.

"A lot of American scripts allow the reader enough space to actually fall into the story, rather than trying to give the reader all the information possible. Like any profession you need to look at the work of people who have excelled and learn from it. I think there's also a lot of good to be had - in training or in practice - from being able to sit down and spend some time with the practitioner and the execs who are commissioning it, understanding what they need out of the process.

"A writer/director needs to know what to put down on the page in order to get their film sold into the market - before they actually make the film. That sounds like a crude distinction but it's quite difficult convincing people of the benefit of this.

"If someone comes through the door here with an original idea that has a spark to it and a passion behind it, they have to bring it to the table but we have to present to them the reality of what they have to do in order to make it. The aim is to get it made and, I would hope, to get it made and have it succeed, whichever way they define success.

"From our side, that's what we try to get people to work on, to define what they regard will make this film a success. Whether it's huge box office acclaim or huge critical acclaim, you then have to look at how that's going to impact upon your story, and ultimately the budget and who you'll want to sell it to.

"Personally I find it shocking that commercialism is treated as a dirty word because actually it should be something to aspire to. It's a very broad subject, you'd hope a success meant huge critical and commercial success. *There's Something About Mary*, which is a very broad comedy, is also critically interesting in terms of what it is doing with the genre. You don't have to lose quality for the sake of commercial success, I think you just have to embrace both."

APPLICATIONS

"In the guidelines we set out the chance for people to come to us with a treatment. That's obviously because one of the caveats of being set up is that we can accept applications from all over the country, and indeed all over Europe. We have to set some boundaries because there aren't enough hours in the day to take a pitch from everybody.

"People can come to us with a treatment or with a book that they've optioned with some notes from the adapter on how they are going to take it forward. That's the earlier stage and beyond that you can come at any point. The interesting thing about this fund is that you can come for creative development at any point but also, when the project is fully developed creatively, you still need to go out and raise the finance. There's a mechanism here to give you the money to go onto that next phase. That's a critical point in a film's progression, the point where an extra £10,000 will help you go out and get hold of a line producer for example, something to keep the ball rolling.

"We'll steer people in whichever direction we can, whenever possible. It depends on the producer. Some have a clear idea but just need a little bit of cash to get them over a hurdle. What I think is good here is, wherever possible, that we can encourage or help people go out and find a partner, and with the money and expertise we give that's really useful. Our development fund acts as a leverage for them to attract further finance for a project.

"There are a lot of projects that we are developing very closely in conjunction with the production funds. Either they've identified a project that has come for production finance that isn't deemed ready yet, or we've identified talent that we've found interesting and passed them on. It's essential and I'd be really worried if we worked completely separately because you need to be able to balance an idea. Something might work creatively but when taken to the Premiere Fund they may tell you that the market isn't there for it. You may have been so wound up in the creative side that you haven't seen the other side of it."

FINDING TALENT

"The process of identification is the hardest and we've had to take a step back and ask ourselves where we think the interesting ones are going to come from. Is it worth asking documentary filmmakers whether they'd be interested in moving over into another area, or theatre companies even? Where will we, and not just the Film Council but the industry as a whole, get that interesting creative talent? It's also really difficult finding young producers that are showing a keen entrepreneurial sense, that's fundamental. Someone, maybe us, has to dig even deeper to understand how we are going to train producers. Perhaps it means making it harder for them to become producers.

"There are a lot of people that want to come in and hear about what we are up to and to talk about what they are doing. There are an untold amount of keen producers out there. There's never a day you can't fill with six meetings but I don't want a situation where we spend a lot of time talking and can't move anything forward.

"We spent a lot of time to get hold of a lot of projects and we now have to spend some time on housekeeping to decide which ones we can go with and to move those forward. As always, you make decisions very early on in a new company or organisation, but your experience and knowledge grows and affects those decisions. Development is such a weird area because we all know that the majority of projects never go anywhere, in some ways there's a cultural hurdle that needs clearing. Failing within development can be a good thing, and obviously better there than after production but also there's a huge amount one can learn whilst failing in development so that one can make sure it's not repeated." *NW*

New Cinema Fund

An annual fund of £5m is available to support emerging talent, particularly from the regions and culturally and ethnically diverse backgrounds and to encourage creative and technological innovation in the production (and delivery) of feature films of any genre intended for theatrical exhibition. Funding is also available to pilot projects exploring the potential of a feature idea.

Magdalene Sisters by Antonine Films received £600,000 from the New Cinema Fund and £23,010 from the Development Fund in June 2001. The film was released in cinemas in the UK early 2003 making it a two-year production period between initial investment from the Film Council and release when the film can begin recouping its costs.

Director Dave McKean and producer Keith Griffiths (Illumination Films) got funding from the New Cinema fund to shoot a pilot film for their feature *Signal To Noise*, and found the process entirely positive. "This idea of developing a project by investing in a pilot, or sample of technique/style etc. is a wonderful opportunity to experiment and play. To try and get a little of what is in your head out onto the screen so the project comes clearer into focus for everybody involved. Obviously it is not going to deal with all aspects of the film, not the least of which is 'plot', so having a clear brief as to the questions you want answered by the pilot is important... Almost every aspect of the pilot showed ways to improve it when we get to make the real thing." **Dave McKean**

Guidelines specific to the New Cinema fund

DETAILS

The UK Film Council will generally invest between 15% and 50% of the film's budget. A pilot film is eligible to receive up to £10,000 to contribute to above the line costs.

CONDITIONS

Investment in pilot films must be repaid once a feature based on the pilot goes into production. The UK Film Council may insist on making an experienced professional available as a mentor to guide the producer and director through the production process if they are both first-timers. The costs for this must be included in the budget. Where part of the film's finance is contributed by broadcasters, the UK TV rights must be valued at a reasonable price.

NEW CINEMA FUND AWARDS

Film	Company	Award	Date
Wooden Camera	Oliver Delahaye, ODP	£205,000	16-Jan-02
Night we called it a Day, The (pilot)	Scala Productions	£10,000	27-Feb-02
Helen of Peckham	Gayle Griffiths Productions	£375,000	13-Mar-02
Entering Blue Zone	Common Features Ltd	£237,500	20-Mar-02
Live Forever	Passion Dox	£190,000	20-Mar-02
One for the Road	East Midlands Media Initiative (EMMI)	£240,000	3-Jul-02
A.K.A. Run with the Foxes	Third Rock Ltd	£100,000	10-Jul-02
Home Movie	Bent Films	£9,999	24-Jul-02
Signal to Noise (pilot)	Illumination Films	£10,000	31-Jul-02
Sportsman of the Century (pilot)	Staccato Films	£10,000	31-Jul-02
Intermission	Company of Wolves	£550,000	7-Aug-02
Blind Fight	Parallax Picutres	£450,000	4-Sep-02
Helen of Peckham	Gayle Griffiths Productions Ltd	£102,250	18-Sep-02
Talent Campus	Talent Campus - Berlinale	£100,000	19-Sep-02
One Love	One Love Films	£459,182	31-Oct-02
A Way of Life	AWOL Films Ltd	£10,000	20-Nov-02
Big Blue and the Humanoid	Cafe Productions	£178,117	20-Nov-02
At Uncle Idriz's Place (aka Sex Planet) - pilot	Autonomous	£10,000	22-Jan-03
Stones In His Pockets (pilot)	Stones In His Pockets Ltd	£11,638	12-Feb-03
The Purifiers (pilot)	Tartan Works	£10,000	19-Feb-03

Source: UK Film Council

PAUL TRIJBITS — **NEW CINEMA FUND**

As head of the New Cinema Fund, Paul Trijbits has become one of the UK's keenest – and most influential - supporters of digital cinema through schemes such as Digital Shorts and a pilot programme which allows filmmakers to shoot tests ahead of their feature.

"DV seems to have a vision of its own. My girlfriend produced *The King is Alive* and I went out on to the film's set in Namibia a couple of years ago, I was incredibly fortunate to see a film being made like that. The change in the filmmaking process is extraordinary and I'm sure that had it been made in the traditional sense it would have cost four or five times that amount. The freedom that it allowed was wonderful and the language of cinema seems to have changed and moved with this new, incredibly lightweight machinery.

"I then came back and exec produced *My Brother Tom*, a digital film and I was also involved on another film called *Harry On The Boat* which was shot on DigiBeta, so I've had my fair share of experiences with digital. It really taught me a lot. The attitude of 'never mind about the script or the process, we'll just shoot it on DV' - is the kind of attitude that doesn't reflect what it's all about. I think what's going to be interesting is whether digital video in particular - not talking about HD here - is going to quite stand up as a form in its own right.

"My guess would be that in the next five to seven years large numbers of feature films will be generated not only digitally but on HD. We know that digital video and its results are fine but I think it works for a fairly limited kind of film. You can't just replace the 35mm camera and say that you can do it for less. The beauty of it is, in a country that has been quite rigid in its production process, as DV technology is changing rapidly you can now go and shoot things differently with a smaller group of people, for a longer period and so on. As long as the films are interesting I think the audience will watch them regardless of what they've been shot on.

"What we are really after is a great script, I'd say the quality is not necessarily so bad but the ambition is poor. I've read a lot of American scripts, and although the story is often very dull the actual quality of the writing is usually higher. People are more capable of writing scripts over there. They have a history of good screenwriters for film that we don't have in the UK. There really are a lot of derivative, really rather uninspiring stories out there that don't play in cinemas and are unlikely to play on television either. When it's derivative and poorly written and dull it's really depressing because someone has put a lot of effort into it.

"I think you have to be very careful here. It's too simplistic to say, 'let's go out and make a mass market film'. It still has to be good but I think what has to work is the combination of elements - a particular script with that director and that cast, in that genre, for that audience. You need to work out why it should cost what it cost, not to just fix a budget and then try to raise the money, which is what many producers do."

"Robert Jones, Jenny Borgars and I apply our own experience. We believe we have skills to apply and we are using them as each team is making funding decisions, selecting projects that we want to invest in creatively and working very actively with the producer. There is a training fund that targets key areas that need help, but all the funds are actively trying to promote better practice." *NW*

Premiere Fund

This programme delivers an annual fund of £10m to support the development, production and distribution of feature films intended for worldwide theatrical exhibition and distribution. The priority for this scheme is to produce commercially viable films with international sales potential. The intended knock-on effect is to improve the sustainability and expertise of the industry in the UK through supporting the long-term growth of production companies by strategic investments.

This fund tends to make bigger investments than the Development Fund or the New Cinema Fund in more obviously commercial and high profile projects. *Gosford Park* by Zestwick Ltd is an example of a Premiere Fund film, receiving a particularly large investment of £2m in 2001. *L'Homme du Train* by Cine B received £500,000 in 2001 from the Premiere Fund, while *Mike Bassett: England Manager* was granted over £1.2m for production, and then a further £870,000 to Entertainment Film Distributors for prints and advertising.

Guidelines specific to the Premiere fund

DETAILS
The Film Council will invest up to 35% of the budget of a Premiere Fund project. Larger contributions will be considered on projects with commercial sector financiers in place.

ASSESSMENT
A film's commercial strength and potential returns, as well as recoupment of the Film Council's investment are key priorities for the Premiere Fund. This means that the confidence of other financiers and the level of partnership funding is also important.

CONDITIONS
In addition to the approvals listed in the general guidelines, the Film Council must have approval on additional elements of Premiere Fund projects. These include the post-production stages, the release campaign for the UK and major territories, the running time of the film, the locations of the studios and the film stock.

Should the Film Council or the production company make any sales on the project they may claim an agreed sales commission.

ROBERT JONES **PREMIERE FUND**

Robert Jones believes in backing talent first and foremost and, as the man who produced the first major films from Paul Thomas Anderson (Hard Eight), Bryan Singer (The Usual Suspects) and Ben Hopkins (Simon Magus), the head of the UK's biggest public fund £30m over three years) is well placed to back it when he's found it.

"What the Premiere Fund is trying to do, along with the development fund, training fund and the other production funds, is help the British film industry support itself by helping production companies become stable businesses. To develop the film industry into something attractive for people to view as a viable career option, which I don't think many people do at the moment. Although many of these aims are long term we need to get film on the agenda and make it appear more exciting.

"We've got particular problems as an industry that we have to try and get over, and they are not easy ones. A major problem is the cost of making a film in this country. The budgets we are getting here are averaging at £3.5m to £4m and apart from the no-budget FilmFour Lab type films, that's a low budget film in this country. When you compare that with what you can make them for in North America and in Europe, it makes us one of, if not the most expensive filmmaking countries in the world. I think that is a huge problem.

"We aren't getting the people coming through and wanting to work as crew members. In America you've got great numbers of people coming through all the time who want to get into the industry at every level. I'm not saying one should exploit people at all, I'm just saying that if we want to move forward we need to take risks and attempt to bring down the cost of making films.

"There's a lot work that needs to be done in terms of training. We've a lot of writers with good ideas but not that many who have mastered the technique of screenwriting. Our traditions are that of theatre and literature whereas America really has a cinematic tradition. I think the training fund that we've got has to work very closely with the production funds - we've just got to attract more people at every level into the industry. And I don't think we do that by saying 'look at all the money you can make'. We get artists into the industry by offering an environment that is creatively exciting - in a way that the fashion world and the art world and the music world have succeeded in doing so. We need to do that in this country.

"What is our culture? We speak the same language as the Americans and, unlike a number of European countries, we haven't actively preserved our culture. We are a little bit adrift. Whilst the pressure is on me to make a return - not necessarily to make a profit - but to make a return on this money, I am very mindful of the fact that I'm not just looking for the next *Bridget Jones* or the next *Full Monty*. Those will always be financial mainstays but if we only pursue those types of films then we shall have a very dull, bland industry."

"What I wanted to get away from is an industry where you have Working Title and then everyone else. If in three years time we've helped 10 or 15 real production companies establish themselves like, in TV the Tiger Aspects and the Talkbacks, then we'll have done something worthwhile."

"It would be good to have a production sector that was as professional as other sectors, and I don't mean that in a bad way. At times I was as amateurish as everyone else. But if we are going to have a more constant supply of good projects we have to have a more stable production sector." *NW*

PREMIERE FUND AWARDS

Film	Company	Award	Date
Gosford Park	Zestwick Ltd	£2,000,000	31-Jan-01
Importance of Being Earnest, The	Fragile Films Ltd	£1,244,697	14-Feb-01
Water Warriors	Silver Fox Films	£500,000	1-May-01
Five Children and It	The Jim Henson Company Ltd	£500,000	25-Jul-01
Mike Bassett: England Manager	Entertainment Film Distributors	£620,000	30-Aug-01
L'Homme du Train	Cine B	£500,000	17-Oct-01
Kiss It	Kiss It Productions	£500,000	23-Jan-02
Young Adam	Recorded Picture Company Ltd	£500,000	6-Feb-02
Proposition, The	Autonomous	£200,000	13-Feb-02
Untitled Love Story	Ruby Films	£1,000,000	20-Mar-02
Sex Lives of Potato Men	Devotion Films	£750,000	19-Jun-02
Freddie Randall Story, The	Peter Chelsom Productions	£250,000	4-Sep-02
Code 46	Revolution Films	£1,565,063	4-Dec-02
Valiant	Fragile Films	£2,580,645	4-Dec-02

Source: UK Film Council

Guidelines

For all feature funds

DEADLINES

All funds with the exception of the 25 Words or Less scheme are rolling programmes so applications may be made at any time.

ELIGIBILITY

Where individuals are eligible to apply, they must be over 18 years old and resident in the UK, EU or European Economic Area (EEA) Where organisations are eligible to apply, they must be limited liability companies resident in the UK, EU or EEA. The company must show the ability and intention to produce feature films in the medium-long term with the potential to benefit the UK film industry. Individuals may apply with the intention of forming a company should their funding application be successful.

All projects must be feature length films made in English (with appropriate exceptions) with a strong chance of achieving cinematic UK release and intended for worldwide distribution. The finished film must be able to obtain classification for release. There is no restriction on genre, except for the 25 Words or Less scheme. The UK Film Council accepts applications from co-productions and foreign filmmakers as long as the projects are capable of achieving British Film Status. Projects based on pre-existing works must have an option in place or available to them.

If appropriate, applications may be referred by one of the lottery funds to one of the other two for assessment by them. Re-submissions are only accepted if the script has changed substantially or if the key personnel attached have changed.

DETAILS

Applicants may receive an up-front commitment from the UK Film Council to fund each stage of the project. Successful applications that do not receive this commitment may apply for further funding but there is no guarantee of success. The contribution from the Film Council must be paid into a separate trust account.

APPLICATIONS

It is advised for applicants to make initial contact with the UK Film Council at an early stage before negotiations with other financiers. In addition to the application form, all projects must be submitted as scripts, along with the other materials requested by each funding scheme. The scripts must be written in the Film Council's preferred format (available for viewing at www.filmcouncil.org.uk/funding/?p=samplescript). Any applications based on pre-existing works must include them with the application materials. Any re-submissions must include an explanation of the changes to the original project.

ASSESSMENT

The top priority for assessment is the quality of the script and its creative merit. The commercial strength of the project is also a major concern.

CONDITIONS

The UK Film Council usually funds projects by way of investment, sharing in the revenues from sales and exploitation of all ancillary rights. The chain of title for all rights must be clear. The production company must comply with regulations concerning trainees and training levies such as the Skills Investment Fund. This might include Film Council staff working with the less experienced personnel on the project. The production company must also work with the UK Film Council's Business Affairs and finance departments throughout the process. These terms and conditions may change according to each individual project.

For the New Cinema Fund and the Premiere Fund

Applications must come from companies or individuals intending to form a company for the project. The New Cinema Fund, the Premiere Fund and Franchise Companies may not fund the same project. Applicants should have the director and principal cast on board upon application.

DETAILS

The UK Film Council does not fully fund projects and generally expects partnership funding to be in place upon application. Should this not be the case, the Film Council may assist the production company over an agreed period of time in securing other funding partners. Funding will usually only be forwarded to the company once and if this is successful, but the Film Council may forward 10% of their agreed contribution to the company for pre-pre-production work before third-party funding is secured if the risk is deemed acceptable. The Film Council sees sale and leaseback as an acceptable form of film finance as long as certain guidelines are met.

Once the UK Film Council has recouped a certain percentage of its investment, it will endeavour to pay 10% of its revenues back to the production company to allow the company to pursue agreed future projects, such as training and business development. This payment will begin once 50% of the contribution from the New Cinema Fund has been recouped and 75% of the contribution from the Premiere Fund has been recouped. It will stop once the Film Council's full investment has been recouped.

APPLICATIONS

Applicants for both Funds must submit detailed information with their application form. This includes details on key cast and crew, examples of the director's work, synopsis, cash flow schedule, finance and distribution structures, sales estimates, and any provisions for cultural, social or economic diversity priorities.

ASSESSMENT

In addition to the creative merit of the project, the production company should demonstrate their ability to deliver the project, considering key areas such as creative vision, financing, distribution and marketing.

CONDITIONS

All UK Film Council contributions are usually made in the form of an investment to recoup the funding award and to share in the profits. The Film Council retains at least 2.5% of the investment it makes in the project until they receive an independent audit upon completion, indicating that the terms of the investment have been met. Once the award has been recouped, the Film Council's share of rights will revert to the producer. The Film Council must receive an approved front and end screen credit.

The budget should be demonstrated to be realistic and to industry norms and market rates. It should be in proportion to the film's projected recoupment and must include provision for certain elements. These include publicity, test screenings, insurance, completion bonds (with the UK Film Council as a named party), the clearance of world wide rights, the payment of the Skills Investment Fund levy and other trade fees, and the production of required screening formats for world wide cinematic distribution. The Film Council's contribution may cover agreed overhead costs and producer's fees, but will not generally cover interest payments, though exceptions do exist. The budget should also make provision for payment of the Film Council's legal fees. This will amount to at least £12,000 for New Cinema Fund projects and £15,000 for Premiere Fund projects. Should there be a budget underspend, the producer and the third party financiers may share a repayment of the balance at 50% each, with a ceiling of £50,000.

The UK Film Council has approval rights over the major elements of production for example, the script, key cast and crew and their fees, co-financiers, budget and schedule, distribution and sales companies and terms, collection agreements, insurance, accounting and the final audit, screen ratio, edits and assemblies, and post-production facilities.

During production the UK Film Council is entitled to receive certain information and up-dates, this includes for example, copies of rushes, progress reports, financial information, books and statements, any changes to script, cast, crew or schedule. Film Council staff must also be granted access to all stages of production. Travel and accommodation for two visits by two members of Film Council staff must be included in the budget.

The producer must deliver certain items to the UK Film Council once the film is complete, such as a print of the film, VHS and DVD copies, film posters and stills, marketing plans, shooting script signed by director and leading cast, soundtrack, and audited statement of costs.

Short Film Schemes

The New Cinema Fund runs two short film schemes: Cinema Extreme for experienced short filmmakers, and Digital Shorts for lower budgeted shorts shot on DV from new filmmakers. Past schemes that may be revised in the future include Comedy Shorts, which offered up to £30,000 plus a development training programme and was managed by Shine production company; the Completion fund, which made available £50,000 for short films that were at a rough cut stage but not completed; and the New Cinema Fund / CNC Short Film Competition which jointly produced pairs of shorts, each with a French and British director filming the same script. The short film department can be contacted via shorts@ukfilmcouncil.org.uk

Cinema Extreme

The Bureau,
PO Box 4242,
London W1A 6FP.

www.ukfilmcouncil.org.uk/shorts/?p=extreme
www.thebureau.com

Cinema Extreme is aimed at filmmakers with significant previous short film or documentary experience ready to springboard their career into feature film production. The scheme is managed by production company, The Bureau, and selections are made by the New Cinema Fund, Film Four Lab and The Bureau.

DEADLINE

There are two deadlines a year but submissions may be made at any time.

ELIGIBILITY

Applicants must have experience of short filmmaking, with applicants likely to have had films shown in festivals or broadcast. The aim is to support filmmakers looking to move into feature film production. Applications must come from directors or teams working with a director.

DETAILS

Five films a year will be commissioned and successful applicants will be teamed with production companies.

APPLICATIONS

Applicants must send in a script, a director's statement, examples of the director's previous work (full films rather than a showreel), CV's of key personnel and details of the designated contact person.

ASSESSMENT

The applications will be assessed on their creative merit with particular attention paid to the expression of vision and passion, original story-telling and projects which push the boundaries of contemporary cinema.

Digital Shorts

www.dvshorts.com

This initiative from the UK Film Council's New Cinema Fund has invested £500,000 a year to enable short film production by new filmmakers using digital technology and providing them with the opportunity for their film to be screened in cinemas. 2003 is the second year of Digital Shorts, which is delivered through the regional and national film bodies and other partner organisations. They are responsible for organising their own deadlines and managing the fund in their area. As a result the deadlines, conditions and scheme titles can vary from region to region.

At the beginning of 2003 the organisations listed to the right were confirmed as the agencies responsible for delivering the scheme over the year. Some areas of the UK are yet to confirm the responsible agency and filmmakers not accounted for in the list below should contact their regional screen agency for further details.

DEADLINE

The deadlines vary between the agencies.

ELIGIBILITY

Writers, directors, writers/directors, artists and producers may apply to the Regional Film Agency that represents their region of residency. Writers must own the rights to their work. There is no requisite theme or genre and the films must be suitable for a theatrical release. Applicants will be assigned to filmmaking teams.

DETAILS

Each agency will offer up to £10,000 to 8 short film projects lasting between 1 and 6 minutes to be shot on DigiBeta. The scheme will also offer training, script development support and production support for each film. The UK Film Council works with the appointed distributor for the scheme, Short Circuit, which selects films from the scheme for sales and distribution.

CONTACTS

London - LFVDA - Honnie Tang
Tel: 020 7383 7755
Email: lfvda@lfvda.demon.co.uk

London - B3 Media (working with Black & ethnic minorities) - Marc Boothe
Tel, 0208 674 1804
Web: www.23-59.co.uk
Email: info@b3media.co.uk

Scotland - Glasgow Media Access Centre Ltd - David Smith (Cineworks), Paul Welsh (Digicult)
Tel: 0141 553 2620
Email: admin@g-mac.co.uk

East of England - Screen East - Nicky Dade
Tel: 01603 756879
Email: production@screeneast.co.uk

East Midlands - EMMI/Intermedia Film & Video
Rebecca Mark-Lawson
Tel: 0115 955 6909
Email: rebecca.marklawson@em-media.org.uk

South of England - Lighthouse - Dean Howard
Tel: 01273 384222
Email: film@lighthouse.org.uk

West Midlands - Screen West Midlands - Jane Slater
Tel: 0121 643 9309
jane@screenwm.co.uk

North West of England - Moving Image Development Agency - Helen Bingham
Tel: 0151 708 9858
Email: helenb@northwestvision.co.uk

North of England - Northern Film and Media
Helen Stearman
Tel: 44 (0) 191 269 9200
Email: helen@northernmedia.org

South West of England - South West Screen
Sarah-Jane Meredith
Tel: 0117 927 3226
Email: sarah-jane@swscreen.co.uk

Yorkshire and Humberside - YMPA - Ann Tobin
Tel: 0114 249 2204

Chapter 4
NATIONS & REGIONS

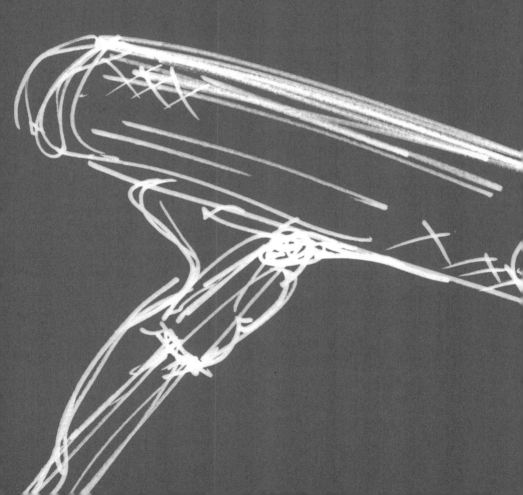

UK Film Funding Map

1. Scottish Screen
2. Sgrin
3. Northern Ireland Film & TV Commission
4. Northern Film & Media
5. Northwest Vision
6. Screen Yorkshire
7. EM Media
8. Screen East
9. Film London
10. Screen South
11. South West Screen
12. Screen West Midlands
13. Isle of Man Film Commission

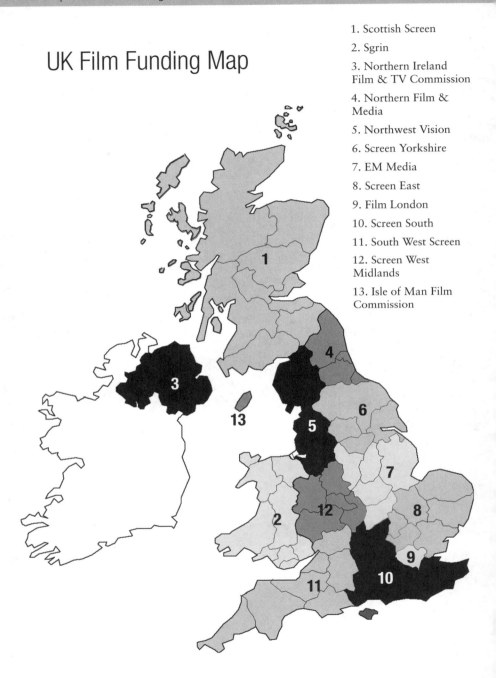

England
Regional Screen Agencies

The Film Council operates the Regional Investment Fund for England (RIFE) with a budget of over £6m a year, which is administered through the appointed regional film agencies in the UK. These were set-up over 2002-2003, typically bringing together existing regional film bodies, commissions and media development agencies; much in the way the Film Council brought together a number of existing national funds and agencies. At time of publication the details of London's agency, Film London, had only announced the basic plans for taking over the remit of the LFVDA, while South West Screen's management were still confirming exact plans and details.

Each agency is self-governing, establishing regional schemes aimed at assisting the film industry in the key areas of training, company support, development, production and exhibition/distribution. Each agency sets priorities for its area in response to the needs of the region, and structures their lottery programme to best suit these needs. For example, in poorer parts of England with high unemployment, the regional agency's priority may be to boost media sector employment and stimulate the local economy. In other regions the main job of the agency may be supporting films coming in from outside the region and ensuring that the local workforce is skilled enough to work on these projects; or attempting to foster an audience for local films through the support of film festivals.

For those looking to cherry pick regional schemes and settle in a region with the most supportive funding structures it is worth bearing in mind how widely the regional priorities differ. Screen South, for instance favours training and company support over production investment, while other areas are committed almost entirely to production and development funding. That said, the film agencies ultimately have the same goal: to develop, strengthen and promote their region's film culture and industry by maximising potential for talent and crews, for audiences, for education, for production and distribution, and for resources in the film and media sector. But making sure that each application is carefully in tune with the agency's specific priorities greatly increases the chances of success in application.

REGIONAL SCREEN AGENCY OVERVIEW

East of England (Bedfordshire, Cambridgeshire, Essex, Hertfordshire, Norfolk and Suffolk) – Screen East

East Midlands (Derbyshire, Leicestershire, Lincolnshire, Northamptonshire, Nottinghamshire and Rutland) – EM Media

London (London Boroughs) – Film London

North (Tyne & Wear, Northumberland, Durham, Tees Valley) – Northern Film & Media

North West (Cheshire, Cumbria, Greater Manchester, Lancashire, Merseyside) – North West Vision

South of England (Kent, Buckinghamshire, Oxfordshire, Hampshire, Surrey, Berkshire, East and West Sussex, and the Isle of Wight) – Screen South

South West (Gloucestershire, Wiltshire, Bristol, Somerset, Dorset, Devon and Cornwall) – South West Screen

West Midlands (Herefordshire, Staffordshire, Shropshire, Birmingham, Coventry, Walsall, Wolverhampton, Warwickshire, Worcestershire, Herefordshire, Telford and The Wrekin) – Screen West Midlands

Yorkshire & Humberside (North Yorkshire, South Yorkshire, West Yorkshire and Humberside) – Screen Yorkshire

Screen East

2 Millennium Plain, Norwich, Norfolk, NR2 1TF.
Leavesden Studios, South Way, Hertfordshire, WD25 7LZ.
Tel: 01603 776920
Fax: 01603 767191
Email: info@screeneast.co.uk
Web: www.screeneast.co.uk

Covering: Bedfordshire, Cambridgeshire, Essex, Hertfordshire, Norfolk and Suffolk.

Screen East's regional priorities are focused on the need to develop regional talent and promote this nationally and internationally, to serve and nurture the industry and to develop audiences. The agency's lottery programme is therefore organised into three priority streams; covering development and production support; company development and investment; and exhibition and audience.

Laurie Hayward, Chief Executive on applications

"1. You have to communicate to us that you know your business in a comprehensive business plan.

2. Show you understand your market, your customers and how to get to them.

3. Assemble the team that can deliver the business plan.

4. Show us what other funding has been raised or can be raised including your own investment.

5. Show us clearly what the benefits are to our regional media profile and content, job creation, social inclusion, sustainability and training,"

"Apply these principles against our three priorities; Innovation; Company Development and Cultural Partnerships.

"Innovation is currently targeted on script development. We are looking for unique ideas that have a market potential. The writer needs to show that the work will benefit from development and that they are open to advice and guidance. We're spending a lot on this at the moment at £5,000 a time.

"Company Development. It's got to be a great plan by people who can deliver. Applications can be for research and development; slate development for TV and film; pilots for new interactive content; projects which attract film finance, broadcaster investment or games publisher money up front. Up to £40,000 is available for the right stuff.

"Cultural Partnerships: We are very interested in digital projection for rural communities; media education working with young people and disadvantaged communities. £10,000 seems to be the maximum so far.

"In 2002 we funded 40 applications out of 102; the figure 102 applications came after receiving and responding to 286 requests for information/application packs.

"The biggest mistake is not to have met with us and discussed the project before application. Applications benefit from advice and guidance, and it is free!"

Priority 1 - Innovation

DEVELOPMENT FINANCE

This award supports script and project development prior to the pre-production stage for low budget feature films (intended for theatrical release), documentaries, animation and digital media. Applicants must apply with a project that has reached at least the full treatment stage. Priority is given to applicants based within the region, however an organisation or team based outside the region may apply as long as their project is strongly associated with the Screen East region. Freelancers must be based in the Screen East Region.

PRODUCTION FINANCE

An award which supports short film production, post-production and distribution, in the fields of fiction, documentary, digital media, or animation which are intended for theatrical release. Collaborations between traditional and new media organisations and broadcast companies are welcomed. Applicants must include a distribution plan. Organisations may apply for up to £20,000.

Priority 2 – Company Development

COMPANY DEVELOPMENT INVESTMENT

This award supports promising regional production companies to develop a slate of projects. An applicant organisation must have more than one project in their slate and demonstrate financial support from broadcasters, film financiers, or distributors. The funding limit for this award is £20,000. Freelancers are not eligible to apply.

SMALL SCALE CAPITAL AWARDS

This award supports an applicant's investment in hardware and software to develop their business. Applicants must include a distribution plan. The funding limit for this award is £5000. Match funding is not required, but the equipment must be competitively priced and demonstrated to significantly improve the applicant's business.

Priority 3 – Cultural Partnerships

INVESTMENT TO SUPPORT ACCESS FOR AUDIENCES

This award supports specialist and mainstream exhibitors to bring diverse cinema to a wider audience. This is focused on four main areas: increasing the availability and international promotion of film produced in the Screen East Region; bringing the moving image to rural audiences; expanding specialist screening activity through festivals, societies and other groups; and supporting training in

important skills for independent exhibitors and cinema operators. Freelancers are not eligible to apply.

EDUCATIONAL PROJECTS AND INITIATIVES

This award supports film education in schools, colleges and the community, particularly through cinemas and new regional film education organisations. This is focused in four main areas: forming regional film education consortia; enabling access of diverse communities to the moving image; training in schools and communities; improving and promoting film education and careers services.

ARCHIVE SERVICES AND ACCESS FOR AUDIENCES

This award supports the film archive and conservation services of the region, particularly improving promotion and access.

General Guidelines for these schemes

DEADLINE

Applications may be made at any time.

ELIGIBILITY

Unless otherwise stated, applicants are expected to be based in the region. Organisations must be limited companies, charities, consortia, schools, societies, colleges, libraries, universities, or legally constituted sole traders. Regional focus is an important priority for Screen East so a project which is backed by another regional company or local authority would increase an applicant's chance of success.

DETAILS.

Unless otherwise stated, organisations may apply for up to £10,000, freelancers may apply for up to £5000 and all applicants must secure at least 30% match funding for the project.

APPLICATIONS

In addition to the application form, and where relevant, applicants must submit a copy of the most recent accounts, a copy of the management accounts and a copy of the organisations constitution or rules. Applications will only be accepted on hard copy by post or courier.

ASSESSMENT

Each application will be assessed against the following criteria: the pubic benefit in meeting Screen East's objectives; creative and commercial quality; impact on social inclusion and cultural diversity; financial viability and partnership funding; and the ability of the applicant to deliver the project.

CONDITIONS

Contributions from Screen East are in the form of an investment which will be recouped from income generated by the project. Screen East also requires a credit on any materials associated with the project.

Production Schemes

FEATURELAB TENDER

This training and development scheme is for screenwriters living or working in the region to produce first draft scripts. Screen East pays the full cost of the screenwriting course at the University of East Anglia. Finished screenplays will be read by the low budget arm of Working Title Films, WT2, and exceptional candidates may receive an MA in screenwriting.

DIGITAL SHORTS

Writers, directors, artists and producers living in the Screen East region may apply for the New Cinema fund DV shorts scheme which offers up to £8000, training and development and production support for each film. For further information see the Film Council section or contact Nicky Dade on 01603 756879.

EM Media

35-37 St Mary's Gate
Nottingham NG1 1PU
Tel: 0115 934 9090
Fax: 0115 950 0988
Email: info@EM-Media.org.uk
Web: www.EM-Media.org.uk

Covering: Derbyshire, Leicestershire, Lincolnshire, Northamptonshire, Nottinghamshire and Rutland.

EM-Media has set its regional priorities as a need to develop business, talent and opportunities for audiences. It organises its lottery programme into three priority streams.

Carol Clarke, Assistant Development Officer, on applications

"Applications which stand out are those that clearly demonstrate they meet EM Media objectives and address regional, local authority cultural and economic development plans. Where applications tend to fail is where applicants have had no dialogue with RIFE personnel and have not discussed their application in detail.

"In this our first year the majority of applications have been from regional delivery partners such as regional film theatres and production agencies, but have also included strategic developments around rural cinema exhibition and festivals."

Priority One: To develop viable film and media businesses

RESEARCH, FEASIBILITY AND COMPANY DEVELOPMENT STUDIES

Long-term sustainability is the motivation behind this award, which focuses on access to market intelligence, market research and testing of ideas and company development plans. The scheme will require evidence of market need and support from industry partners.

DEVELOPMENT OF LOCAL SECTOR PARTNERSHIPS FOR MEDIA BUSINESSES

This award supports the development of industry partnerships and networks on regional and national scales supporting regional industry.

ORGANISATIONAL AND CAPACITY DEVELOPMENT PROJECTS

This award supports projects that increase and develop the market intelligence, business skills, and research capacity of organisations. It will also consider funding the development of a slate of projects over an extended time period.

Priority Two: To develop and promote regional talent

DEVELOPMENT OF SCREENWRITING TALENT AND CONTENT INNOVATION

This award supports new and established screenwriters and creative personnel in the research, writing, and development of scripts, storyboards and ideas. It will also evaluate the previous works of the applicant, the experience and potential of the personnel involved, the treatment and the significance of the project for the region.

INNOVATION IN THE DISTRIBUTION OF DIGITAL MEDIA

This award supports research and development in the use of digital media in production and distribution, to encourage partnerships between traditional production companies and new media companies and to secure investment in projects from regional organisations.

INNOVATION IN SHORT FILM AND TELEVISION PRODUCTION ACROSS A RANGE OF GENRES AND CONTEXTS

This award supports producer, director and writer teams in the development and production of short drama in any genre intended for cinematic release or broadcast, by funding up to 70% of the project's costs, with a ceiling of £10,000. The aim

is to improve related skills to aid career development.

DEVELOPMENT AND ASSISTANCE TOWARDS THE PRODUCTION AND DISTRIBUTION OF LOW BUDGET FILMS

This award supports the development of small and larger scale feature films that have clear market potential and established writers and producers on board, by funding up to 70% of the project's costs, with a ceiling of £10,000. The emphasis is on projects with partners that cross regional and national borders which will benefit the EM-Media region.

Priority will be given to companies based in the region, however, applications from companies based outside the region will be accepted and evaluated for their impact on the region's culture and industry. Additional assessment will be based on track record of the producer and writer, the quality of the project, the distribution and exhibition plans, and the audience and market potential.

Priority Three: To develop access and opportunity for the end user

DEVELOPING ACCESS TO ARCHIVE SERVICES AND MATERIALS

This fund supports schemes that promote the use of archive materials and the understanding of film culture and heritage, potentially using commercially viable methods.

DEVELOP EXHIBITION PROVISION, ACCESS AND CHOICE

This supports increasing access to, and audiences for, specialist cinema, paying attention to the cultural diversity of the region and areas lacking in specialist cinema facilities.

DEVELOP INTEGRATED EXHIBITION, EDUCATION, PRODUCTION AND DISTRIBUTION OPPORTUNITIES

This fund supports schemes that link education, production and distribution together, possibly in collaboration with other areas identified by EM-Media's priorities such as increasing access to archive materials.

DEVELOPMENT OF REGIONALLY, NATIONALLY AND INTERNATIONALLY SIGNIFICANT FESTIVALS, BUILDING AUDIENCES AND ACCESS

This supports festival initiatives that aim to overcome geographical and cultural boundaries.

SMALL SCALE CAPITAL AWARDS

This fund supports capital awards to benefit audiences and the end user. Assessment will be made of the costs involved in terms of the potential financial benefit and the potential sustainability of purchases.

General Guidelines for these schemes

DEADLINE

Applications may be made at any time.

ELIGIBILITY

Individuals are only eligible to apply for the schemes listed under Priority 2. Unless stated otherwise, all applicants, whether individuals or organisations, must be based in the region. Where organisations are eligible to apply they may be new or established and must be registered as limited companies, charities, consortia, schools, societies, colleges, libraries, universities, or local authorities.

DETAILS

Except where stated, EM-Media will fund organisations up to two-thirds of the project's costs, with a minimum of one third from match funding. Funding in kind is allowed at a maximum of one third of the project's costs. Where freelancers are eligible to apply, a ceiling of £5000 will be awarded to them.

APPLICATIONS

It is advised that applicants speak to EM-Media before submitting an application. The application process is carried out in two stages. Stage one involves completing a RIFE application form, which can be downloaded from the EM-Media web site. If an applicant is successful in being selected for stage two, they will be asked to provide further information.

ASSESSMENT

Each application is assessed against the following criteria: the cultural and industry benefits, impact and relevance, the improved access to film and moving image, the extent to which the project meets the regional priorities, the financial viability, and the ability of the applicant to manage the project.

CONDITIONS

EM-Media will inform applicants of the conditions attached to the lottery funding at the appropriate stage.

Digital Shorts

EM Media also operates the Digital Shorts scheme in association with the Film Council New Cinema Fund. For more information please refer to the Film Council section, or contact New Talent Executive Rebecca Mark-Lawson on 0115 955 6909 or rebecca.marklawson@em-media.org.uk

East Midlands Media Investments

EM-Media offers further funding in the form of investment through East Midlands Media Investments (EMMI), a partnership with the European Regional Investment Fund and private and public sector organisations, to support development and production of feature films, television singles and series, animation, radio, new and interactive media projects, and short films. There is no restriction on genre. Specific targets for production and development are features with budgets up to £4m, digital features with budgets up to £1m, television series or pilots with potential to sell to multiple markets, new media projects such as computer games, iTV, on-line projects, and mobile applications and services.

DEVELOPMENT

This fund supports individual projects in development and a slate of projects in development, which in turn aid the development of the company. Applicants are eligible to apply for up to £15,000 for individual project costs and up to £25,000 for a development slate, or a maximum of 50% of the costs.

PRODUCTION

This fund supports production including feature films, TV programmes and new media projects. Applicants are eligible to receive no more than 25% of the production cost from EMMI with a ceiling of £250,000.

SHORT FILM PRODUCTION SCHEMES

Occasionally, EMMI will consider funding production of individual short films under this programme, but more usually, short film production is delivered through production schemes such as the Digital Shorts.

General Guidelines for the EMMI lottery funding schemes

DEADLINE

Applications may be made at any time.

ELIGIBILITY

Individuals must be based in the region. Companies must be based in the region, or their production based in the region, or working with a partner based in the region, or creating opportunities for regional media and creative talent.

APPLICATIONS

Applicants must discuss their project with EMMI before submitting a formal application. In addition to the application form a formal application must include a treatment or script, a budget and schedule, details of other financiers and partners and CVs of key personnel and partners.

ASSESSMENT

Projects will be assessed on the following criteria: quality and distinctiveness of the project; the ability of the applicant to deliver the project; the level and type of benefit to the applicant company; inward regional investment; employment; the other financiers and the commercial viability. In addition other factors will be considered such as the distribution and exhibition plans, the necessity of receiving funding from EMMI, and the future economic benefit for the region.

CONDITIONS

Contributions from EMMI are made in the form of a loan, repayable only once the project goes into production. In addition EMMI will expect a premium to be paid or, if it contributes to the production finance, to receive an equity share.

Film London

20 Euston Centre
Regents Place
London
NW1 3JH
Tel: 020 7387 8787
Fax: 020 7387 8788
www.filmlondon.org.uk

Film London's activities incorporate the distribution of lottery money through the Regional Investment Fund for England and from the other funding programmes of the Film Council, as well as taking on the responsibilities of the LFVDA and the London Film Commission. Adrian Wooten, former director of the LFF is Chief Executive and producer Sandy Lieberson is chair. Film London receives funding from the Film Council's National Lottery programmes, the Regional Investment Fund for England (RIFE), the London Development Agency (LDA) and European Regional Development Funds. Film London's areas of responsibility include: encouraging and supporting filming in London; promoting access for all to watch, participate and enjoy moving image culture through exhibition and education; developing the industry, through support for production, training and economic initiatives; researching and making the case for film and media in London.
Film London currently has 8 films in production in the Pulse! digital shorts scheme run in partnership with the UK Film Council's New Cinema Fund. This scheme encompasses intensive training and script development for all the awardees.

The new agency continues to support artists working with film and video through the London Artists Film & Video Awards which is funded by Arts Council England London. The deadline for the 2003/4 awards is the end of November 2003 and information on how to apply is available at www.filmlondon.org.uk The ELMII initiative will run until December 2003

in collaboration with partners offering business advice, mapping of the area's industry and production schemes. The partners include Africa at the Pictures, Black Filmmakers Magazine, Community Media Association, East London Chamber of Commerce, Four Corners, Greenwich Films and Team Pictures. Some North and East London Boroughs run small production schemes as part of the initiative such as Enfield, Newham, Hackney and Tower Hamlets. Similar production funds which fall outside the ELMII initiative are supported by Film London Details of these schemes are in the London Boroughs section on page 138.

Film London is currently developing an integrated strategy across production, training and personal and company development which will maximise limited resources, complement existing provision and partnerships and encourage production that genuinely mirrors the complexity and diversity of London. They hope to announce their initial range of funding schemes and programmes early in 2004 with finance available from April 2004.

NORTHERN
FILM ✛ MEDIA
investing in people and ideas

Northern Film & Media

Central Square
Forth Street
Newcastle upon Tyne , NE1 3PJ
Tel: 0191 269 9200
Fax: 0191 269 9213
Email: info@northernmedia.org
Web: www.northernmedia.org

Covering: Tyne & Wear, Northumberland, County Durham, Tees Valley

Northern Film & Media has set its regional priorities as economic sustainability and creative quality in media businesses, encouraging investment, innovation in the use of digital technologies, improving international relationships and increasing opportunities for audiences.

Development of People

This scheme is aimed towards developing training and vocational development opportunities for individuals in the film and media sector. The kinds of projects likely to receive funding are industry standard training courses, industry placements for career development and for graduates, and mentoring schemes. The fund will support both those looking to deliver these schemes and those wishing to benefit from them. Up to £5000 is available for individuals and up to £10,000 for organisations.

Development of Content

This scheme is aimed towards developing, producing and delivering creative content projects with a commercial market in mind. The kinds of projects likely to receive funding are treatment and script development, production of moving image projects in a range of genre and platforms, completion and post production of moving image projects, and marketing of a developing project or a completed project. Up to £10,000 is available for individuals and up to £40,000 for organisations.

Development of Companies

This scheme is aimed towards growth and development of regional media companies. The kinds of projects likely to receive funding are business development, business mentoring, marketing, training support and skills and talent attachment. Up to £25,000 for organisations which have been established for at least 36 months are eligible to apply.

Development of Audiences

This scheme is aimed towards development of size and diversity of audiences for specialist film and moving image media, as well as development of education and opportunities for audiences. The kinds of areas likely to receive funding are festivals, venues, technology, access and inclusion, participation, education and archives. Up to £5000 is available for individuals and up to £20,000 for organisations.

Development of Networks

This scheme is aimed towards the sharing of resources, skills and information regionally, nationally and internationally. The kinds of projects likely to receive funding are regional networks, partnerships, attendance of events, regional conferences, trade visits and screenings. Up to a maximum of £1500 is available.

General Guidelines

DEADLINE
Applications may be made at any time.

ELIGIBILITY
Organisations and individuals living or working in the Northern region are eligible to apply for all the awards, with the exception of the Company Development scheme.

DETAILS
Match funding of more than 25% of the total cost of the project is required.

APPLICATIONS
In addition to the application form, the monitoring form and the data protection preferences, individuals must submit a CV and organisations must submit copies of their accounts, and their rules, constitutions or memoranda & articles. Applications will only be accepted on hard copy by post.

ASSESSMENT
Each application will be assessed against the following criteria: the quality of the proposed project; the contribution to Northern Film & Media's strategic objectives; the ability to fulfil the planned proposal; the financial viability and the value for money.

CONDITIONS
For further information see the website www.northernmedia.org

Digital Shorts

Northern Film & Media also operates the Digital Shorts scheme in association with the Film Council New Cinema Fund. For more information please refer to the Film Council section, or contact Helen Stearman on 0191 269 9200 or email helen@northernmedia.org

North West Vision

233, The Tea Factory
82, Wood Street
Liverpool, L1 4DQ
Tel: 0151 708 2967
Fax: 0151 708 2984
General email: jacquir@northwestvision.co.uk
Production & Funding: tomg@northwestvision.co.uk
Web: www.northwestvision.co.uk

North West Vision is the regional screen agency for the North West of England set up to champion the region's film and TV industry, celebrate the region's talent and diversity and build on the region's production success. North West Vision distributes Regional Investment Fund for England (RIFE) Lottery funding on behalf of the UK Film Council to develop an innovative and sustainable film industry. This funding is split into three strands.

Organisational & Individual Development

The minimum award available is £500 to a maximum of £5000.

TRAINING
This strand covers professional development and skills training for writers, directors

and producers, careers advice, training for trainers, projects that support the training and development of members of the population currently under-represented in the screen media industries, training for skills shortages, training support for new talent.

SECTOR SPECIFIC SUPPORT FOR COMPANIES OR ORGANISATIONS

This strand covers hiring of expertise to assist skills development, market research, collective marketing initiatives, trade shows, markets and festivals attendance, training and skills development courses.

PROFESSIONAL DEVELOPMENT OF INDIVIDUALS

This strand covers hiring of expertise to assist skills development, trade shows, conferences and festivals attendance, training and skills development courses.

Production & Development

North West Vision intends to invest in creative people and products that are diverse, distinctive and dynamic; that originate from a broad range of cultures, backgrounds and experiences and that contribute to the economic, social and cultural prosperity in the North West. They will support:

DEVELOPMENT (ADVERTISED QUARTERLY)

Feature Film Script development (applications up to £5,000); Development of feature film projects. This can include feature film seed funding to secure further finance (up to £5,000);

FILM PRODUCTION (APPLICATIONS CAN BE MADE AT ANY TIME)

Completion awards for short films (applications up to £5,000); Innovative feature film production projects which exploit the unique properties of new media technologies (up to £20,000);

SCHEMES

Virgin Shorts - £1,000 bursaries for first time film makers; Production of short narrative films; North West Vision's Digital Short Film scheme run in conjunction with the UK Film Council's New Cinema Fund

Recoupment on development projects that convert into productions (including script development) must be repaid out of the budget plus a 20% premium, once a project secures production funding. This will be due on the first day of principal photography.

Audience Development

Projects are eligible to receive between £5000 and £20,000.

North West Vision seeks to ensure audiences throughout the region have access to a wide and diverse range of cinema and moving image product: and that there is a spread of learning opportunities that develop people's understanding of the creation of moving images. They also seek to support conservation of and access to the region's audio visual heritage. They will support:

- Festivals or similar activities that display a high level of quality which include one of the following priorities:

  • Celebrate Black and Asian culture and actively involve Black and Asian communities.

  • Work with and excite young people.

  • Have something to offer rural communities.

  • Promote and celebrate the work of practitioners from the North West to a wider audience

- Projects that develop exhibition and distribution opportunities in particular those utilising new media technologies;

- Education projects with young people or that improve access into the film industry

- Projects that support the conservation of audio visual material and increasing public access to archive collections.

General Guidelines for the lottery funding schemes

ELIGIBILITY

Applications are eligible from legally constituted organisations, and in some cases individuals, living or operating in the North West region of England, comprising Cheshire Cumbria, Greater Manchester, Lancashire and Merseyside.

ORGANISATIONS

North West Vision welcome applications from film and moving image media organisations and from organisations whose normal activity may not be film and moving image media related but whose specific proposal deals with this area. These can include private companies, voluntary organisations, community groups, local authorities and other public organisations and registered charities.

If you are an organisation you must have a written constitution or set of rules that show how your activities and finances are managed. To be eligible to apply for Lottery funding, your organisation must be based in the North West region.

National organisations can apply for lottery funding if the beneficiaries are resident in the North West region. North West Vision welcomes applications from national organisations running pan regional schemes that benefit the North West's film and moving image industry.

INDIVIDUALS

Freelance individuals resident in the North West region can make applications for specific strands. Please contact the Lottery Department at North West Vision for further information. If you are an individual you will need to provide NWV with proof of your address.

Individuals cannot apply for lottery awards to purchase capital items such as equipment. Awards to individuals are limited to a maximum of £5,000. Students, staff and

Board members of North West Vision are not eligible to apply for funding.

ASSESSMENT

Each applicant must meet the Mission and priorities of North West Vision and the UK Film Council to be eligible. Then they will consider the following four criteria:

-The quality of the proposed activity (the project must be of the highest standard)

-Public benefit (the project must benefit the region, the industry and the public and contribute to social inclusion, cultural diversity and access to film and moving image activity)

-Ability and commitment (you must provide evidence of ability and demonstrate your commitment to the regional film industry)

-The financial viability of the proposal (this must show that the project is financially viable, represents value for money and will lever a suitable level of partnership funding)

CONDITIONS

North West Vision expects to receive a credit on any related promotion materials for any project they fund.

Partnership/match funding should consist of

-For projects up to £2,000, the minimum amount of partnership funding must be 25% (£500) of which at least half (£250) must be in cash from external sources.

-Projects in excess of £2,000 must secure a minimum of 30% partnership funding of which at least two thirds must be in cash.

-Awards for script development and individual training bursaries may not require partnership funding (please check this with North West Vision's Lottery Department prior to applying).

North West Vision Schemes that are funded through the Lottery but advertised separately (such as funding for short films) have their own partnership/match funding requirements that will be published alongside the scheme's guidelines.

Screen South

Folkestone Enterprise Centre
Shearway Road
Folkestone, CT19 4RH
Tel: 01303 298 222
Fax: 01303 298 227
Email: info@screensouth.co.uk
Web: www.screensouth.co.uk

Covering: Kent, Buckinghamshire, Oxfordshire, Hampshire, Surrey, Berkshire, East and West Sussex, and the Isle of Wight

Screen South has set its regional priorities as the need for a sustainable media industry, to increase opportunities for audiences, and to develop talent. Its lottery programme is structured in three priority streams. Filmmakers can apply to Screen South through one of its production schemes or through the open funds where projects should fit with the agency's priorities.

Priority One: To develop viable film and media businesses

This priority supports the development of a sustainable media industry. The kinds of projects likely to receive funding are development of business partnerships, organisational and capacity building, and events that promote networking, collaboration and co-production.

Priority Two: To develop audiences and cultural partnerships

This priority supports development of accessibility to film and moving image media, education for audiences, and opportunities to participate in a film culture. The kinds of projects likely to

receive funding are bringing diverse cinema to audiences, bringing film and media education to audiences and taking film archives and heritage to audiences.

Priority Three: To develop and discover regional talent

This priority supports development and promotion of regional film and media businesses and individuals. The kinds of projects likely to receive funding are script development schemes, advice for developing scripts and projects, production and distribution of film, media and new technologies in a range of genres.

General Guidelines for the lottery funding schemes

DEADLINE

Applications may be made at any time.

ELIGIBILITY

Individuals and organisations based or working in the region are eligible to apply. Organisations must be registered as limited companies, charities, consortia, schools, societies, colleges, libraries, universities, or sole traders.

DETAILS

Organisations can apply for a maximum £10,000. Individuals can apply for a maximum of £5000. Partnership funding is required.

APPLICATIONS

In addition to the application form, individual applicants must submit CVs for all personnel involved. Organisations must submit CVs for all personnel involved, a set of the most recent accounts, a set of the management accounts and the constitution or rules of the organisation.

Other items are also required depending on the project. Feature film applications must include a full treatment, a full script and a cash flow projection. Short films or TV

GINA FEGAN, CHIEF EXECUTIVE   SCREEN SOUTH

"Our ethos goes against the subsidy culture – we're not hand-out, but hand-up.

"Usually people will come to us wanting to make a short film - 80% of applications are for short films, but we actually try not to fund them - we prefer to offer support and skills training. The application process is one where the filmmakers learn to professionalize. Through the funding round they will pitch to a panel of people from different sides of the industry and those people will give their own advice as well as our staff, so you're getting quite high level feedback just by the process of applying. We've worked with Scott Meek of Indigo Productions, Alex Marshall of Spice Factory, Dawn Sharpless at the Short Film Bureau, Linda James at Alibi.

"We also run a workshop for everyone wanting to apply to us. We go through the process of funding – does the project have legs; how should you view your own project; the various budgeting info you need to know. So by the time the filmmaker gets to the panel, they should have a budget, a treatment and an outline that could convince any investor in the validity of the project. They've been encouraged to prepare a written statement and have had an experience of making an oral presentation – so they've had proper industry experience.

"The open funds are where we have a much more open view. Sometimes people will propose a project which is about how to move them on in the industry. Such as 'I want to present my feature film proposal to the industry'. And this is where we fund the lunch and they do the work in getting the industry to come along, So we allocate a sum of money to their project – they in turn include perhaps another three projects attempting to do the same from the region who will also join in and get their industry contacts along, so each is bringing something in. We've used their time and energy and given the money to present the screening – and they've gained the skills in presentation. Of course to do this they would need to have a viable and developed project - we wouldn't pick someone who hadn't applied to us in the past.

"We don't give development money, we give the tools to develop the project – if there are a number of filmmakers then we will back something appropriate such as help with international sales estimates, preparing to present to financiers, or packaging or pitching as we can see there's a list of things you need in your toolbox as a filmmaker. It's very much about the skills based needs of the filmmaker, and we try to respond with appropriate projects. We recently sent a group of filmmakers with features to sell out to LA for 10 days – we covered flights and accommodation, helped them prepare their pitch and they did the legwork. The most common failure is people not treating themselves as professionals. We expect everybody to be a professional.

"Our maximum award is £10,000 – we've given out £600,000 in the past year. £200,000 goes on our community programme and we've given out £280,000 in individual awards. The written application comes in and that goes to an external assessor, who passes that on to all of the panel, so when the applicant comes to us its in a context that we've actually read about the project beforehand. We get further information from an oral presentation, and take all of that together and the panel will make a recommendation which will go to the board and at that point the decision is taken in connection with the funding we have available. So for example at the last funding round we had applications for £350,000, and we made awards of £38,000. You may apply for £10,000 and we may give only £1,000."
NW

production applications should include a full script and a detailed budget. Festival applications should include a detailed cash flow projection, a detailed budget, a programming schedule and a full festival description.

ASSESSMENT

Each application will be assessed against the following criteria: the technical and artistic quality; the ability of the project to meet Screen South's regional priorities; the benefit to the general public of the Screen South region; financial viability; the applicants ability to manage and deliver the project.

CONDITIONS

Screen South's contributions are made in the form of an investment, which will be recouped from income generated by the project. Screen South also requires a credit on any materials associated with the project.

Production Schemes

DREAMCATCHER

In collaboration with Kent Hothouse this scheme supports script development for screenwriters in the Screen South region. In a similar way to the 25 Words Or Less scheme from the Film Council Development Fund, screenwriters are selected to develop their ideas to first draft script stage. Applicants must submit a pitch line of 25 words or less outlining the story idea, a one page outline of the story idea and narrative structure, a 10 page sample scene preferably from the story, name and contact details, a covering letter outlining the ambitions for the project and an indication of the target audience. Fifteen writers will be chosen to attend a workshop to develop ideas. Five of the writers will be awarded £1500 to develop the treatment and the help of a script editor. Writers from two of these projects will go on to receive £5000 to write the first draft with the support of the script editor.

FREE FOR ALL

This initiative searches for stories from underrepresented voices, such as rural communities and senior citizens. It is for people with no experience who will be supported by mentors. For further details, contact Screen South.

ONE-TO-ONE

This is a mentoring scheme for producers to take a short project into co-production with European partners. It is delivered through the Kent Hothouse. For further details, contact Screen South.

FIRST CUT

This is an annual broadcast production scheme for 5-10 minute factual-based films focused on contemporary regional stories. The films are commissioned by Carlton TV. It is open to individuals with no previous broadcast credit, living in the region. The projects must aim to use crew and resources in the region.

There is a budget guideline of £1000 per broadcast minute. Carlton Television will support the successful applicants in the completion of their project by providing an induction workshop to the technical, legal and marketing aspects of producing, as well as offering technical and editing facilities, paid for from the film's budget.

South West Screen

St Bartholomews Court
Lewins Mead
Bristol, BS1 5BT
Tel: 0117 952 9977
Fax: 0117 952 9988
Email: info@swscreen.co.uk
Web: www.swscreen.co.uk

Covering: Gloucestershire, Wiltshire, Bristol, Somerset, Dorset, Devon and Cornwall.

South West Screen has set its regional priorities to develop a strong and sustainable infrastructure and media industry, to develop talent and to increase opportunities for audiences. The agency is re-organising its lottery funding schemes into three priority areas and at publication full details of awards were not yet available.

Sarah Jane Meredith, Screen Development and Lottery Manager

"South West Screen is the public agency responsible for leading the strategic development and promotion of the film, TV and digital content sector in the South West of England. We aim to improve the competitiveness and sustainability of the sector, developing a dynamic and innovative culture where creativity flourishes and businesses thrive and which is strengthened by being both inclusive and diverse.

"We won't be offering our funds in the same way as in 2002/03. Our funds will cover applications for: moving image education, exhibition/access, moving image archives, marketing, short film production, feature length project and script development, company/business development, individual training bursaries. Alongside general guidelines, we will also offer particular schemes, such as the Digital Shorts scheme, but this has yet to be confirmed for 2003/04."

Strand 1: Developing the film, television and digital content sector.

The focus will be on developing a sustainable sector with a strong physical and human infrastructure. It will work in five specific areas:

1   Development of regional and sub-regional sector partnerships.

2   Provision of robust data and information about the sector in the region.

3   Development of regional organisations and businesses.

4   Promotion and/or development of the South West's profile as a centre of excellence for film, television and digital content.

5   Contribution to the region's provision of training and vocational education so that the South West's workforce is able to meet the needs of employers, both now and in the future.

Strand 2: Developing talent and innovation

This strand will support regional talent, encouraging innovation, creativity and dynamism in the moving image business and culture of the region. It will work in three ways: script development of feature film projects; project development of feature projects; and professional development.

Strand 3: Developing film and moving image culture and increasing access.

This strand's priority is to encourage participation and education in moving image creation, culture and history.

It will work in five specific areas:

1　Investing in regional, national and international film festivals .

2　Supporting audience development projects.

3　Investing in the development of Moving Image Education Hubs.

4　Developing exhibition provision across the region.

5　Supporting the conservation of audio visual material and increasing public access to archive collections.

Screen West Midlands

31/41 Bromley Street
Birmingham, B9 4AN
Tel: 0121 766 1470
Fax: 0121 766 1480
Email: info@screenwm.co.uk
Web: www.screenwm.co.uk

Covering: Herefordshire, Staffordshire, Shropshire, Birmingham and The West Midlands, Warwickshire, Worcestershire & Telford and The Wrekin.

Screen West Midlands invests public funding to create a vibrant, dynamic, productive and constantly evolving screen culture and industry in the West Midlands.

Regional Lottery Fund

The Screen West Midlands Regional Lottery Fund aims to financially support high-quality film and screen media activity throughout the West Midlands. Screen West Midlands has set its regional Lottery priorities in key areas of training, education, audience development and sub-regional development.

Priority is given to projects that:

1.　Promote and reflect the diversity of the region

2.　Encourage social inclusion into film and screen media industry and culture

3.　Offer high quality ideas with good standards of design and planning, and which can be practically achieved within the resources available.

ADVANTAGE BROADCAST FUND

Screen West Midlands has a stream of funding for helping to create a strong broadcast infrastructure in the West Midlands. The Advantage Broadcast Fund aims to stimulate more commissions from the region and contribute to a sustainable broadcast industry in the West Midlands.

TRAINING FREELANCE DEVELOPMENT FUND

Screen West Midlands is working to increase the level and quality of training for freelancers and companies through facilitating access to career development advice and providing funding to help with the costs of training and development. We can provide a contribution of up to 70% of the cost of short courses, funded in partnership with Skillset.

GRADUATE TRAINING PROGRAMME

Screen West Midlands is offering 20 Birmingham based graduates the opportunity to spend 3 months on placement in a busy production company gaining hands on experience and an NVQ in Health & Safety. Funded by Birmingham and Solihull Learning and Skills Council, companies prepared to offer this experience will get a significant contribution towards the salary of their graduate trainee.

PRODUCTION FUNDING

Screen West Midlands is currently developing a Production Loan Fund which will fund script and feature film development. Further information will be available later in 2003.

Steve Chapman, Funding & Policy Manager on Lottery applications

"What characterises a good funding application is that it is like a mini business plan. Good thought has gone into the design and planning of the project, how it is managed, who is involved, and how it is delivered. Enough detail has gone into the budget to show that all costs have been considered. A common mistake is to rush an application and give the bare bones, it's really a full days work – we take at least 4 hours to assess each one. Make sure you address the criteria for the scheme, and your project falls within its priorities; we can't fund everything and so we have to make choices. Get advice and information – applications to our main Lottery programme have had an 80% success rate because of the help we have given in their preparation."

General Guidelines for these schemes

DEADLINE

All of the funding strands have set deadlines, check the website for further info.

ELIGIBILITY

All applicants must be based in the Screen West Midlands region.

DETAILS

For Lottery projects grants are provided up to a maximum of £20,000 except in exceptional circumstances. Match funding is required.

APPLICATIONS

Applicants should contact Screen West Midlands at least one month before the scheme deadline. They will then be booked into an appropriate advice surgery, ahead of which applicants must send a draft application for the project. In addition to the application form, applicants must enclose a detailed budget for the project. If the applicant is an organisation, they

must additionally supply a copy of the organisation's most recent accounts and a copy of the organisation's constitution. Applications will only be accepted as hard copy by post.

ASSESSMENT

Each Lottery application will be assessed against the following criteria: the quality of the project; the public benefit; the ability of the applicant to deliver the project; the extent to which the project fits with the priorities of Screen West Midlands; the financial viability.

CONDITIONS

For every project funded Screen West Midlands must be credited on all film, video, website or other related promotional material. They also require prior approval of any press releases.

Production Schemes

DIGITAL SHORTS

Screen West Midlands operates the Digital Shorts scheme in association with the Film Council's New Cinema Fund. For more information please refer to the Film Council section or contact Jane Slater on jane@screenwm.co.uk

FIRST CUT

First Cut is a regional broadcast production scheme for 5-10 minute films focused on contemporary regional stories. The films are commissioned by Carlton Broadcasting and Screen West Midlands. It is open to individuals living in the region with no previous broadcast credit as Director. The projects must aim to use crew and resources from the region.

There is a maximum budget guideline of £8500 per project and each year the West Midlands will commission 40 minutes of programming (4 or 5 films). Screen West Midlands and Carlton Broadcasting will support the successful applicants in the completion of their project by providing

an induction workshop to the technical, legal and marketing aspects of producing. Screen West Midlands also provides training opportunities and Production Executive support.

Screen West Midlands is committed to developing production support and constantly working on new methods to support filmmakers, for information on new or updated production schemes please refer to the website.

screen
YORKSHIRE
Screen Yorkshire

40 Hanover Square
Leeds, LS3 18Q
Tel: 0113 294 4410
Fax: 0113 294 4989
Email: info@screenyorkshire.co.uk

Covering: Humberside, North Yorkshire, South Yorkshire and West Yorkshire

Screen Yorkshire has set its regional priorities to develop talent, to develop a sustainable media industry, and to develop opportunities for audiences. Its lottery programme is organised into three priority streams.

Priority 1: Investing in development and promotion of regional talent

SCRIPT DEVELOPMENT AND SCREENWRITING TALENT

This award supports new and established screenwriters and creative personnel in the research, writing and development of scripts, storyboards and ideas. Organisations may apply for up to 70% of the development costs or up to £10,000. Partnership funding must be at least 30% and 10% of this can be in kind.

Applications from organisations outside the region will be considered as long as the project takes place within the region, but applicants resident in the region will be given priority. The previous works of the applicant, the experience and potential of the personnel involved, the treatment and the significance of the project for the region are key to assessment.

SHORT FILM DEVELOPMENT, PRODUCTION AND DISTRIBUTION

This award is to develop the skills and experience and careers of creative teams of writers, directors and producers with the aim of producing short dramas, documentary or animation broadcast or cinematic exhibition. Organisations may apply for up to 70% of the production costs or up to £10,000. Partnership funding must be at least 30% and 10% of this can be in kind. The distribution plans will also be taken into consideration.

DEVELOPMENT AND DISTRIBUTION OF LOW BUDGET FILMS

This award supports development and distribution of small or mid scale feature films which have a clear market potential by focusing on script and project development, and securing production finance on a local, national and global scale. Organisations may apply for up to 70% of the development costs or up to £10,000. Partnership funding must be at least 30% and 10% of this can be in kind.

Applications from organisations outside the region will be considered as long as the project takes place within the region with a significant cultural and industrial impact. Applicants resident in the region will be given priority.

Priority 2: Increasing the size and competitiveness of the film and moving image sector

RESEARCH, FEASIBILITY, AND COMPANY DEVELOPMENT STUDIES

This award supports business and sector development schemes, such as increasing access to market information, market research and testing of ideas and company development plans for new and established businesses. The award will fund up to 80% of the project costs, requiring partnership funding of at least 20%. 5% of this can be in kind. Projects will be assessed for their need in the market place and the support from the industry.

EVENTS AND SCHEMES WHICH ENCOURAGE COLLABORATION AND PARTNERSHIPS

This award supports the development of partnerships and networks for the screen industries. It will fund up to 80% of the project costs, requiring partnership funding of at least 20%, and 5% of this can be in kind.

ORGANISATIONAL DEVELOPMENT AND CAPACITY BUILDING

This award supports projects that increase and develop the market intelligence, business skills, and research capacity of organisations. It will also consider funding the development of a slate of projects over an extended time period. The award will fund up to 80% of the project costs, requiring partnership funding of at least 20%, and 5% of this can be in kind.

Priority 3: Building audiences, participation, knowledge and culture

This award supports improvement of access for audiences to film and the moving image and their understanding and involvement through access to archive services and materials, supporting sustainable and diverse exhibition provision, the promotion of festivals, and increasing the availability of media education. The award will fund up to 80% of the project costs, requiring partnership funding of at least 20%, and 5% of this can be in kind. Individuals may not apply.

General Guidelines for the lottery funding schemes

DEADLINE

Applications may be made at any time.

DETAILS

Individuals may apply for up to £5000.

ELIGIBILITY

Individuals may apply for all awards except those under Priority 3. Organisations may apply for all awards if they are registered as limited companies, charities, consortia, schools, voluntary organisations, colleges, libraries, universities, or sole traders. Applicants must be based within the region, unless stated otherwise.

APPLICATIONS

It is possible to speak to staff from Screen Yorkshire before applying. In addition to the application form, applicants must enclose a copy of the organisation's most recent accounts, a copy of the management accounts, a copy of the organisation's constitution and a cash-flow projection. The applicant will be notified if their application is eligible within two weeks and a likely decision date given.

ASSESSMENT

Each application will be assessed against the following criteria: the quality of the project; the public benefit; the ability of the applicant to deliver the project; the extent to which the project fits with the priorities of Screen Yorkshire and the financial viability.

CONDITIONS

Screen Yorkshire invests in projects requiring repayment of their investment and a percentage of revenues in most cases. Any project must be credited to Screen Yorkshire.

London Boroughs

City of Westminster

City of Westminster Arts Coucil
Room 70, Marylebone Library
Marylebone Road
London, NW1 5PS
Tel: 020 7641 1017 or 020 7641 1018
Email funding@cwac.org.uk
Web: www.cwac.org.uk

WESTMINSTER FILM, VIDEO AND MOVING IMAGE BURSARIES

The City of Westminster Arts Council
is funded by the Westminster City
Council. The bursary is run by the City of
Westminster Arts Council and the London
Film and Video Development Agency. The
annual award with a deadline in March
supports the production of new work
in film, video or digital multimedia. In
2003 individuals and organisations that
work, study or live full time in the City
of Westminster were eligible to apply for
£1000 to produce a short film. Applicants
may apply for funding to cover the full costs
of the production as long as this is below
the ceiling of £1000. In addition to funding
successful applicants will be given free
editing time at Paddington Arts and City
of Westminster Art Council will organise a
screening of the films.

Croydon Council

Croydon Media Awards
Croydon Clocktower
Katharine Street
Croydon CR9 1ET
Tel: 020 8760 5400
Email: paul_johnson@croydon.gov.uk
Web: www.croydon.gov.uk/clocktower

The annual Croydon Media Awards with
a deadline in March supports up to 8
short films of drama, documentary or an
experimental nature of no more than 8
minutes long. Applications may be made
by directors or director-producer teams.
Submissions must include a treatment,
application form and showreel for the
directors. Shortlisted applicants will be
selected through an interview process.
Residents within a seven mile radius of the
Croydon Clocktower are eligible to apply
for between £500 and £1500. Successful
applicants will also be given the use of
MiniDV camera kits and postproduction
facilities, along with consultancy sessions
from a professional producer and script
advisor.

Enfield

Enfield Film Fund
London Borough of Enfield
Arts Unit
Forty Hall
Forty Hill, EN2 9HA
Tel: 020 8363 8196
Fax: 020 8367 9098
Email: fortyhall.lbe@fsmail.net
Web: www.enfield.gov.uk

The Enfield Film Fund with an annual
deadline in March offers two levels of film
and video awards to produce short films of
any genre or theme. The first award offers
£1000 to young inexperienced filmmakers
between the ages of 16 and 24. The second
offers two awards of £2000 to more
experienced filmmakers over the age of 18
with at least one short film behind them.
Applicants must come from production
teams with at least one member resident in
Enfield. Young filmmakers based in Enfield
may receive support from the Enfield Youth
Service in preparing their application. In
addition to the cash award, the filmmakers
will receive guidance from a professional
script editor and production advisor as well
as free or preferential rates on production
and editing facilities.

Newham

Newham Film Fund
London Borough of Newham
Regeneration & Partnerships Division
330 Barking Road
East Ham
London, E6 2RP
Tel: 020 8430 3312
Email: carol.thomas@newham.gov.uk
Web: www.newham.gov.uk/filmfund

This annual award with a deadline in March/April supports the production of short films, drama, or artistic videos lasting no longer than 10 minutes, or 25 minutes for documentaries. Newham-based production companies or professional freelancers who have not received more than £60,000 from public grants or schemes over the previous 3 years are eligible to apply. The maximum grant is £5000. Match funding is not required unless the project costs exceed the maximum grant available.

Tower Hamlets & Hackney

Tower Hamlets Film Office
Brady Centre,
192 Hanbury Street,
London, E1 5HU.
Tel: 020 7364 7920
Email: filmsoffice@dial.pipex.com.

The Tower Hamlets Film and Video Production Fund supports new and emerging filmmakers with 8 awards a year made up to a value of £4,000 to make a short film. Formats accepted are experimental/animation/drama (no longer than 10 minutes), and documentary (no longer than 30 minutes). The application deadline is in March each year. Filmmakers must include a script, treatment and budget.

Film Officer Sarah Wren explains the thinking behind the scheme: "The film industry has traditionally been based in the West End and, I think I can say this, it's pretty much based on who you know. Doors open through your contacts. If you are going to make short films you have to beg and borrow from everyone you know and people in the East End just haven't got that access to hand because people in the industry never worked out here. It's still a big problem so we are trying to make it easier for them to take their first step into the industry.

"We are trying to be quite professional about it for the filmmaker's sake. We'll draw up a shortlist, scale that down and then ask people to come in and pitch, give people an experience of what it's like to go through that process. They've got to write a decent script and a decent treatment. Sure we'll give them a script editor but we aren't going to do all the work for them."

Waltham Forest

Waltham Forest Arts
William Morris Gallery
Lloyd Park, Forest Road
London, E17 4PP
Tel: 020 8527 8750

HITCHCOCK PRODUCTION FUND

The Hitchcock Fund provides £15,000 a year with contributions of £5000 each from the LFVDA, the Waltham Forest Arts Council and the London borough of Waltham Forest. Three filmmakers or groups of filmmakers resident or working in Waltham Forest receive £5000 each, enabling them to film in the area. Applicants must send in a script by July. The selected projects are chosen on their creative merit and the likelihood of being produced within the budget.

London Borough of Wandsworth

Arts office
Room 224A
the Town Hall
Wandsworth High Street
London SW18 2PU
Tel: 020 8871 8711
Email: arts@wandsworth.gov.uk
Web: www.wandsworth.gov.uk

WANDSWORTH FILM & VIDEO AWARDS

The annual award with an April deadline is run by the Wandsworth Arts Office, the Wandsworth Film Office and the London Film and Video Development Agency. Individual filmmakers or filmmaking organisations that work, study or live full time in Wandsworth are eligible to apply for up to £5000 to produce or complete a short film. The film must have a budget of no more than £25,000.

LAB KY MO   NINE DEAD GAY GUYS

Lab Ky Mo's debut feature was one of the few major controversies of Cannes 2002, clocking up serious column inches this side of the pond – all on a micro-budget with a profile cast including Steven Berkoff, and a heavy dose of political incorrectness.

"I spent a year writing the script and got very excited by all the silliness and the blowjobs and things. I was very optimistic and so I gave it to my agent who's quite well known - she hated it and wouldn't represent it. If your agent won't work with your script there's not a great deal you can do with it and secondly, a lot of people were turned off by the subject matter, because they thought that it would be a hard core porn movie. So I did approach some organisations but I didn't get very far.

"My only mistake was with the budget. I started off with a small outfit and ended up with a very large, professional shoot and the money didn't tally. Case in point: If you have four wardrobe people that are all used to working in TV and used to taking tons and tons of Polaroid's, if they come on your shoot they'll continue to and that's all money.

"The shooting budget was £80,000 and we over shot by about the same amount, we got our money's worth really. It was a good set up, 50 people every day but I got them from all sorts of places. One of the assistant producers works on Family Affairs and we got a lot of our HoD's from soaps who'd had a lot of experience running large teams. This film was inspired by my mate who went out and shot a film for £25,000 on DigiBeta and I was heading down that route - a 10 man guerrilla shoot on a similar budget. I ended up shooting a million pound film on Super16 and on a lot less money.

"There's a point where you've got to spend money to have a product that's a little more saleable. For instance, our transport budget was about six or seven grand, our catering budget was around twenty grand but every little detail helps.

"You can knock Hollywood forever, however, it's an industry town and British people won't understand what that means. Every single person in the city has something to do with film and it's a respected industry so everyone gets well paid. LA's great for the technicians. My BAFTA sponsored neg is still there, it's stored in the same vault as the Terminator 2 neg and the place looks like the Pentagon! In Hong Kong they cut my neg with cellotape so you saw a white flash with every cut but they are so immune to the fucking poor quality that they didn't see it." *TF*

Other English regional funds

City Eye Media Centre

The City Eye Production Award
Swaythling Neighbourhood Centre
Rear 200 Burgess Road, Swaythling
Southampton, SO16 3AY
Tel 023 80 677167
Email: takeone@city-eye.co.uk, or, taketwo@city-eye.co.uk
Web: www.city-eye.co.uk

City Eye Media Centre is funded by Southampton City Council, Southern Arts and Screen South to support local filmmakers and film production through hire of equipment, access to resources and production schemes. They run two short film production awards called Take One and Take Two.

Take One Production Award

This award supports first time filmmakers to produce short films of original drama, documentary or experimental content.

ELIGIBILITY

The filmmaker must not have any previous experience.

DETAILS

Applicants receive training on City Eye's filmmaking equipment, use of the equipment to make their short film and presence of a "mentor" for guidance and assistance throughout. The Take One scheme allows 3 days shooting and 4 days editing. This is not a monetary award.

APPLICATIONS

In addition to the application form, Take One applicants must submit a project outline and a treatment.

Take Two Production Award

This award supports filmmakers with some experience to produce short films of original drama, documentary or experimental.

ELIGIBILITY

The filmmaker must have some previous experience of short filmmaking.

DETAILS

Applicants receive training on City Eye's filmmaking equipment, use of the equipment to make their short film, and a "mentor" for guidance and assistance throughout. The Take Two scheme allows 14 days shooting and 14 days editing. This is not a monetary award.

APPLICATIONS

In addition to the application form, Take Two applicants must submit a project outline, a treatment, draft script, a draft story board and details of the creative elements.

General Guidelines for both awards

DEADLINE

Applications can be made at any time.

ELIGIBILITY

Filmmakers, video, digital and fine artists, photographers and anyone interested in the moving image who lives in the Southampton or Hampshire area are eligible. Full time students are not eligible. Filmmakers living outside Southampton may be considered if the majority of the crew live in the area.

ASSESSMENT

Each application will be assessed for imagination and creativity, a clear and realistic vision and aims, and the benefit of the opportunity for aspiring directors, producers and crew.

CONDITIONS

City Eye will receive 60% of any profit made on income from the film and share in the copyright until the agreed value of the award has been recouped. The full copyright will then return to the filmmaker. If there is no income from the film, repayment will not be necessary. The filmmaker is responsible for securing any rights relating to the production.

City Eye must receive a credit on the film, and stills photographs from the production. City Eye must be advised of any changes during production and reserves the right to withdraw due to significant changes.

Cornwall Film Fund

Pydar House
Pydar Street
Truro, TR1 1EA
Tel: 01872 322886
Fax: 01872 322887
Email: director@cornwallfilm.com
Web: www.cornwallfilm.com

The fund supports local filmmaking and has contributed to feature film development, short film production and screenwriting. Phase 1 of the initiative is now over, and Phase 2 is expected to begin in 2003. Contributions are intended to be up to 10% or £200,000 towards production costs of feature films and major TV programmes. The fund is supported by South West Screen, Cornwall County Council, Cornwall Enterprise and the European Union. The web site will be up-dated with information once developments have been confirmed.

The Ignition Network

The Ignition Network
9-12 Middle Street
Brighton, BN1 3RH
Tel: 07773 634328
Emal: ignition_net@hotmail.com

This initiative was set up in 2000 to support new filmmakers to produce short digital films lasting no longer than 7 minutes in any genre in drama, documentary or animation. Each year a theme is given, for example, in 2003 the theme was "Memory". The scheme is supported by Screen South.

DEADLINE

There is an annual deadline in December

ELIGIBILITY

First time filmmakers based in Brighton are eligible to apply. Applicants must be over 16 and students are not eligible.

DETAILS

The award covers equipment loan, script, production and post-production support, paid expenses, technical support and a guaranteed screening as part of the Brighton Festival. Four proposals are selected a year.

APPLICATIONS

Application forms may be downloaded from the web site. In addition to the application form, applicants must submit a treatment, a first draft of the script, a C.V. and a summary of expected expenses.

ASSESSMENT

Applications are assessed for interesting and original ideas and judged on creative merits.

CONDITIONS

The Ignition Network retains the right to use the film as they choose, in festivals and screenings, for example, but the director will retain the copyright. Films must be credited to The Ignition Network, Screen South and the Film Council.

Lighthouse

9-12 Middle Street
Brighton
BN1 1AL
Tel: 01273 384222
Fax: 01273 384233
Email: info@lighthouse.org.uk
Web: www.lighthouse.org.uk

Lighthouse supports the development of individuals working in film and digital media through training, partnership-building, production and distribution support and guidance, offering various short film production schemes.

As one of the agencies commissioned by the Film Council's New Cinema Fund to deliver the Digital Shorts scheme (see the Film Council chapter), Lighthouse works with digital filmmakers in the Screen South region.

Take Two - Dance for Screen is a joint initiative between Lighthouse and South East Dance. It provides £8000 and facilities for a filmmaker and choreographer to collaboratively produce a dance film.

The Pool: Lincoln

3 Campus Way
Lincoln, LN6 7GA
Tel: 01522 532959
Fax: 01522 532957
Email: info@thepoolonline.co.uk
Web: www.thepoolonline.co.uk

The Pool is a not-for-profit organisation to support recent graduates, practitioners and companies in the screen and media industries in Lincoln. It will soon be a membership organisation with annual fees of £10 for students and concessions, £15 for individuals and £30 for companies. Members will have access to services and The Pool aims to organise events throughout the year, projects with students, the community and corporate clients as well as providing funding and training.

Yorkshire Media Production Agency

The Workstation, 15 Paternoster Row
Sheffield, S1 2BX
Tel: 0114 249 2204
Fax: 0114 249 2293
Email: admin@ympa.workstation.org.uk
Web: www.ympa.org.uk

The YMPA's responsibility for dealing with grant aided film production and support in Yorkshire has passed over to the new Regional Film Agency, Screen Yorkshire.

The company now trades under its original name of Independent Media Investments Ltd and has added sister companies Studio of the North ltd and Independent Media Rights ltd to its portfolio of companies. Together these companies offer production support, executive and co-production, project management and funding and also act as the central UK contact point for Cre.Net a web based collaboration and rights management tool (www.creafilms.net)

Arts Council England

14 Great Peter Street
London, SW1P 3NQ
Tel: 020 7333 0100
Fax: 020 7973 6590
Email: enquiries@artscouncil.org.uk
Web: www.artscouncil.org.uk

Since the foundation of the National Film Councils, distribution of film funding for film projects intended for distribution is no longer the responsibility of the National Arts Councils. However, there are certain funds that are available to film and video artists and the creative industries.

The Arts Council and its Regional Arts Boards merged into one entity over 2002, streamlining English arts lottery funding into three England-wide schemes: Grants for the Arts – Individuals, Organisations and National Touring; Grants for the Arts – Stabilisation and Recovery; and Regular Funding for Organisations. Though the awards are England-wide, applicants must apply through their regional office. Production companies would not be eligible to apply for these awards. However, an individual film and video artist with a proposal for productions intended for gallery installation and not distribution would be eligible for the Individual award stream. For this reason, details of the Grants for the Arts – Individuals, Organisations and National Touring are listed below.

Grants for the Arts – Individuals, Organisations and National Touring

Individuals applying for this award can receive funding to support projects and events, commissions and productions, research and development, capital items, professional development, training and travel grants, bursaries and residencies.

DEADLINE

This scheme is open to submissions between 1 April 2003 and 31 December 2004, applications can be made at any time within this time frame.

ELIGIBILITY

Artists, performers, writers, promoters, presenters, curators, producers and other individuals working in the arts who live in England are eligible to apply. The activity must be based in England (except professional development applications which may take place outside England) and be arts-related. Film-based projects must be intended for gallery installation, not commercial distribution.

DETAILS

Individuals are eligible to receive between £200 and £30,000 for activities lasting up to three years. Partnership funding of at least 10% is required.

APPLICATIONS

Applicants must submit an application form and a proposal outlining the activity, including information about themselves and their work, how they will make the activity happen, the finance and budget, the benefits, how the proposal meets the Arts Councils aims and how the they will evaluate their project.

ASSESSMENT

Applications will be assessed for the artistic quality or its impact on the applicant's work, the management of the project, the financial feasibility, the public benefit and the way the project meets the aims of the Arts Council. They will also be compared to other applications received.

Other Funding

The Arts Council has other funding schemes in operation, some of which support the creative industries. As film is a qualifying creative industry, production companies are able to benefit from these schemes as long as they are based in the region that offers them. These initiatives are listed here.

Arts Connection

East England Arts
Eden House
48-49 Baterman Street
Cambridge, CB2 1LR
Tel: 01223 454400
Fax: 0870 2421271
Email: east@artscouncil.org.uk
Web: www.artsconnection.co.uk

Covering: Bedfordshire, Cambridgeshire, Essex, Hertfordshire, Norfolk, Suffolk.

This initiative is aimed at supporting young people (under 25) to establish themselves in the creative industries. The scheme offers start-up funds, guidance, mentoring, advice, networking opportunities and access to the arts funding system. The Prince's Trust supports the scheme.

Creative Advantage Fund

West Midlands Arts
82 Granville Street
Birmingham, B1 2LH
Tel: 0121 631 3121
Fax: 0121 643 7239
Email: fred.brookes@west-midlands-arts.co.uk
Web: www.creative-advantage-fund.co.uk

Covering: Herefordshire, Worcestershire, Shropshire, Telford and Wrekin, Staffordshire, Warwickshire, Stoke-on-Trent and the West Midlands Metropolitan Districts.

This is an investment fund to provide venture capital to smaller size creative businesses in the region. It invests in commercially viable growth businesses with a view to making a profit to be fed back into the fund. The project is co-ordinated by West Midland Arts, managed by Birmingham Venture Capital Ltd and financed by the European Development Fund, the Arts Council, Advantage West Midlands, West Midlands Arts and Birmingham City Council.

DEADLINE

This is a rolling programme and applications may be made at any time.

ELIGIBILITY

Creative businesses based in the West Midlands region with a range of activities or a slate of films in development. Individual projects will not be seen as viable investments. The company must have a fully developed business plan.

DETAILS

Sums invested are expected to range from £5000 to £130,000. Match funding from other sources such as banks will normally be expected. This is not a grant or an award but a commercial investment in a creative business so commercially exploitable projects will be the focus of the scheme.

APPLICATIONS

Applications are made by submitting a fully developed business plan. These will be accepted by post and email. Companies may seek support from their local Business Link to develop their plan.

ASSESSMENT

Each application will be assessed on the potential of the proposal to be a commercial success and on the quality of the business plan. The business plan should contain the following details to be considered: summary / introduction; key facts; key individuals; business description; products & services; the market; competitors; market research; prices; production & facilities; suppliers; risks; SWOT analysis; organisation; past accounts; projections; cash flow, profit and loss, accounts and balance sheet; sensitivity analysis; finance required.

Cultural Business Venture

North East
Central Square
Forth Street
Newcastle upon Tyne, NE1 3PJ
Tel: 0191 255 8500
Fax: 0191 230 1020
Email: info@northernarts.org.uk
Web: www.artscouncil.org.uk

Covering: Tees Valley, County Durham, Northumberland, Tyne and Wear.

This award is to support small and medium sized businesses working in the cultural sector. It is provided in collaboration with The Prince's Trust. The kinds of projects likely to receive funding are legal costs, office or workspace fit-out/improvement, purchase of equipment, marketing and promotion.

DEADLINE

This is a rolling programme and applications may be made at any time.

ELIGIBILITY

Applications must be from new or established creative or cultural businesses which have a bank account set up in the name of their business; employ/will employ less than 35 members of staff and which have an annual turnover of less than £100,000. Applicants must be based in the Northern Arts region.

DETAILS

Awards will be between £1000 and £10,000, with an average grant likely to be between £4000 and £5000. Match funding of at least 25% is required.

APPLICATIONS

Along with an application form, applicants must submit a business plan, latest annual accounts (if applicant is an existing business), a three-year cash flow including the project to be funded, evidence of business advice or business training, evidence of 25% match funding and quotes/estimates for equipment, refurbishment or marketing costs.

ASSESSMENT

Each application will be assessed against the following criteria: the quality of the proposal; the public or industry benefit; the ability of the applicant to deliver the proposal; the financial viability and the extent to which the proposal meets the priorities of Northern Arts.

In addition, there are more specific criteria for the proposal to meet: the benefit to developing the business; research showing the need for the proposal; the coherence between the proposal and the business plan; a realistic business plan; a realistic budget; the financial viability; the opportunity for creating employment; realistic targets; evidence of alternative sources of funding; the appropriateness of the training and advice required.

Scotland
Scottish Screen

SCOTTISH SCREEN

Second Floor
249 West George Street
Glasgow, G2 4QE
Tel: 0141 302 1700
Fax: 0141 302 1711
Email: info@scottishscreen.com
Web: www.scottishscreen.com

Scottish Screen was established in 1997 as the national body for film, television and media in Scotland. Its stated objectives are to:

1) Develop world class production business in Scotland.

2) Attract major productions to Scotland.

3) Champion a culture of investment in screen industries.

4) Nurture and develop talent and audiences.

5) Preserve and present Scottish screen production.

6) Encourage and support international outlook.

7) Drive screen policy from school to statute.

Scottish Screen is a significant investor in Scottish talent and has continued to support acclaimed filmmakers such as Lynne Ramsay and Peter Mullan through their careers as well as pushing new talent schemes. Other priorities include investment in film development and distribution; training bursaries; provision of information resources and archives; and production assistance.

Steve McIntyre, Chief Executive

"Scottish Screen operates a range of schemes and funding programmes to support filmmaking at every level and filmmakers at every stage of their careers. It can invest up to £500,000 into feature films. Recent productions include *Magdalene Sisters*, *Sweet Sixteen*, *Morvern Callar*, *Last Great Wilderness*, *Young Adam* and *Wilbur Wants to Kill Himself*. On average we would invest in about 6 feature films per year (of the dozen's of applications received).

"We fund feature film development (both fiction and documentary) and in any one year will put about 40 projects into development representing about 10% of the applications received. New talent schemes include the long standing and respected Tartan Shorts with the BBC and New Found Films with Scottish Media Group.

"There are a number of core criteria when assessing projects: Quality - is this script any good?; viability - is this film likely to get financed?; and Scottish relevance - is this project and the production team associated helping to develop a healthy and sustainable film industry? Most of the projects we support come from Scottish production companies with projects usually shooting in Scotland."

Lottery Funding

Full general guidelines for each of the awards and schemes appears at the end of the section.

Feature Film Production Funding

This fund supports Scottish feature films and feature length documentaries, and animated feature films aimed at theatrical exhibition.

DEADLINE

There are five deadlines per year.

DETAILS

Scottish Screen will fund up to 25% of a production's costs with a ceiling of £500,000.

Twenty First Films

This fund supports low budget Scottish feature films with budgets of no more than £600,000 which are intended for theatrical exhibition, encouraging innovation combined with commercial viability.

DEADLINE

There are five deadlines per year.

DETAILS

Scottish Screen will fund up to 75% of a production's costs, with a ceiling of £300,000. Partnership funding in kind is acceptable, as long as it is matched by partnership funding in cash to the same value. The fund will also provide training and development.

Short film Production Funding

This fund supports the production of Scottish short films, documentaries and animation intended for theatrical release.

DEADLINE

Applications for awards of over £25,000 have four deadlines over the year May, August, December and February.

Applications for awards of below £25,000 can be made at any time as they are assessed on a rolling basis.

DETAILS

Scottish Screen will fund up to 50% of a production's costs. Partnership funding in kind is acceptable, as long as it is matched by partnership funding in cash to the same value.

Script Development Funding

This fund supports the development of Scottish feature films, documentaries and animation projects intended for theatrical release.

DEADLINE

Applications for under £25,000 can be made at any time as they are assessed on a rolling basis.

DETAILS

Scottish Screen will contribute between £2000 and £25,000 and up to 90% of the development costs.

CONDITIONS

In addition to the usual terms, Scottish Screen must be paid a 50% premium on their investment.

Project Development Funding

This fund supports the advanced development of Scottish feature films, documentaries and animation projects intended for theatrical release.

DEADLINE

Applications for awards of over £25,000 have four deadlines over the year May, August, December and February. Applications for awards of below £25,000 can be made at any time as they are assessed on a rolling basis.

DETAILS

Scottish Screen will contribute between £5000 and £75,000 for the advanced development of feature films and between 10% and 50% of a project's costs. Exceptions may be made for contributions of up to 75 % of the project's cost.

CONDITIONS

In addition to the usual terms, Scottish Screen must be paid a 50% premium on their investment.

Distribution and Exploitation Support

This fund supports print and advertising costs of Scottish feature films intended for theatrical release in Scotland, UK and worldwide.

DEADLINE

Applications for awards of over £25,000 have four deadlines over the year May, August, December and February. Applications for awards of below £25,000 can be made at any time as they are assessed on a rolling basis.

ELIGIBILITY

Distributors seeking to release a film or producers with a distributor attached.

DETAILS

Scottish Screen will contribute up to 50% of distribution and exhibition costs. Partnership funding in kind is acceptable, as long as it is matched by partnership funding in cash to the same value.

Company Development Programme

This fund supports companies in developing a slate of projects for feature film and documentary intended for theatrical release, television drama and factual projects aimed for broadcast, animation and new media, interactive joint ventures.

DEADLINE

There is an annual deadline.

ELIGIBILITY

Companies with the capacity to develop a viable mixed slate of projects in feature

film, television and new media. Applicants should be based in Scotland but some of the slate projects may be developed outside of Scotland and with non-Scottish partners. Applicants need to show a feature or television production track record and a slate of projects with financiers attached.

DETAILS

Scottish Screen will contribute up to £75,000 or 50% of the slate development costs. Exceptions may be made for contributions of up to 75 % of the project's cost. Partnership funding in kind is acceptable, as long as it is matched by partnership funding in cash to the same value.

General Guidelines for these schemes

ELIGIBILITY

Individuals are not eligible to apply for the awards. Organisations must be commercial companies or organisations with formal constitutions and based in Scotland. Sometimes organisations based outside Scotland intending to deliver their project in Scotland or with direct benefit to the Scottish film industry will be considered.

DETAILS

Partnership funding in kind is acceptable, as long as it is matched by partnership funding in cash to the same value.

APPLICATIONS

In addition to the application form, other documents must be submitted including a script, synopsis and character descriptions, budget, schedule and financing plan, CVs, details of rights, company accounts and other information.

ASSESSMENT

Each application will be assessed against the following criteria: the benefit to the Scottish general public; the benefit to the Scottish film industry; the development stage of the project (the more advanced the better); the commercial and creative quality; the ability to reach audiences in Scotland and beyond; the added value lottery funding gives to the project; the ability of the applicant to deliver the project; a realistic budget and schedule; the other financing in place and the eligibility of the film registering as British under the Films Act 1985.

CONDITIONS

Scottish Screen's contributions are made in the form of an investment to recoup their contribution and share in revenues from income generated from the project. Their share will be in proportion to the level of investment. Scottish Screen must also receive a credit on the finished film and related publicity.

The budget for any of the production funds (except the short film awards) should make provision for payment of levies to PACT and the Skills Investment Fund, as well as providing a print and promotional material for the Scottish Screen Film & Television Archive. The producer must give Scottish Screen regular progress reports and provide financial and other documents as required.

Production Schemes

Scottish Screen works with partners to deliver production schemes for short filmmakers in Scotland. The deadlines for 2003 had closed at print, to be added to Scottish Screen's database to receive an application form and guidelines for the next round contact Tricia McCormack on 0141 302 1742.

New Found Land & New Found Films

New Found Land has been running for three years to enable production and commission of six contemporary, digital Scottish TV dramas, lasting twenty five minutes with a budget of up to £50,000 each. In 2002, the scheme was adapted to enable development of ten to twelve low budget feature films leading to the production of two selected projects receiving up to £200,000. Scottish

Television and Grampian Television support the scheme.

Tartan Shorts

Tartan Shorts is run in collaboration with BBC Scotland to produce short cinematic films of no longer than 9 minutes by writers directors and producers who have not yet made a feature. There is an available budget of £65,000 for each of the three films selected. They must be shot on Super16mm for blow up to 35mm for theatrical exhibition and transfer to digibeta for television broadcast.

Tartan Smalls

Tartan Smalls is run in collaboration with CBBC Scotland to produce short films of no longer than 9 minutes for a child audience between the ages of 6 and 13 years. The scheme is aimed towards new filmmakers or experienced filmmakers new to the youth audience. Individual writers and writer/producer/director teams are eligible to apply for an available budget of £40,000 for each of the three films selected.

This Scotland

This is a scheme run in collaboration with Scottish Television and Grampian Television to commission twelve digital documentaries for broadcast and theatrical distribution. The budgets are £17,750 for each programme and the running times are twenty four minutes.

First Writes

Run in collaboration with First Light, this scheme commission three five minute scripts from young people between the ages of 11 and 16 years.

Archive Live

This new scheme is designed to promote creative approaches to the wealth of archive material held by the Scottish Screen Archive. Five projects will be developed for £5,000 each and two will be commissioned with budgets of £25,000.

LESLIE LOWES

THE BLACKENING

The Blackening, a low-cost feature from new outfit Fresh Paint Pictures, was intensively developed through Scottish Screen and Scottish Media Group (SMG). One of the co-producers, Leslie Lowes tells how development can be used as a tool to pull private investment into production.

"My co-producer Alec Bruce is a graduate of Moonstone Screenwriting Labs and has been working on an outline of the project for several years, I joined him two years ago. Scottish Screen and SMG have a 30-minute TV drama strand for filmmakers called New Found Land which has been very successful. Early last year, following a film recoupment windfall they decided for just one year to up New Found Land to feature length. They renamed it New Found Films - Modern Scottish stories created by new Scottish talent for an international cinema audience.

"They called for outlines, which had to have international cinema appeal, a creative team behind them and good potential for international cinema distribution and could be made for £200,000. We had about 3 weeks to get a bid in and were among the ten projects they selected for development from about 80 received. Two only out of the ten could be offered production funding, so competition was bound to be serious. Coffee break at the first development session had everyone sniffing each other out, circulating like a pack of dogs. We had researched the competition. We like to know what we are dealing with. We were new on the scene and the rest all seemed to be old pals. Most of them had been through Scottish Screen schemes before and we were outsiders. I don't think they were too worried about us. Someone told me quite confidently that we must be mad for planning to shoot a feature up in the Shetland Islands. They quoted the cost of transport there and arctic-type weather that would make it impossible, but went amazingly quiet when I said we had just wrapped a feature there in January.

"We were quietly confident though. Most of the competition seemed to be grant-dependent but we already had an expression of interest from a Scottish financier, so that boosted us. In private session with the development executives we were told the £200K production funding we were in competition for was a floor, not a ceiling. We could bring in extra finance with their prior approval. That meant we were free to use the status of being developed through Scotland's screen agency and SMG to lever in private finance. We could use this method even if we were not finally selected for production funding for New Found Films. For us it was a win-win situation, a tremendous confidence builder.

"We had to attend a development by treatment method seminar in Glasgow, then deliver a first draft treatment. If they liked it we would get £750. We funded ourselves entirely until development money came through but it was welcome. The New Found Films plan was to move all the selected projects forward, through two treatments to first draft script, scheduling and budgeting on the way, dropping any that might prove unsatisfactory. Finally, two scripts would be recommended to Scottish Screen's production panel. The projects could attract up to £1,500 in total and the creative teams also got some very useful seminars and training weekends on the way. We used that money to lever in more. Shetland Arts Trust were keen to assist with the project development. They knew transport costs for recce put us at a disadvantage compared with projects shooting in Glasgow or Edinburgh. They came up with another £750, so we pulled in £2,250 to assist development. It was development on a shoestring, and it still is, but we now have a little money to help us prepare the Blackening for gaining private finance.

"Having been though this development process gives the project credence that helps open doors. There's no doubt in my mind that the project is in much better shape although the pressures to meet tough deadlines was intense, but then that's not a bad thing either. A little pressure cooking can produce some very good ideas and has certainly increased self-confidence. Intensive treatment development also builds investor confidence. We now have four financiers with expressed interest and we are now in a far healthier position to be able to deal." *JM*

IRVINE ALLEN   DADDY'S GIRL

It must have given Irvine Allen considerable satisfaction to have the £45,000 Scottish Screen backed short he shot from the script so many had rejected accepted at Cannes and put into competition. And even more when he got a call from Cannes to say his film had landed the Palme D'Or.

"It's a universal story about a neglected child waiting outside a pub for her daddy. It follows her subsequent misadventures as she is left prey to the whims and fancies of passing strangers. The themes are neglect and loss of innocence and she learns the cunning needed to survive the street, among some other unsavoury ideas, before being rescued by a local shopkeeper. Her rescue is only temporary though as her father soon appears. It's set over 8 1/2 minutes real time, in the rain. The style is spare and simple, nothing fancy; no cranes, dolly or track. Just a lot of rain machines.

"It was shot for £45,000. BBC2 Bristol 10x10 series 12 gave me £18,000, Scottish Screen provided £20,000, the BFI £2000, and the Glasgow film Office another £5000; all acquired in that order. When it was finished Scottish Screen were on the case quick, and really supportive. They struck a new print which was subtitled into French by a friend of mine. They also gave me a "Go-and-See" grant for a flight to Cannes. They also produced posters and handled publicity. The British Council had been supportive of the film before Cannes and during it.

"The pressure I did feel concerned whether I should go or not. My partner Annie was expecting our first child that week so I decided to stay but it wasn't an easy decision. At first I kidded myself that it was too important for my future not to go, but I soon realised that I was fooling myself for the sake of an ego massage. To do a film about a neglected child, and not be there for my own family at such an important time would have been an absolute hypocrisy.

"I have spent a lot of time at short film festivals over the last 2 years. I must have seen over five hundred short films and I feel qualified to comment on the biggest mistakes short filmmakers make, so here goes: forgetting you need a good script; not reigning in the actors trying for the Oscar; miscasting; trying to be Quentin Tarantino with a budget of 5 bob. Also, relying on style rather than substance.

"To short filmmakers I'd say apply to every short film scheme going. Bust a gut or the budget to stay on film, or at least print to 35mm at the back end. That way you can get into the best festivals; that's where you're going to make your name. Also, don't give up, I spent two years trying to get Daddy's Girl made. Find a good crew who you can get on with, and a DoP who'll give you your place. If all else fails get a handcam and just do it. Taking pictures is easier than getting good sound so don't skimp on the sound requirements." *TF*

Other Scottish Funds

ALT-W

Leisure and Arts Department
Floor 13, Tayside House
Dundee, DD1 3RA
01382 433042
info@alt-w.com
www.alt-w.com

This award supports the production of digital experimental and interactive productions intended for delivery through the web. Scottish Screen, Dundee Council, Scottish Enterprise, Dundee College, University of Abertay and the School of Television and Imaging at the University of Dundee support the scheme.

DEADLINE

There is an annual deadline in December.

ELIGIBILITY

Individuals, students, artists groups and teams of professionals are eligible to apply. Applicants must be based in Scotland and may come from backgrounds including the visual arts, design, film, audio, music, games and programme developing. Projects may be at any stage of development.

DETAILS

Up to ten people will be awarded up to £2,500 each as a contribution to production costs. They will also have the opportunity to receive training and mentoring to enable them to make the most of their idea.

APPLICATIONS

Applicants must submit a completed application form. Short listed applicants will be invited to interview to discuss their idea and asked to bring examples of current and past work.

ASSESSMENT

Each application will be assessed for the intended use of new media, quality and originality, the ability of the applicant to deliver the project and the realistic employment of the web as a distribution tool. The films should be tailored to the web as a medium, making the most of the interactivity the web offers and most probably employing a non-linear structure.

CONDITIONS

ALT-W does not hold any of the film's rights but the filmmaker must allow ALT-W to screen their film online. ALT-W should also receive a screen credit for their support.

Bridging the Gap

Edinburgh College of Art
Lauriston Place
Edinburgh EH3 9DS
Email: bridgingthegap@eca.ac.uk

Bridging the Gap commissions five, twenty minute digital documentaries for theatrical distribution. Awards are £16,000 and the projects are developed and produced over a nine-month period. The filmmakers are supported by mentors and through practical and theoretical workshops. The scheme is supported by Scottish Screen, Scottish Enterprise Tayside, Angus Digital Media Centre and Edinburgh College of Art.

Cineworks

Glasgow Media Access Centre
Third Floor, 34 Albion Street
Glasgow, G11 1LH
Tel: 0141 553 2620
Fax: 0141 553 2660
Email: info@cineworks.co.uk
Web: www.cineworks.co.uk

Cineworks commissions five short films a year in the genres of drama, documentary and animation by new filmmakers. The scheme was initiated by Glasgow Media Access Centre and Edinburgh Media Base and supported by Scottish Screen, The Film Council's New Cinema Fund and BBC Scotland. In 2003 the scheme formed part of the Film Council's Digital Shorts scheme which is also delivered through Digicult (see below).

DEADLINE

There is an annual deadline in autumn.

ELIGIBILITY

Applicant writers, producers and directors must not have a previous broadcast credit for the role in the application. Individual writers and writer/directors, as well as writer/director/producer teams may apply. Producers and directors without projects may apply to be teamed up with a developed drama or documentary project.

DETAILS

Each film is eligible to receive between £10,000 and £15,000 for production, as well as receiving support from industry professionals who will act as mentors throughout development. Training may be provided for the applicants before production and the productions supported by GMAC and the Mediabase.

APPLICATIONS

For documentaries; submit a proposal. For drama; submit a script, synopsis, and optional supporting material. For animation, submit an outline of story, visual style and 12 storyboards. Producers and Directors without a project must submit a CV and covering letter.

ASSESSMENT

Each application will be assessed for its quality, vision and originality and whether it is realistic to achieve within the allocated fund without additional finance.

CONDITIONS

Cineworks takes a screen credit and in some cases takes all the films rights.

Digicult

Glasgow Media Access Centre
Third floor, Albion Street
Glasgow, G1 1LH
Tel: 0141 553 2626
Email: info@digicult.co.uk
Web: www.digicult.co.uk

Digicult is a scheme to create a pool of new and established filmmaking and creative talent in Scotland to enable short film production through the pooling and sharing of skills, ideas and knowledge. It invites creative people to become members. The organisation is responsible for delivering part of the Digital Shorts scheme in Scotland in 2003, along with Cineworks.

ELIGIBILITY

To become a member, applicants must be based in Scotland and be involved in various areas of film and related arts, such as opera, theatre, graphic design, animation, fine art, film directing or other film production areas. Members of established production teams must apply separately.

DETAILS

Digicult aims to produce at least five short digital films per year, commissioned from the members and developed from the members' ideas. Members also have the opportunity to benefit from debate, screenings and master classes.

APPLICATIONS

To become a member of Digicult, applicants must submit, in addition to the application form, a pitch, a CV, two short film ideas of no longer than 10 minutes (including scripts, treatments and other optional material) and a selection of previous work (including showreel, photographs, storyboards, and so on).

ASSESSMENT

The priority is to attract talent in a variety of disciplines.

Edinburgh Mediabase

25a Southwest Thistle Street Lane
Edinburgh, EH2 1EW
Tel: 0131 220 0220
Fax: 0131 220 0017
Email: info@edinburghmediabase.com
Web: www.edinburghmediabase.com

Edinburgh Mediabase is a membership
organisation providing access to affordable
and professional filmmaking equipment,
facilities, resources and support. There are
three levels of membership at £12/year for
students and the unemployed, £20/year for
those on a low wage and £30/year for those
on a high wage.

48 Hours

This no budget production scheme is
launched once a month at the Blue Room
short film showcase at the Cameo Cinema.
An application form and brief for the 48
hours scheme is left on each seat at the
beginning of the showcase. Each member of
the audience has until the end of the evening
to submit their idea and application forms,
one of which will be selected by Edinburgh
Mediabase to go into production. Over
the next month, the winner will receive 48
hours of free equipment and editing time
plus guidance and support to produce
a film of no longer than 5 minutes. The
film will be screened at the following Blue
Room event. Anyone can apply as long as
they become members of the Edinburgh
Mediabase if they are chosen.

Box Room

This scheme brings together new filmmakers
and new music producers to produce
a music video. Ten tracks have been
chosen by Edinburgh Mediabase, which
can be downloaded from their web site.
Filmmakers may submit an idea for a music
video to match one of the tracks. Edinburgh
Mediabase will select ideas to be produced,
donating 24hrs use of equipment, extended
use of editing facilities and production
guidance from the team. The finished films
will be screened on the web site.

Glasgow Film Office

Glasgow Film Office
City Chambers
Glasgow, G2 1DU
Tel: 014 1287 0424
Fax: 014 1287 0311
Email: film.office@ced.glasgow.gov.uk
Web: www.glasgowfilm.org.uk

Glasgow Film Office has supported 40 film
productions in Glasgow since 1997. The
aim in Phase 2 of their initiative is to assist
the growth and development of independent
production companies based in Glasgow so
they can deliver TV with a high value (i.e. a
primary value of at least £50k per hour) or
high impact productions (with budgets in
excess of £200k and committed to spending
at least £100k in Glasgow) intended for
television broadcast or cinematic exhibition.
Most of the projects they become involved
in will have been referred to them by
business development agencies, such as
Scottish Enterprise Glasgow. GFO are aware
of all production companies operating or
with the potential to operate in high value
and high impact TV and film production
in Glasgow. Any new companies moving
to the area, are advised to contact Scottish
Enterprise Glasgow to make their presence
known.

New Writer Integration

This award is to encourage production
companies to work with new screenwriting
talent by supporting script and project
development for feature films, feature
documentaries, commercials, and other
forms of productions.

ELIGIBILITY

Local independent production companies intending to work with new writing talent are eligible to apply.

DETAILS

There are three levels of development grants at £1000, £3000, and £5000. Applicants must raise at least 50% match funding.

New Director/Producer Integration

This award is to encourage young filmmaking teams to produce short films with established production partners. The films should be shot digitally under 25 minutes long.

DEADLINE

This is a rolling award, so applications may be made at any time.

ELIGIBILITY

Local independent production companies sponsoring a team of local young filmmaking individuals are eligible to apply.

DETAILS

Grants up to £7500 are available for an average production budget of £30,000, with an average award of £5000. Applicants must raise at least 50% match funding.

Product Commercialisation

This award is to aid the growth of production companies by pinpointing buyers that might be interested in investing in development projects, formats, franchises and completed programmes.

ELIGIBILITY

Production companies based in Glasgow with a strong business plan.

DETAILS

Rather than a monetary award this will offer professional advice and guidance. In some cases, grants may be awarded where appropriate.

General Guidelines common to all schemes

DEADLINE

There is no deadline so applications may be made at any time and assessed individually.

ELIGIBILITY

Productions should have budgets of over £200,000, or a commissioning value of over £50,000.

APPLICATIONS

There is no application form and GFO prefer not to receive unsolicited material. Projects may be referred to the GFO by Scottish Enterprise Glasgow. Production companies may also email or telephone the GFO to discuss the project.

ASSESSMENT

All projects will be assessed for the commercial potential and the benefit to the company. The harmony between the company's business plan and the proposed project will also be examined, as the intention is to drive forward the company's business.

CONDITIONS

The Glasgow Film Office must receive a screen credit indicating the development support if a project from the New Writer or New Director/Producer schemes goes into production. In the case of the New Writer programme, the grant must be repaid once production begins so this can be fed back into future development projects. The GFO do not hold any rights in the projects they support.

SAUL METZSTEIN   LATE NIGHT SHOPPING

Saul Metzstein and Jack Lothian created Film Four Lab's Late Night Shopping, a comic play on life on the comfortable but boring life choices of the consumer generation – it was part-funded by the Glasgow Film Office who wanted to encourage a film to be shot in Glasgow out-of-season.

"We'd written about a hundred short scripts together, sometimes two a day. We made a film about a fight between a psychotic Santa Claus and a monster that lives under a child's bed. Anyway, we made that and no one ever gave us money to make another short so we decided we'd better write features instead! It seemed easier to get money for a feature than for a short, mysteriously.

"Glasgow is not big enough to be a cottage industry but they make a lot up there, which is a good thing. Everyone knows each other and it's not nearly so pressured - not at all like London. It's also really sporadic - Late Night Shopping was the only Scottish film made there in 2000, one film a year isn't exactly an industry. But then the Glasgow Film Office initiated the thing in the first place and put in, I think, £100,000. It was their idea to get a film made in Scotland out of season. They have great crews up there, much better than down here in London, because they are quite a small community up there. If someone is no good at their job they won't get any work. In the winter they have to go and work elsewhere because the light is so terrible. Anyway, we decided to make a film at night so we wouldn't need any daylight - of course when the film was finally made it was June!

"Jack and I have got three films on the go. We just sit around my parents' house eating pizza and coming up with bad film ideas. The one thing that is very, very deliberate is we always try to make films that we would like to see as an audience. Not films we'd like to make, films we'd like to see and there's a huge difference between them. We ditch great ideas because we couldn't be bothered to go and see the finished film and in a way it's a filter for the shit that we would probably come up with. Films have very distinct relationships; what the filmmaker makes of the film and what the audience makes of the film." *TF*

4 Minute Wonders

4 Minute Wonders
Centre for Contemporary Arts
350 Sauchiehall Street
Glasgow, G2 3JD
Tel: 0141 332 0005
Email: bronagh@bigemedia.com
Web: www.4minutewonders.com

Once a month, this scheme supports new directors in Scotland (and Wales – see relevant entry under Wales) to make music videos for new music tracks by awarding funds and production facilities to the successful applicant. In Scotland, 4 Minute Wonders is assisted by Scottish Screen, Scottish Enterprise and Glasgow Film Office.

DEADLINE

There is a deadline line at the end of every month.

ELIGIBILITY

The scheme is open to any applicant, including previous applicants, who produce the video in Scotland.

DETAILS

There is up to £5000 available to produce each music video in one month, with access to production facilities and support as part of the budget. The video will be streamed through the web site for feedback from visitors to the site. At the end of the year all the videos will be screened and judged at a presentation evening for industry professionals. The winner will be awarded a prize.

APPLICATIONS

An application is based on a new music track that can be downloaded from the web site each month. The applicant uses the track to develop their music video concept for it. This must then be submitted via the online application form for assessment, along with support material, which could be a showreel of previous work or a visual treatment the idea. The successful applicant will be given the opportunity to make the video concept into a real production.

ASSESSMENT

All applications will be assessed for quality and innovation and their ability to be produced within budget.

CONDITIONS

4 Minute Wonders will be executive producers of each video to assist delivery of the video on schedule and budget and meeting technical requirements. A second production company may be brought in to assist if the project appears to be in danger of not being completed. 4 Minute Wonders will be the sole distributor of the video receiving all revenues.

South West Scotland Screen Commission

South West Scotland Screen Commission
Gracefield Arts Centre, 28 Edinburgh Road
Dumfries, DG1 1JQ
Tel: 01387 263666
Fax: 01387 263666
Email: screencom@dumgal.gov.uk
Web: www.sw-scotland-screen.com

The screen commission administers £5000 in April each year from the Dumfries & Galloway Council to support short film development and production to local filmmakers. This sum will be split between two to three films each year. Partnership funding is required and the local enterprise agency may be able to assist with this in the future, depending on the success of the scheme in bringing filmmaking to the region.

They are looking for emerging filmmakers, ideally with one short film behind them and experience of low-budget filmmaking. Applicants may be graduating students, ex-students or professional filmmakers.

Films must be shot in the region, which provides largely rural and small-scale urban locations.

The commission is able to assist in finding locations, cheap accommodation and local crew, provision of which should be included in the applicant's budget. The filmmaker should be able to demonstrate plans for exhibition and/or distribution. The commission will not hold any rights to the film but they must be credited on screen and the film must be screened in the region.

Scottish Arts Council

12 Manor Place
Edinburgh, EH3 7DD
Tel: 0131 226 6051
Fax: 0131 225 9833
Email help.desk@scottisharts.org.uk
Web: www.scottisharts.org.uk

The Scottish Arts Council distributes lottery funding across the Arts through streams covering Crafts, Dance, Drama, Literature, Music, Visual Arts and Capital funds. Within each stream the two priorities are for individual artists and non profit-making arts organisations. Film and video artists are eligible to apply for the Individual Awards under the Visual Arts stream, which support Creative Development and the Amsterdam Studio Residency. Projects must be intended for gallery exhibition and not commercial distribution.

Creative Development

Artists may apply for funding as a form of income enabling them to develop work over an extended period of time, to support research and development of new projects, and the costs involved in creating and presenting new work.

DEADLINE

Deadlines vary depending on the sum awarded. For grants between £100 and £2000 deadlines are in May, July, November and January. For grants above this, the deadline is in November.

DETAILS

This fund will award grants of between £100 and £2000 for costs related to production and presentation of new work, £5000 for research and development and £15,000 to replace an existing income.

Applicants are generally expected to contribute 10% of the costs through partnership funding. This may be funding in kind or in cash.

Amsterdam Studio Residency

The selected artist will have the opportunity to research and develop work in Amsterdam for one year.

DEADLINE

The deadline is in July.

DETAILS

The artists will receive a monthly-paid grant of £15,000 and rent-free accommodation in the Council's flat near the city centre.

General Guidelines

ELIGIBILITY

Visual artists including film and video artists at any stage of development in their work, with a body of work outside formal education and who are based in Scotland are eligible.

APPLICATIONS

Applications must include evidence of the applicant's past work. Film and video artists may submit a VHS tape of one whole work or samples of various works.

ASSESSMENT

Applications will be assessed for the quality of the applicant's past work and that the award will have significant impact on the applicant and their work, providing an opportunity to develop that is otherwise not available.

Wales

Sgrîn Cymru Wales

The Bank
10 Mount Stuart Square
Cardiff Bay
Cardiff, CF10 5EE
Tel: 029 20 333300
Fax: 029 20 333320
Email: sgrin@sgrin.co.uk
Web: www.sgrin.co.uk

Sgrîn was established in 1997 as the national body for film, television and new media in Wales. It is responsible for developing strategic film policy in Wales, and administers the Lottery film fund on behalf of the Arts Council for Wales to support film production in the region. Sgrîn's current objective is to encourage a sustainable Welsh media industry through development of business skills and understanding of international markets; and development of audiences and skilled personnel through cultural and educational programmes. A typical investment would be Peter Greenaway's trilogy *The Tulse Luper Suitcase*.

Judith Higginbottom, Head of Production on features applications

"We provide two production awards and about ten development awards each year. Numbers are approximate because we can re-invest profits/ unspent funds and move money between the categories. We receive a very large volume of applications so we can afford to pick the strongest projects. We fund about 20% of the applications we receive. If you are thinking of applying for Welsh Lottery funding, then please do discuss your project with us first"

APPLICATIONS

"You must be a limited company to apply to us (this is a precondition for most Lottery funding). All kinds of companies apply from very large, long-established ones to new micro-businesses. In order to succeed with Welsh Lottery funding, companies should either be Welsh-registered or be employing Welsh people in key creative roles (writer, producer or director) on the project."

PREFERRED PROJECTS

"The best projects for us are highly original stories with very strong scripts. It's really hard to answer this question as we like to support the widest possible range of films from the straightforwardly commercial to the avowedly art-house and independent. We look at each project on its merits."

COMMON MISTAKES

"Applicants simply fail to read our guidelines and take our eligibility criteria on board. The common mistakes tend to be really basic: people apply to us with projects which have no connection at all with Wales and no Welsh involvement. We simply can't support these. Budgets don't add up, key information is omitted from the application (all the information about a project that we ask for is essential to our assessors and omitting key information means your application will be delayed). We are happy to provide applicants with pre-application advice and I strongly advise anyone applying to us to discuss their application with us first."

Lottery Funding

Script Development

This award supports development of features in various genres, including fiction, documentary and animation intended for theatrical release. Exceptions may be made for development of animated short films due to the expense of this genre.

ELIGIBILITY

Partnership funding must be in place when the application is made.

DETAILS

Sgrîn will contribute up to £20,000 or 75% of the development costs. Partnership funding in kind must form no more than 12.5% of the overall budget.

Short Film Production

This award supports the production of short films of no longer than 10 minutes in various genres, including fiction, documentary and animation intended for theatrical release. Sgrîn intends to distribute the short films.

DEADLINE

There is an annual deadline in April.

DETAILS

Sgrîn will contribute between 50% and 90% of the production costs with a ceiling of £36,000.

APPLICATIONS

Applicants must make a formal application with the application form. More than one application may be submitted.

Feature Film Production

This award supports production of fully developed features in various genres, including fiction, documentary and animation intended for theatrical release.

ELIGIBILITY

If partnership funding is not in place, applications might receive a conditional offer from Sgrîn as long as interest from the proposed financiers can be proven.

DETAILS

Sgrîn will fund up to £250,000 or 50% of the production costs.

General Guidelines for these schemes

DEADLINE

Unless otherwise stated applications can be made at any time.

ELIGIBILITY

Limited companies are eligible to apply for these awards with projects that are eligible to qualify as British under the Films Act 1985 (ammended 1999).

APPLICATIONS

Applicants are advised to discuss their application with Sgrîn and are asked to fill in an Advanced Notification Form as an initial application for features. Once this has been approved a formal application must be made.

ASSESSMENT

Applications will be assessed against the public benefit, the artistic quality, the need for lottery funding, the financial viability, partnership funding, the demand and the ability of the applicant to deliver the project.

CONDITIONS

Sgrîn contributes funding in the form of an investment, which must be recouped through revenues from income from the film, in relation to the proportion of the investment. Sgrîn must receive screen and publicity credits and be kept up-to-date with cost and project reports.

Production schemes

Sgrîn aims to offer production schemes to support short filmmakers throughout the year. Future schemes are listed on the website, in 2002 these included:

Animated Shorts

This scheme has enabled ten short animated films, of three minutes long and six minutes long, to be produced in partnership with S4C. It may be repeated and details will be published on the website.

Digital Visions

This scheme gives often unheard voices the opportunity to produce short digital films. In 2002 the priority was to support filmmakers from ethnic minorities. In 2003 the priority is likely to be for disabled filmmakers. Three awards are given each year offering up to £10,000 to each for a film of no more than ten minutes in length.

Screen Gems

This scheme, which has been running for four years, supports the production of short films on 35mm film and on DV or High Definition. Director and writer teams are invited to apply with a script lasting no more than 3 minutes. Ten of these are selected to go into production. The scheme will select two new producers who will each produce five of the films and eight trainees to work as crew members. Screen Gems is supported by the Arts Council of Wales and ITV1 Wales.

Other Welsh Funds

Arts Council of Wales

Central and South Wales Office
9 Museum Place
Cardiff, CF10 3NX
Tel: 029 20 376500
Fax: 029 20 221447
Email: information@artswales.org.uk
Web: www.artswales.org.uk

Mid & West Wales Office
6 Gardd Llydaw
Jackson Lane
Carmarthen, SA31 1QD
Tel: 01267 234248
Fax: 01267 233084
Email: information@artswales.org.uk
Web: www.artswales.org.uk

North Wales Office
36 Prince's Drive
Colwyn Bay, LL29 8LA
Tel: 01492 533440
Fax: 01492 533677
Email: information@artswales.org.uk
Web: www.artswales.org.uk

The Arts Councils of Wales will not fund film production intended for distribution but film and video artists are eligible to apply for support in developing professional skills and producing and promoting art works intended for gallery installation. Screenwriters are also eligible to receive funding from the Arts Council.

Professional Development: Creative Wales Awards

This fund supports new and established artists working in any discipline by offering bursaries to develop skills and produce new and experimental work without needing to consider audience development concerns.

Funding will cover salaries, travel, training, networking, research and other costs relating to the project being undertaken.

DEADLINE

The deadline for applications for under £10,000 is annually in May. The deadline for applications between £10,000 and £25,000 is annually in November.

ELIGIBILITY

Individual artists resident in Wales who plan to undertake their project in Wales are eligible to apply. The applicant may collaborate with other artists.

DETAILS

Applicants may apply for between £500 and £25,000, though the average award is £10,000. Partnership funding of at least 10% must be secured.

APPLICATIONS

In addition to the application form, an applicant must submit a CV.

ASSESSMENT

Each application will be assessed against the following criteria: sincerity and ambition; creative quality; the need for funding; support from arts organisations and/or artists; previous work and track record, budget and other finance, benefit for the applicant and the Welsh public, the contribution to the discipline of the applicant and the Arts in Wales, comparison to other applications in terms of cultural and artistic diversity and social inclusion and meeting the Arts Council's priorities.

In addition, other priorities exist for this scheme such as artists working across disciplines, working with young people, working in the Welsh language and artists from ethnic communities.

Capacity Building and Development Fund

This award supports the development of artists and arts organisations to encourage growth and sustainability. The awards are intended to be able to meet individual applicants' needs, including grants for start-up organisations and company development, support for arts bodies and forums, research grants, improving professional standards and practice, encouraging community development and support for sector representatives. Funding will cover operational, development, research and travel costs for individual projects within a time limit.

DEADLINE

Applications for under £5000 may be made at any time. Applications for over £5000 must meet one of two deadlines per year in May and December.

ELIGIBILITY

Individuals and organisations based in Wales are eligible for this award.

DETAILS

Individuals are eligible to apply for between £25 and £5000. Organisations are eligible to apply for between £250 and £50,000. Partnership funding of at least 10% must be secured.

APPLICATIONS

It is advised to discuss an application with the Arts Council before applying.

ASSESSMENT

Each application is assessed against the following criteria: realism and sustainability, the ability of the applicant to deliver the project, the demand; the fulfilment of a lacking in the Arts, the benefit for the applicant and the Arts in Wales, the need for funding; budget and partnership finance, track record and potential of the applicant, the contribution to improving sustainability in the Arts, meeting the Arts Council's priorities.

In addition, other priorities exist for this scheme such as strengthening the Arts infrastructure, sustainable community development, the involvement of young people, the welsh-speaking population and ethnic minorities, arts bodies, employment and promotion of craft in Wales.

Individual Screenwriters Awards

This award offered in collaboration with SGRIN, supports new and established screenwriters to develop fiction, documentary, animation or experimental screenplays intended for theatrical release and/or public exhibition.

DEADLINE

There is an annual deadline in December.

ELIGIBILITY

Applicants must be resident in Wales or be developing a screenplay that is culturally-significant to Wales. The film must be eligible to receive British Film status under Schedule 1 of the Films Act 1985.

DETAILS

The maximum fund available is £5000.

APPLICATIONS

In addition to the application form, applicants must submit various items depending on the genre. Feature applications must include a pitch line, a synopsis, a treatment and sample dialogue. Animation applications must include a pitch line, a synopsis, an outline, storyboard samples and/or sample dialogue. Documentary and experimental applications must include a pitch line, a synopsis and an outline. In addition, established screenwriters will need to demonstrate market understanding and development plans.

ASSESSMENT

Each application will be assessed against the following criteria: public benefit, artistic quality, the need for lottery funding and demand.

CONDITIONS

Contributions from the Arts Council of

Wales and Sgrîn are made in the form of an investment, to be recouped with a 50% premium once the project goes into production. Both councils must be informed of all developments and allowed to monitor the project's finances, direction and management. Both Councils will require a credit on screen and all promotional material.

4 Minute Wonders

Quadrant, 63 Cowbridge Road
Cardiff, CF11 9QP
Tel: 029 20 237333
Fax: 029 20 255514
Email: gwydion-lyn@quadrant.uk.com
Web: www.4minutewonders.com

This scheme that brings together musicians and filmmakers to produce music videos originated in Scotland. In Wales, the scheme is managed by Quadrant, who act as executive producers of each video to assist delivery of the video to schedule and to budget and to technical requirements. Quadrant will be the sole distributor of the video receiving all revenues. See the Scottish 4 Minute Wonders entry on page 158 for full guidelines.

D. M. Davies Award

International Film Festival of Wales
Market House, Market Road
Cardiff, CF5 1QE
Tel: 029 20 406220
Fax: 029 20 233751
Email: enq@iffw.co.uk
Web: www.iffw.co.uk

This award supports emerging filmmakers by awarding the winner of an adjudicated short film competition a cash contribution and production support towards their next film. It is delivered by the Film Festival of Wales and supported by Sgrîn. For further details contact the International Film Festival of Wales.

Northern Ireland

NORTHERN IRELAND FILM AND TELEVISION COMMISSION

Northern Ireland Film and Television Commission

3rd Floor Alfred House
21 Alfred Street
Belfast, BT2 8ED
Tel: 028 9023 2444
Fax: 028 9023 9918
Email: info@niftc.co.uk
Web: www.niftc.co.uk

The NIFC was established in 1997 as the Film Commission for Northern Ireland, with the objective of attracting film production to the region. In 2002, the name was changed to incorporate television, becomming the Northern Ireland Film and Television Commission. The Arts Council of Northern Ireland designated NIFTC with the responsibility of distributing the annual lottery film funds. The commission's objective is to encourage the development of a sustainable film and television industry in Northern Ireland through key areas such as encouraging and facilitating development and production, developing access to moving image heritage, supporting company development and training, providing information services and developing education policy. Investments include a substantial £200,000 from the feature film scheme in *Straight to Video* by Parallel World and £30,000 from the short film scheme in *Shane* by Hot Shot Films.

Andrew Reid, Head of Production

"The NIFTC received over one hundred applications in 2002 and supported twenty eighgt projects. To break this down, we invested £658,826 in twelve production projects, £142,625 in eleven development projects and £10,000 in two distribution projects. The production awards included four features, one TV drama, five short films and two documentaries.

"It is very difficult to say what makes an application stand out as each one is assessed on its own merits. The two main priorities for us when granting an award are to invest in projects which are culturally significant for Northern Ireland and which encourage inward investment, so a proposal should take both these factors into account.

"The difficulties we often encounter when assessing applications is that the form just hasn't been filled in properly or all the enclosures are not submitted. We can't process an award if this is the case no matter how interesting the proposal might be. Another issue for applicants to consider is when to apply for an award. Many approach us too early while the script is being developed and the project researched, so that neither they nor we are clear on the nature of the proposal, in which case, we won't be able to make a fair assessment."

"We get a diverse range of applicants from emerging filmmakers and producers to those with a track record in lower budget feature filmmaking."

Lottery Funding

The Lottery funds are intended to support local film and television production and distribution through three schemes.

Feature films and television drama production

This fund supports the production of feature film, short film, documentaries, animation and television drama.

DETAILS

The fund will award up to 50% of the total cost of production with a ceiling of £150,000. Generally, the contribution the NIFTC will offer is 10% or less of the cost of production.

Script Development

This fund supports the development of feature films and television drama. This includes rights and option payments, fees for key personnel, recce expenses, scheduling and budgeting, legal and accountancy fees and office costs.

DETAILS

The maximum development loan will be no more than 50% of the total costs or £20,000, whichever is the least ammount. Office costs must be no more than 10% of the total development costs.

CONDITIONS

The NIFTC will fund development in the form of a loan, to be repaid with a 50% premium once the project goes into production.

Local cultural production and distribution

This fund is to support the local industry in production and distribution of feature films, short films, television drama series, singles, documentaries, animations and digital media content. In addition to production costs, this will include support for short films, and distribution and promotion costs such as 35mm prints, telecine transfers, tape masters and VHS or DVD copies, entry fees for festivals, shipping costs, and design and print costs. Any distribution funding is aimed at production companies looking to secure a distributor, rather than to the distributor themselves.

DETAILS

In general, the fund will contribute no more than 50% of the cost of production with a ceiling of £50,000. Low budget productions, defined as having production costs of less than £30,000, are eligible to receive up to 75% of the cost of production. Ultra low budget productions, defined as having production costs of less than £5000 are eligible to receive up to 90% of the cost of production. The distribution and promotion of a single film will be eligible for no more than 10% of the production costs with a ceiling of £5000.

ASSESSMENT

Priority for distribution applications will be given to films that have spent a high proportion of their production costs in Northern Ireland.

General Guidelines

DEADLINE

Applications for awards of over £25,000 have four deadlines per year. Applications for awards of below £25,000 can be made at any time as they are assessed on a rolling basis.

ELIGIBILITY

Companies are eligible to apply for all funds. Applicant organisations do not have to be based in Northern Ireland but at least 50% of the film must be shot in Northern Ireland and at least 40% of the budget must be spent in Northern Ireland.

APPLICATIONS

Applicants are advised to apply early. In addition to the application form, applicants must submit various items including a copy of the constitution, recent accounts, statements on the artistic merits, management and financial aspects of the production, a synopsis and script, budget and schedule, details of the rights, CVs, distribution and promotion details, partner finance and other information.

ASSESSMENT

Priority will be given to projects that are filmed entirely in Northern Ireland using Northern Ireland residents. Applications will be assessed against the following criteria: benefit to the general public in Northern Ireland; the artistic quality; the demand; the capability of the producers to manage the project and the viability; other financing in place; the project's need for lottery funding and benefit from receiving it.

CONDITIONS

With the exception of the script development award, the NIFTC will fund projects in the form of investment, with their agreed recoupment based on the NIFTC's contribution in relation to the other investors.

Also, with the exception of the script development award, the project must spend over 40% of the budget in Northern Ireland and the production must adhere to the Northern Ireland Industry Code of Practice. The producer is also expected to contribute 0.5% of the budget with a ceiling of £35,000 towards the Skills Investment Fund. The films must be intended for distribution and broadcast in Northern Ireland.

Production Schemes

The NIFTC aims to offer production schemes to support short filmmakers throughout the year. In 2002 Deviate, part of the digital shorts scheme from the Film Council's New Cinema Fund, awarded up to £8000 for short projects with production support from the Nerve Centre and North West Visions Centre in Belfast.

Other Northern Ireland Funds

Creativity Unit at the Dept of Culture, Arts and Literature

Creativity Unit
Interpoint
20-24 York Street
Belfast, BT15 1AQ
Tel: 028 90 258975
Email: dcal@dcalni.gov.uk
Web: www.dcalni.gov.uk

The Creativity Unit's aim is to encourage initiatives that cross commercial, cultural and educational sectors to support and promote the creative industries in Northern Ireland. The Unit works with four government departments: the Department of Culture, Arts and Leisure, the Department of Education, the Department of Employment and Learning, Invest Northern Ireland.

Creativity Seed Fund

This fund aims to support initiatives encouraged by the Creativity Unit through contributing to costs for sustainable projects. The scheme is intended to provide the trigger for companies in Northern Ireland to develop innovative, creative and dynamic initiatives that will support arts and culture, employment, enterprise and education.

DEADLINE

The application process involves two stages each year. The deadline for Stage 2 follows two months after the deadline for Stage 1 which is usually in January or February.

ELIGIBILITY

Companies and organisations are eligible to apply. They must be private businesses, companies limited by guarantee, not-for-profit organisations, registered charities, or education providers. Applicants should be based in Northern Ireland with experience and reputation in cultural, commercial or educational fields. The scheme will not fund any project that falls under the NIFTC remit.

DETAILS

The total available fund for one project is £50,000, or 50% of the project costs. Partnership funding of at least 50% is required.

APPLICATIONS

Applicants must initially submit an Expression of Interest Form including information about the project, its aims and finances for stage 1. Short listed applications will go through to Stage 2 to make a formal application.

ASSESSMENT

Each application will be assessed for creativity and innovation, extending or crossing boundaries, access and dissemination, feasibility and sustainability.

CONDITIONS

The project must credit the Creativity Unit with their logo on all promotional material (and on screen if applicable). Once the award has been offered, there are certain terms and conditions relating to information provision and submission of invoices.

Arts Council of Northern Ireland

The Arts Council of Northern Ireland
MacNeice House, 77 Malone Road
Belfast, BT9 6AQ
Tel: 028 90 385200
Fax: 028 90 661715
Email: publicaffairs@artscouncil-ni.org
Web: www.artscouncil-ni.org

The Arts Council of Northern Ireland will support film and video artists in their development to produce artwork for gallery installation. Production companies and filmmakers seeking to produce and distribute film projects are not eligible for funding.

General Art Awards Scheme

This award is for artists resident in Northern Ireland seeking support for specific projects, research, artistic development and payment for professional services, materials and equipment. The emphasis is on challenge and innovation, particularly with new technology.

DEADLINE

There are two annual deadlines in February and September.

ELIGIBILITY

Individuals working in any art form or discipline resident in Northern Ireland for at least one year, and with an artistic track record in Northern Ireland. Exceptions may be made for Northern Irish applicants living elsewhere. Projects that involve collaborations of

DETAILS

Applicants may apply for up to £5000. No more than £4000 will be awarded for the purchase of equipment. Professional services include facilities and equipment hire which are necessary for completing the project.

APPLICATIONS

In addition to an application form, applicants must submit a CV and an example of recent work.

ASSESSMENT

Each application will be assessed against the following criteria: previous artistic achievement; viability; impact on advancement of skills, expertise and career; involvement with events and courses; artistic quality.

CONDITIONS

The Arts Council requires the individual to evaluate their project once completed and to submit this to the Council

Major Individual Award Scheme

This fund supports established artists of any discipline in Northern Ireland to enable them to work on extended or ambitious work. Five awards are granted, two of which are discipline-specific; in the year 2003 the disciplines are traditional arts and literature.

DEADLINE

There is an annual deadline in June.

ELIGIBILITY

Same as General Art Awards Scheme.

DETAILS

Applicants may apply for up to £15,000. Five awards at this level are available.

APPLICATIONS

In addition to an application form, applicants must submit a CV and an example of recent work.

ASSESSMENT

Each application will be assessed against the following criteria: continuing professional practice; national or international recognition for artistic achievement; viability; impact on advancement of skills, expertise and career; involvement with events and courses.

CONDITIONS

The Arts Council requires the individual to evaluate their project once completed.

PETER MULLAN

SHORT FILMS

"A problem with short films up to now is new directors have been using them as calling cards and have been putting all their goodies into one bag, one exquisite love scene that works for what it is. Because they are so anxious to show all their tricks, they'll get the crane shot in and whizz bang cut to show that they can edit. The approach to a short film should be the single off the album, the full album is the rest of your fucking life. I've done 15 drafts for a 10 minute film, 15 drafts! Someone will tell you one thing and another will tell you something else and they do seriously think that they are educated. All you are doing is screwing up the single - the filmmaker's not happy and nor is the company. They bury it at 2am and your pals say, 'I thought you were going to be on the telly!' Its a miserable experience to make a film if people really really don't like it. It doesn't mater if its 2 minutes long or 2 hours long, if your mates tell you its shit its going to take a long time to get your confidence back." *NW*

Isle of Man

Isle of Man Film Commission

First floor
Hamilton House
Peel Road
Douglas
Isle of Man, IM1 5EP
Tel: 01624 687173
Fax: 01624 687171
Email: filmcomm@dti.gov.im
Web: www.gov.im/dti/iomfilm/home.html

The Isle of Man is self-governing with its own laws. The government has made available equity funding for films shot on the island to encourage film production and to boost the local economy.

Isle of Man Film & TV Fund

The Isle of Man Film and Television Fund offers equity investment for films and television productions that are shot at least in part on the island.

DEADLINE

This is a rolling scheme so applications may be made at any time.

ELIGIBILITY

Production companies resident in the UK or the Isle of Man, intending to shoot their film in whole or in part on the Isle of Man are eligible to benefit for this fund. At least 50% of the principal photography must take place on the Isle of Man and at least 20% of below-the-line budget on local services. The company must have a sales agent or distributor on board, and a completion bond secured.

DETAILS

Eligible productions may receive up to 25% of the production costs from the fund as a recoupable equity investment with no upper or lower limits on the investment. Producers may also benefit from assistance with financial structuring of budgets. In addition to this, film and TV productions may be able to benefit from production credits if a broadcaster is attached, through it is preferred that the broadcaster does not fund the full budget. This will make up to £350,000 available to the production and it may be combined with equity investment.

APPLICATIONS

It is advised to submit applications as early as possible including details of the investors, the finance plan, budget, distribution plans, details of ownership of rights, sales estimates, a cashflow and a script.

ASSESSMENT

Each application for funding must meet certain criteria such as secure partnership funding, an agreement with a sales agent or distributor, and a completion bond. The commercial viability of the project is a key priority.

CONDITIONS

The Isle of Man contributes to projects in the form of an investment, recouping their investment and shares from the net profits. If the production does not secure UK theatrical release within eighteen months of completion, the Isle of Man may exhibit the film at its own cost and would receive all net profits as a result. The Isle of Man must be kept informed with access to financial and management reports and a final audit after completion. The Isle of Man must receive a screen credit, copies of production stills and two DVD and two VHS copies.

Chapter 5
OTHER SOURCES

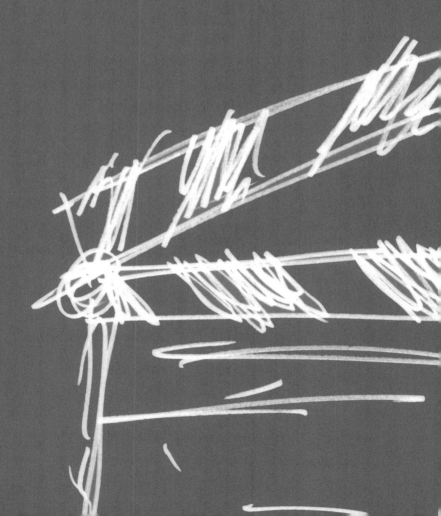

Business Support

Department of Trade and Industry

DTI Enquiry Unit
1 Victoria Street
London, SW1H OET
Tel: 020 7215 5000
Email: Enquiries@dti.gsi.gov.uk
Web: www.dti.gov.uk

The DTI offers support to UK businesses through various programmes and initiatives, usually administered at a local level. Funding and finance for small and medium enterprises is delivered though the Small Business Service, Regional Development Agencies, Business Links and Government Offices. Full contact details for these organisations are available in the Chapter 7. The general guidelines to the schemes on offer are below, and it is important to note that there may be regional variations.

The Enterprise Grant Scheme

Apply to the government office in your region (page 215)

Enterprise Grants are administered through the Regional Government Offices, who are supported by the Regional Business Links and Regional Development Agencies. The grants provide financial support for small and medium sized enterprises, in areas of the UK which are eligible according to EU regulations. The grants are funded by the EU's Enterprise Fund. They The criteria and assessment priorities vary from region to region. The grants will cover fixed assets, for example camera or post-production equipment.

ELIGIBILITY

Small and medium sized enterprises (SME's) in the eligible areas may apply for the grants. Businesses must meet the EU's definition of SME's. Small enterprises are defined as employing fewer than 50 staff, with an annual turnover of 7m Euros (approx. £4,745,000) or less, or a balance sheet total of E5m (approx. £3.4m) or less. Medium enterprises are defined as employing between 50 and 249 staff, with an annual turnover of E40m (approx £27.6m) or less, or a balance sheet total of 27m Euros (approx £18.1m) or less.

DETAILS

Small enterprises are eligible to benefit for up to 15% gross of fixed capital costs. Medium enterprises are eligible to benefit for up to 7.5% gross of fixed capital costs. This may be up to 15% in Assisted Areas (areas identified by the EU as in need of economic development). The maximum grant available is £75,000 for projects, and £500,000 for capital investment.

ASSESSMENT

All applications are assessed against quality, need, viability and job displacement.

APPLICATION

All applicants are advised to talk to the local Government Office or Business Link before applying. In addition to the application form, applicants must submit accounts, details of other funding, trading forecasts, and cash-flow projections.

CONDITIONS

Once an offer is made to an applicant, an accountant must check the claim. The grants may be publicised.

Small Firms Loan Guarantee Scheme (SFLGS)

Small Business Service
Kingsgate House
66-74 Victoria Street
London, SW1E 6SW
Tel: 0845 600 9006
Email: gatewayenquiries@sbs.gsi.gov.uk

Companies with sound business proposals, that are unable to secure loans due to a lack of security or track record, may apply to the DTI for a loan guarantee. The loan will come from one of the DTI approved lenders, and is guaranteed by the Small Business Service. UK companies with annual turnovers of £1.5m or lower are eligible. This is raised to £5m for manufacturers. There are some restrictions on business activities.

Businesses that have been trading for under two years are eligible to receive a government guarantee for up to 70% of the loan amount, which will generally be between £5000 and £100,000. Businesses that have been trading for more than two years may apply for a government guarantee of up to 85% of the loan amount, which may be up to £250,000. The repayment period lasts between two and ten years.

Applicants must apply directly to the lender for a loan. The Small Business Service has a list of approved lenders involved in the Small Firms Loan Guarantee Scheme.

Regional Selective Assistance

Apply to the Regional Development Agency in your region (page 217)

This scheme provides financial assistance for projects in Assisted Areas. It must be clear that the project needs the support from the RSA, encourages employment and costs are more than £500,000. Funding will cover: starting up new businesses, existing business growth, research and development facilities and allowing business to move from development to production. The priority is to raise productivity and to improve the skills base.

ELIGIBILITY

Business in manufacturing and service industries are mainly eligible to apply. Their markets must be national, rather than local. Companies, partnerships and sole traders may apply. The project must last for at least five years and spend more than £500,000 on capital expenditure such as property and machinery.

DETAILS

Generally, grants will be between 5% and 15% of the project costs. The minimum amount that can be awarded is £75,000.

ASSESSMENT

Applications are assessed against the following criteria: location (projects should be in Assisted Areas, some of which will have restrictions based on UK and EU policy, such as the European Commission's sectoral restrictions for synthetic fibres, vehicles, food production, agriculture, fisheries, shipbuilding, coal, iron and steel), need, eligible investment, jobs, quality, national and regional benefit, no prior commitments, and partnership funding.

Further assessment might be based in the following priorities: wage and salary levels, creation of highly skilled sustainable employment, research and development, training and development.

APPLICATIONS

Applicants are advised to contact the local Regional Development Agency, to establish if their project will be in an Assisted Area. In addition to the application form, applicants must submit financial documents and a business plan to the local Regional Development Agency. Applications for over £2m will be required to submit further information.

Following this, Appraisal Officers may discuss the project with the applicant, request further details, and visit the location of the project.

The Prince's Trust

Head Office, 18 Park Square East
London, NW1 4LH
Freephone: 0800 842 842
Fax: 020 7543 1200
Web: www.princes-trust.co.uk

The Prince's Trust is a UK charity that has been helping young people overcome barriers and get their lives working since 1976. Through practical support including training, mentoring and financial assistance, The Prince's Trust helps 14-30 year olds realise their potential and transform their lives. The Trust focuses its efforts on those who've struggled at school, have been in care, are long-term unemployed or who have been in trouble with the law.

Most programmes operate in the majority of areas, although there are some variations. The contact details for the regional offices are listed in Chapter 7.

DEVELOPMENT AWARDS

These awards help 14-25 year olds to access education, training and work. Participants can receive a cash award of between £50 and £500. The scheme supports individuals most in need of support and priority will be given to those with a lack of qualifications, who have been in care, long term unemployed or who have been in trouble with the law. The award does not fund NVQ, SVQ level 4, HNC, HND, degree or post-grad or courses of an equivalent level.

GROUP AWARDS

These awards are given to groups of young people working within the community. Groups of 3-12 UK residents aged 14-25 are eligible to apply and the size of the award depends on the size of the group and the cost of the project. The Prince's Trust is currently not providing grants for groups of young people. It is looking for a funding partner and hopes to provide more support for groups shortly. Visit the website to find out more.

EUROPEAN PROGRAMME

The Prince's Trust European Programme offer 2-3 week opportunities to work in Europe and helps develop skills, confidence and employability. Work Away is a three-week work placement in countries including Sweden, France, Poland, Italy and Greece. The European Team Challenge is a two-week team based community project in Eastern Europe. As well as the overseas element, participants go through structured programme of preparation and follow up. This includes a pre-departure training residential. The Trust provides personal support in the UK and abroad, help in achieving goals, accreditation through City and Guilds, personal travel insurance, return flights and travel to airports, accommodation and food.

BUSINESS PROGRAMME

The Prince's Trust offers funding and support to help 18-30 year olds to start their own business. Support can include a low interest loan of up to £5,000, a grant of up to £1,500 in special circumstances, a business mentor, marketing support and specialist advice including a free legal helpline.

Competitions

Britshorts / Nike Young Director's Awards

Britshorts Limited
25 Beak Street
London, W1F 9RT
Tel: 020 7734 2277
Fax: 020 7734 2242
Email: contactus@britshorts.com
Web: www.britshorts.com

This competition, organised by leading short film distributor Britshorts, invites young writer-directors to submit an idea for a short film about sport that lasts up to 3 minutes. There is an annual deadline (tbc), and applicants must be older than 18 and younger than 29, with no more than two broadcast credits as writer/director.

Three winners receive £8000 to make the submitted idea into a short film on digital video. While making the film, they also receive support in the form of coaching and mentoring from industry professionals. The panel at the awards ceremony judges the films and an overall winner is picked. The winning film is distributed by Britshorts and screened at NikeTown.

In addition to the application form, applicants must submit a treatment and a CV. The treatments and the films are judged on: style, emotion, message, originality, performance and relevance to sport. Nike reserves the right to interview or photograph the applicant for advertising purposes, but the intention is not to use the treatments for advertising purposes.

Euroscript

Euroscripts
Suffolk House
1-8 Whitfield Place
London, W1T 5JU
Tel: 020 7387 5880
Fax: 020 7387 5880
Email: info@euroscript.co.uk
Web: www.euroscript.co.uk

The company supports screenwriters by offering consultancy, development programmes, workshops and promoting scripts. It is run on an international level, funded initially by the Media II European funding programme. Euroscripts also runs a biannual international scriptwriting competition for features, single TV drama and TV series in any genre. The selected scripts go on to benefit from script development to reach first draft stage.

There are two deadlines per year and applications must be post-marked by either 30th April or 31st October. The competition is open to international applicants but the screenplays must be in English. Adaptations of pre-existing works are accepted as long as an option has been acquired. Selected submissions are short-listed for further development over the following nine months with an experienced script consultant, encouraging each project to reach first draft stage.

There is an entry fee of £35. In addition to the application form, applicants must submit an outline of an idea, a CV, and sample pages from a screenplay. Short listed writers may be asked to submit a full-length script. Each project developed by Euroscripts must be credited on the first page and on screen if the screenplay is produced. The full copyright will stay with the writer.

Nicholl Fellowships

Nicholl Fellowships in Screenwriting
Academy of Motion Picture Arts and Sciences
8949 Wilshire Blvd.
Beverly Hills
CA 90211-1972
USA
Email nicholl@oscars.org
Web: www.oscars.org

The Nicholl Fellowships in screenwriting is an international competition run by the Academy of Motion Picture Arts and Sciences for emerging screenwriters. It began in 1986 and in 2002 received over 6000 entries. All entries must be postmarked by May 1st of the year of application and are judged by a panel of industry professionals.

Applicants must not have earned more than $5000 (approx £3,150) by writing for film or TV, or have received a prize which includes an option or first look clause. Individual writers or two co-writers may apply. The competition is open for international submissions but all screenplays must have been written in English. The screenplays must not be based on pre-existing works. Students may apply, but should they win, the fellowship year will be deferred until their course is finished.

There is an entry fee of $30 (£18), which is reduced for early applications. In addition to the application form, applicants must submit a full screenplay. Applications will be accepted by post or courier only. Short listed applicants will be asked to write to the fellowship explaining their interests in receiving the award. The fellowship will give a copy of the screenplays submitted to the Academy during the fellowship year, but the Academy will not hold any rights. The competition awards up to five fellowships a year at $30,000 each and the successful writers must produce a feature screenplay during the following year.

The Oscar Moore Foundation

The Oscar Moore Foundation
c/o Screen International
33-39 Bowling Green Lane
London, EC1R 0DA
Tel: 020 7505 8080
Fax: 020 7505 8087
Email: annmarie.oconnor@media.emap.com
Web: www.screendaily.com/omf.asp

The foundation exists to support new European screenwriters. The trade magazine, Screen International, manages the trust in memory of Oscar Moore, former editor-in-chief of the magazine. New European screenwriters are eligible to apply for the competition with a first draft of a screenplay. It must be in the genre chosen for that year's prize and submitted by the annual deadline in September to be judged by the trustees of the foundation.

The award winner receives £10,000 for the best draft screenplay and a place on the week-long Arista script editing workshops. These workshops provide an opportunity to develop the screenplay with European writers, producers, directors and development executives. The winner is also offered a performed reading of the screenplay by the Script Factory.

Shell Live Wire

Shell Live Wire
Hawthorn House
Forth Banks
Newcastle upon Tyne, NE1 3SG
Tel: 0191 261 5584
Fax: 0191 261 1910
Email: shell-livewrie@pne.org
Web: www.shell-livewire.org

The Shell Live Wire scheme began in 1982, to support 16-30 year old residents of the UK to start up and develop businesses. The programme offers factual advice and support programmes, in addition to an annual competition, the Young Entrepreneur of the Year Awards, to reward business start-ups.

Young Entrepreneur of the Year Awards

The awards, with prizes of £10,000 out of a £200,000 pot, are open to business start-ups run by individuals aged between 16 and 30, who are living and running a company in the UK, which has been trading between 3 and 18 months. Applicants must register for the awards, after which a local co-ordinator will help the applicant prepare for entry into the awards. Entrants must submit a business plan, as well as an application form, before the end of January each year.

Straight 8

Godman
10a Belmont St
London, NW1 8HH
Email: ed.ben@straight8.net
Web: www.straight8.net

Organised by the production company Godman, this event asks filmmakers to shoot a 3 minute film on one cartridge of Kodak Super 8mm film. The filmmakers must edit in-camera and hand over the unprocessed film, along with an original soundtrack burned onto CD, to the competition organisers who arrange for it to be processed. All the received films are screened in public on the prize-giving night without the filmmakers having seen the results of their work. The audience votes for their favourite film. Several events of this nature are run throughout the year and filmmakers should subscribe online to receive email updates.

Competitions for completed projects

DepicT!

DepicT!
Brief Encounters Short Film Festival
Watershed Media Centre, 1 Canon's Road

Bristol, BS1 5TX
Tel: 0117 927 5102
Fax: 0117 930 9967
Email: lucy.jefferies@brief-encounters.org.uk
Web: www.depict.org

This competition asks new filmmakers to make a short film of no longer than 90 seconds in the category of live action or animation. There is an annual deadline in September, so the films can be shown at the Brief Encounters Short Film Festival in October and November. The films may be made in any format, but must be submitted on the specified mediums. Emerging filmmakers from anywhere in the world may apply. Applications will be judged on:

originality, style, readability, clarity of idea and impact. Ten short films are chosen to be presented at the awards ceremony, where a panel of judges will select a winning film in each category. The prize for each winner is £3000.

Gone in 60 Seconds

Camcorder User & DVD Movie Maker
Highbury-WV
53-79 Highgate Road
London, NW5 1TW
Tel: 020 7331 1000
Email: letterbox@camuser.co.uk
Web: www.camuser.co.uk

This annual competition, with a deadline in September, is a joint initiative between Canon and What Camcorder and Camcorder User magazines. Applicants are asked to make a video film of no more than 60 seconds following a set theme (in 2003 this was Identity) and submit it on VHS, miniDV or DV. The prize winner will receive a latest model professional video camera and the runner up will receive a digital camcorder. Their entries will also be screened at the closing ceremony. Over the duration of the competition applicants have the chance of being selected to have their film screened on the magazine web sites.

Jameson Short Film Awards

European Coordination of Film Festivals
64 rue Philippe le Bon
B-1000 Brussels,
Belgium
Tel: +32 2 280 1376
Fax: +32 2 230 9141
Email: cefc@skypro.be
Web: www.eurofilmfest.org

Email: info@jameson.ie
Web: www.jameson.ie

Throughout the year, the Jameson Short Film Awards, tours a selection of Film Festivals, which are members of the European Co-ordination of Film Festivals. Short films are selected during each of the festivals, and judged by the festival panel against the brief set by Jameson, which is to: select a film from their country which they think has the best potential for seducing all the different audiences across Europe. Films of all genres are eligible and one winner is chosen from each Festival, receiving E6000 (approx £4000) and a trophy. It is likely for the winning films to be screened at events throughout the year, including the International Critics Week at the Cannes film festival. During 2003, the Awards will be visiting twelve festivals. Over the past two years the Awards have travelled to Finland, Germany, Spain, Portugal, Ireland, Italy, Turin, UK, and France.

Kodak

Kodak Entertainment Imaging
Kodak House
Station Road
Hemel Hempstead, HP1 1JU
Tel: 01442 261122
Email: danielclark@kodak.com for show case
Email: julieann@kodak.com for commercial awards
Web: www.kodak.co.uk

Kodak/BAFTA Short Film Showcase

This competition accepts short films for selection to be screened at the annual showcase at BAFTA in March. All films must: be shot on Kodak stock, be less than 15 minutes long, have been shot in the previous 18 months and have a print on Super16mm or 35mm. The short listed films will be screened at the showcase and judged by the audience of professionals. The winning producer and director will have the opportunity to attend the Cannes Film Festival with Kodak.

Kodak Student Film Awards for Best Commercial

This award, presented in association with the BTAA, invites film student teams to produce a commercial based on a brief given by Kodak's advertising agency, Ogilvy. The students choose from a selection of products, and are given 400ft of Kodak Colour Negative 16mm film stock, to produce the commercial that is judged by a panel of film industry professionals. Three winners are chosen. The winning commercials are screened at the BTAA Industry Award ceremony, and the winning teams receive prizes of film stock, camera hire and processing, worth up to £1500.

Ten Seconds Film Competition

Candide Media Works, Inc
27 West 24th Street, Suite 202
New York, NY 10010,
USA
Web: www.tensecondfilms.com

Applicants must shoot a ten second digital film to enter this online competition. There is a month long submission period each year in February and March, and the films must be submitted by uploading the film to the competition web site. Visitors to the web site vote on the films. The viewers' top ten are selected and judged by a panel for their creativity and aesthetic appeal. The first prize is $1000 (approx £315), the second prize is $500 (approx £500), and the third prize is $250 (approx £160). They hope to begin running more than one competition a year with details published on the web site.

All locations and people that appear in the film must have signed release forms. Copyrighted music must not be played in the film without the copyright. Trademarks cannot be shown unless the applicant owns them. The films must adhere to certain technical requirements to be uploaded to the web site. Applicants must be over 13 years old.

Turner Classic Movies Classic Shorts

Turner House
16 Great Marlborough Street
London, W1F 7HS
Email: nick.hart@turner.com
Web: www.tcmonline.co.uk

Emerging filmmakers, with short films completed between 18th September 2002 and September 2003, are eligible to apply for this competition. The films must be: no more than 20 minutes long, shot on film or a professional video format, made in the UK in English, and cannot have been shown commercially, at a major film festival, or have received a major prize. Applicants must send in a completed application form with the film on VHS, and be sure that they have a screen quality copy available. Eight to ten selected films will be screened at the Awards Ceremony during the Regus London Film Festival, when the panel will choose the winners. Past judges have included Hugh Grant, Ewan McGregor, Stephen Frears and Stephen Woolley. Winning films will be shown on Turner Classic Movies, entered into the BAFTA Awards and the winning filmmakers will receive £5000 for first prize, £3000 for second prize and £2000 for third prize.

National Lottery Funding

Funding hotline: 0845 275 0000
Web: www.lotterygoodcauses.org.uk

Just under a third (27%) of the money raised by the National Lottery goes to 'good causes'. These are split into six areas: arts, charities, heritage, millennium projects, sports, and health, education and the environment. Some of the organisations supported by the National Lottery, which offer grants to filmmakers, are listed elsewhere in this book, such as The Film Council, Scottish Screen, and the Arts Council. A selection of lottery distributors that filmmakers in some cases are able to apply to is listed below.

Awards For All

Head Office
Ground Floor
St Nicholas Court
25-27 Castle Gate
Nottingham, NG1 7AR
Tel: 0115 934 9350
Fax: 0115 934 9355
Email: enquiries.england@awardsforall.org.uk
Web: www.awardsforall.org.uk

North East:
6th Floor
Baron House
4 Neville Street
Newcastle upon Tyne, NE1 5NL
Tel: 0191 255 1100
Fax: 0191 233 1997

North West
Ground Floor
Dallam Court
Dallam Lane
Warrington, WA2 7LU
Tel: 01925 626800
Tel: 01925 234041

Yorkshire and the Humber
3rd Floor
Carlton Tower
34 St Pauls Street
Leeds, LS1 2AT
Tel: 0113 2245300
Fax: 0113 2440363

East Midlands
Ground Floor
St Nicholas Court
25-27 Castle Gate
Nottingham, NG1 7AR
Tel: 0115 9349304
Tel: 0115 9484435

West Midlands8th Floor, Edmund House
12-22 Newhall Street
Birmingham , B3 3NL
Tel: 0121 2003500
Fax: 0121 2123081

Eastern
Elizabeth House,
2nd Floor,
1 High Street
Chesterton, CB4 1YW
Tel: 01223 449009
Fax: 01223 312628

London
9th Floor
89 Albert Embankment
London, SE1 7UF
Tel: 020 7587 6600
Fax: 020 75876610

South West
Beaufort House
51 New North Rd
Exeter, EX4 4EQ
Tel: 01392 849705
Fax: 01392 253105
South East
3rd Floor

Dominion House
Woodbridge Road
Guildford, GU1 4BN
Tel: 01483 462943
Fax: 01483 569893

Scotland
Highlander House
58 Waterloo St
Glasgow, G2 7DB
Tel: 0141 242 1200
Fax: 0141 223 8628
Email: scotland@awardsforall.org.uk

Wales
Tel: 01686 611740
Fax: 01686 621534

Northern Ireland
2nd Floor
Hildon House
30-34 Hill Street
Belfast, BT1 2LB
Tel: 028 9055 9090
Fax: 028 9055 1444
Email: enquiries.ni@awardsforall.org.uk

Awards For All is a rolling (no deadline) awards scheme that funds community projects across the arts, sports, heritage and other areas. The main aims for the scheme are to encourage community activity and participation, to improve skills and creativity, and to improve quality of life. It is a nation wide scheme but guidelines may vary slightly from region to region.

Not-for-profit organisations are eligible to apply for an award of between £500 and £5000 for projects and activities. The organisation must have an annual income of below £20,000 excepting schools, health bodies, and parish or towns, which may apply for awards, as long as the project is related to sport, art, environment, heritage, education or health. It would be wise to contact the local Awards for All office to establish the particular priorities for your region, before making an application.

Heritage Lottery Fund

Corporate & London & South East England offices
7 Holbein Place
London, SW1W 8NR
Tel: 020 7591 6000
Fax: 020 7591 6001
Email: enquire@hlf.org.uk
Web: www.hlf.org.uk

East of England office
Kett House
Station Road
Cambridge, CB1 2JT
Tel: 01223 224870
Fax: 01223 224871
Email: enquire@hlf.org.uk
Web: www.hlf.org.uk

East Midlands office
Chiltern House
St Nicholas Court
25-27 Castle Gate
Nottingham, NG1 7AR
Tel: 0115 934 9050
Fax: 0115 934 9051
Email: enquire@hlf.org.uk
Web: www.hlf.org.uk

North East office
St Nicholas Building
St Nicholas Street
Newcastle upon Tyne, NE1 1RF
Tel: 0191 255 7570
Fax: 0191 255 7571
Email: enquire@hlf.org.uk
Web: www.hlf.org.uk

North West office
9th Floor
82 King Street
Manchester, M2 4WQ
Tel: 0161 831 0850
Fax: 0161 831 0851
Email: enquire@hlf.org.uk
Web: www.hlf.org.uk

South West office
Trinity Court
Southernhay East
Exeter, EX1 1PG
Tel: 01392 223950
Fax: 01392 223951
Email: enquire@hlf.org.uk
Web: www.hlf.org.uk

West Midlands office
Bank House
8 Cherry House
Birmingham, B2 5AL
Tel: 0121 616 6870
Fax: 0121 616 6871
Email: enquire@hlf.org.uk
Web: www.hlf.org.uk

Yorkshire and the Humber office
Carlton Tower
34 St Paul's Street
Leeds, LS1 2QB
Tel: 0113 388 8030
Fax: 0113 388 8031
Email: enquire@hlf.org.uk
Web: www.hlf.org.uk

Scotland office
28 Thistle Street
Edinburgh , EH12 1EN
Tel: 0131 225 9450
Fax: 0131 225 9454
Email: enquire@hlf.org.uk
Web: www.hlf.org.uk

Wales office
Suite 5A, Hodge House
Guildhall Place
St Mary's Street
Cardiff, CF10 1DY
Tel: 029 2034 3413
Fax: 029 2034 3427
Email: enquire@hlf.org.uk
Web: www.hlf.org.uk

Northern Ireland office
51-53 Adelaide Street
Belfast, BT2 8FE
Tel: 028 9031 0120
Fax: 028 9031 0121
Email: enquire@hlf.org.uk
Web: www.hlf.org.uk

The Heritage Lottery Fund was set up in 1993 by the trustees of the National Heritage Memorial Fund, which was established in 1980 to conserve the national heritage, giving grants in the name of people who have lost their lives for Britain. The lottery fund supports projects aimed at conserving national heritage. Film and video projects will be supported as long as they record and increase public access to Britain's heritage, and form part of a wider heritage project.

Between 2002 and 2007 the priority for the Heritage Lottery Fund is focused in three areas: conserving and enhancing the UK's diverse heritage, encouraging more people to be involved in their heritage, and making sure that everyone can learn about, have access to and enjoy their heritage. A representative of the Heritage Lottery Fund has said of filmmaking projects that, "the emphasis should be on the benefits to the heritage and increasing the understanding and involvement in heritage rather than on the particular medium. Performing arts, visual arts and media projects can be supported if they have community involvement and can bring to life a heritage tradition or language for a defined heritage purpose with a defined outcome. We would not support film making for its own sake."

The fund runs its own grant schemes which include Awards for All (see above), Local Heritage Initiative, Your Heritage, Heritage Grants, Repair grants for places of worship In England, Northern Ireland and Scotland, Townscape Heritage Initiative, Public Parks Initiative, Landscape Partnerships and Young Roots, involving young people in Heritage conservation.

Millennium Commission

The Millennium Commission
Portland House
Stag Place
London, SW1E 5EZ
Tel: 020 7880 2001
Fax: 020 7880 2000
Email: info@millennium.gov.uk
Web: www.millennium.gov.uk

The Millennium Awards

The Millennium Awards Fellowship
The Millennium Commission
Freepost Lon10626
London, SWE 5YP
Tel: 020 7880 2072
Fax: 020 7880 2070
Email: starpeople@millennium.gov.uk
Web: www.starpeople.org.uk

Unltd – the Millennium Awards Trust

Head Office/London Office
The Mezzanine Floor
Elizabeth House
39 York Road
London, SE1 7NQ
Tel: 020 7401 5305
Email: paulcarbury@unltd.org.uk
Web: www.unltd.org.uk

Birmingham Office
Unit G2, The Ground Floor
The Arch, 48-52 Floodgate Street
Birmingham, B5 5SL
Tel: 0121 766 4570
Email: dawndcaccia@unltd.org.uk

Bradford Office
Second Floor
Highpoint Building
Westgate
Bradford, BD1 2TT
Tel: 01274 728 525
Email: zulfiqarahmed@unltd.org.uk

Northern Ireland Office
Room 70/71
Scottish Mutual Building
16 Donegal Square South
Belfast, BT15 JG
Tel: 028 9024 4007
Email: stephaniereid@unltd.org.uk

Scotland UnLtd Office
54 Manor Place
Edinburgh, EH3 7EH
Tel: 0131 226 7333
Email: jimbennett@unltd.org.uk

Wales Office
1st Floor, Suite D2
Alexandra Gate, Ford Pengam
Rover Way,
Cardiff, CF24 2SA
Tel: 029 2089 4774
Email: sianthomason@unltd.org.uk

The Millennium Commission is an independent body receiving a share of lottery money to support local communities. The commission enables various projects and schemes to be realised under certain priorities: the environment, science and technology, urban regeneration, education and community. The Millennium Awards are to be replaced in 2004 with the Millennium Awards Trust, a lottery endowment of £100m managed by UnLtd, which aims to make the Millennium Awards available indefinitely.

The Awards

These awards are open to any individual over the age of 16 from the UK. Since 1996, small grants of about £2000 have been given to proposals for community projects. The intention is to encourage the individual who is applying to meet personal goals, and to help them to help their community through the implementation of their idea. The awards are distributed through over 100 designated Award Partners made up of charities and community networks. These Award Partners will continue to distribute lottery awards until 2004.

The endowment allows this scheme to continue through the Trust, which can already accept applications. The Trust is managed by UnLtd, a consortium of seven charity organisations. The lottery awards will be administered through two schemes, or levels. Level 1 awards between £500 and £5000, and will cover development costs such as materials, equipment, room hire and so on. Level 2 awards between £5000 and £15,000 for more ambitious projects, or projects which have already received funding from Level 1 and need further development. Funding at this level will cover living costs in addition to development costs. Groups may work together on a project if they apply for the Level 1 award. People who have been awarded grants from the Millennium Commission, may join other awardees in the fellowship and benefit from events, training, information and useful contacts.

The aims of the awards from the Trust remain in line with the preceding Millennium Awards, intending to support individuals to help the community and themselves through a project based on a good idea. The projects must: benefit the public or a community in the UK, be in need of an UnLtd Millennium Award to ensure their success; offer a learning opportunity for the applicant(s); be either a new initiative or clear expansion of an existing project. According to the Millennium Commission, so far 13% of funding has gone to arts based projects and 6.5% of fund winners have made videos as part of their projects. Film and video projects have been funded where they clearly match the aims of the fund in bringing a group or community together for a project.

NESTA

Fishmongers' Chambers
110 Upper Thames Street
London, EC4R 3TW
Tel: 020 7645 9500
Email: nesta@nesta.org.uk
Web: www.nesta.org.uk

NESTA is the National Endowment for
Science, Technology and the Arts. In 1998,
it was established with a £200m endowment
from lottery money, to support and invest in
British talent to encourage innovation and
invention in the UK. NESTA invests with
the interest from the endowment. There are
several programmes of support.

Invention and innovation

This rolling award scheme (no deadline)
invests in often high-risk original and
innovative projects, which offer potentially
significant monetary, cultural or social
returns. Projects that combine arts, science
and technology are of particular interest
to NESTA. Support is aimed at the early
development stages of an idea and will cover,
for example: research and development,
tests to prove the concept, securing
Intellectual Property Rights, market
research, and salaries.

Any UK resident is eligible to apply if they
have a registered office in the UK, but
particular priority goes to individuals and
small groups. NESTA will invest between
£5000 and £150,000 in each project, with
an average investment of between £30,000
and £85,000. The aim is to recoup the
investment, but it is accepted that because
of their high-risk nature only a small
proportion of the projects will go into
production and see a return on investment.
There may be funding available for projects
that do develop further than this, but there
is no guarantee. As well as investing money,
NESTA will invest time and energy in the
project in the form of a project champion,
an experienced business professional who
can provide advice and expertise as a
mentor.

Applicants are advised to test their idea on
others before applying to NESTA (whilst
ensuring that confidentiality and intellectual
property protection is not compromised
by doing so), and include these results in
the application along with a collection of
materials. These will include: a business
plan, idea description test reports, CV's,
financial statements and market research
reports. Successful proposals will show:
innovation and creativity, commercial
and social potential, protection of the
idea, genuine originality, and a need for
NESTA's support in particular. In addition,
applicants with science and technology
based projects will be judged for their
knowledge of competitors' projects and
patents. Applicants for arts-based projects
will be judged for the evidence of innovation
and creativity provided.

Fellowship

This programme allows talented individuals
to create a personal programme of creative
development, and offers the time and
resources to follow it through. The aim is
to encourage development and exploration
of ideas, particularly in the combination of
arts, science and technology. Support may
cover training, travel, and income to allow
the time to consider, research and test ideas.

Individuals are nominated for the award.
NESTA has established a changing network
of nominators with the experience and
expertise to spot emerging talent. In
addition to this, NESTA has established
talent scouts in the East Midlands, offered
certain organisations the chance to make
one nomination, and may be organising
competitions.

The nominee must have achieved excellence
in their field and be looking to pursue an
unchartered direction. The individual is
assessed on their track record and on the
proposal's merits for, excellence, promise,

creativity, originality, usefulness and commitment. The successful nominee will be awarded between £3000 and £75,000 for a project lasting up to five years. The individual will also benefit from a programme manager and mentor.

Dream Time Fellowships

This pilot award scheme is being repeated in 2003. It is open to outstanding individuals looking for the time and the funds to pursue an idea relevant to their area of expertise, and which has a practical application. The applicant must have at least ten years experience in their field.

Education

This scheme encourages and supports establishment and development of new and innovative education programmes that promote creativity in the arts science and technology. Key priorities are: how people learn and the encouragement of learning across ages and sectors, links between arts, science and technology, and working with a diverse range of organisations.

NESTA researches need, demand and gaps in education provision, then invites or commissions projects from organisations in the UK. One of these projects may be a pilot to test out the idea. NESTA will continue active involvement in any funded project, appointing project supervisors. Organisations are also welcome to approach NESTA with ideas. Projects are assessed primarily for potential and need. Other considerations are: partnership, talent, innovation, impact, management, promotion, strategic approach and exit strategy.

Other

Carlton Metroland

Regional Programmes
Carlton Television
101 St Martins Lane
London WC2N 4RF
Web: www.itv.com/metroland

This documentary production scheme has been running for ten years enabling new documentary filmmakers in London to produce half hour films that reflect the diversity of the region.

DEADLINE

The annual deadline is around January

ELIGIBILITY

Filmmakers must be resident in the Carlton area of Greater London with no previous documentary director credit for television.

DETAILS

Five half-hour documentaries are commissioned by Carlton each year and are transmitted on ITV in the London-Carlton region as part of a documentary series called Metroland. The films should be about London in some way, touching on people, places or experiences that relate to London-Carlton regions.

Before shooting, the filmmakers will go through three weekends of editorial and technical training as well as attending six master classes. The films are shot on Digi-beta with five shooting days allowed and three weeks editing time for each film. The selected directors work with experienced teams. Drama-reconstruction is not eligible and use of graphics, rostrum and archive material should be limited.

APPLICATIONS

Applicants should submit a CV and a page of writing about the applicant's skills and experience in documentary filmmaking and their interest and commitment to the scheme; a page summarising the film idea; and a treatment.

An initial short list of 25 applicants will be asked to attend a seminar where finalists will be selected from interviews.

ASSESSMENT

Assessment of the submitted ideas is based on strong narrative and well-developed characters combined with the practicality of being able to shoot it. If there are specific elements – interviewees or locations - necessary for the film to be successful, an applicant should obtain agreement in principle for them. Also, as the films form part of a series to be broadcast on a mainstream channel, selected projects must have a broad appeal for a wide cross-section of audience. The applicant must be able to demonstrate their ability to handle the project, so previous experience and skills will be assessed.

CONDITIONS

Carlton Television reserves the right to approve each documentary for transmission.

First Film Foundation

9 Bourlet Close
London, W1P 7PJ
Tel: 020 7580 2111
Email info@firstfilm.co.uk
Web: www.firstfilm.co.uk

This organisation exists to assist new filmmakers towards making their first feature film.

First Development

This annual scheme is a development programme for nine feature-length screenplays. It aims to produce projects with commercial potential, by bringing

screenwriters, directors and producers together under a six-month development programme that includes three four-day workshops. At the end of the term, the work will be presented to industry professionals. The scheme is supported by the Film Council, Mission Pictures and the Jerwood Charitable Foundation. The next deadline will be September 2003.

Jerwood First Film

This is an annual prize to develop a slate of short film projects. Writers may apply alone or as part of a writer/producer/director team. The development programme will include three screenwriting workshops and professional advice on creating a package for potential partners or investors. At the end of the term, the scripts will be presented online in print in the annual project book. One of the projects will be selected for production with the support of the BBC.

Comedy Shorts

This award supports the development of short comedy scripts by emerging writers, and partners them with emerging comedy directors. The short listed projects are presented to a panel of judges comprised of industry professionals.

Sci-Fi Shorts

Sci-Fi Shorts is an annual award that supports development and production of short science-fiction films that can be played to theatrical audiences. Writers and directors may apply as teams or separately, for the chance of producing a film that receives nation wide theatrical release in front of a feature. The scheme is supported by the Sci-Fi channel, which will broadcast the finished film.

The Studio Film Completion Fund

This award supports the completion of short films by independent filmmakers, who have no other source of post-production finance.

TIM CLAGUE

JERWOOD PRIZE

A rushed application for the Jerwood prize and Tim Clague got himself a BAFTA nomination, Stephen Daldry as director, and development with Working Title.

"I wrote *Eight* for a Sony prize that had to be shot on miniDV, it was dead new at that point, you had to write a script to use the camera in a new way. I never heard back from them but somebody emailed me about the Jerwood prize but the entry date was in five days time so I dug that script back out again. Trouble was that the Jerwood prize was 10 minutes maximum and this was only 5 minutes long. I posted it off anyway and it came in at the top 20, they mentioned that it was too short so I agreed to lengthen it.

"The good part about this top 20 thing was that we were brought down into a room where there was a group of guests talking about writing and directing, including Guy Ritchie. It was an interesting day and I could instantly see what the trouble was with a lot of scripts, or rather writers. I was really the only person willing to mingle and talk about films; I'd introduce myself to others and suggest that we have a read of each other's scripts to see what we both thought. Most of them didn't want to show theirs and that seemed to be a big problem. Jerwood were looking for that sort of enthusiasm, I brought out a storyboard which no one else had, they weren't just looking for a good script – and *Eight* got through.

"They had £100,000 but it was pre-agreed that you wouldn't be directing it. Stephen Daldry was pulled in on the deal via Working Title. I did some more work on it with the development guy at Working Title before Stephen came on board. You walk in past reception, you see all the posters of the films that have been made by them and you find yourself sitting down talking about your own script. It was a big thing for me as a writer. We discussed everything together and it was great to get that sort of feedback - really valuable and exciting. Then Stephen came on board. He forces you to go through your top ten ideas, get rid of them because they are going to be cliché's and after that they become original and fresh. It really worked and so I've tried to do that a little bit more myself.

"I guess Working Title put it in for the Bafta. Of course anyone can enter a short film and it doesn't have to be attached to a production company and I knew they were coming out but on the day I'd forgotten. I got a phone call at work to say that it had been nominated, I tried to tell people but they didn't really believe me. I couldn't believe it, but in a naïve way I thought that I was made. Of course it didn't win on the night but if it had you move onto the next round where it's Oscar nominations. It's done a lot for me though, not in the stupid ways that I'd imagined, but in a proper way - if you write scripts then people will read and consider them." *NW*

First Light

Hi8us First Light Ltd
Unit 407
The Custard Factory
Gibb Street
Birmingham, B9 4AA
Tel: 0121 693 2091
Fax: 0121 693 2096
Email: info@firstlightmovies.com
Web: www.firstlightmovies.com

First Light aims to promote collaboration between production companies and young people, to develop a creative medium for expression, and to foster a new generation of filmmakers. The priority is to support short film production from script development through to exhibition.

The projects are managed by organisations who want to make films with young people aged between 7 and 18 years who take lead roles in all aspects of the production. The films can be live action, animated or documentary in any genre. Digital filmmaking will be the main medium and exploration of filmmaking techniques is encouraged.

First Light Pilot Awards

This funding strand is for organisations that have experience of working with young people and of filmmaking, but who may not have produced a short film with young people before. The applicant must bring young people between the ages of 7 and 18 and professionals together, to collaborate on producing a short film of no more than 5 minutes over a period of four months. The films must be live action, animation, fiction or creative documentary shot on digital cameras.

ELIGIBILITY

The organisation or partners must have experience of working with young people aged 7 to 18 and some filmmaking experience.

DETAILS

The fund will provide up to 70% of the production budget with a ceiling of £5000.

First Light Studio Awards

This annual award is for organisations that have a track record of filmmaking with young people, and successful outreach capability. The applicant must produce between two and six short films up to 10 minutes long, over a period of six to eight months, with young people aged between 7 and 18. This initiative will act as a kind of mini studio with a slate of productions, allowing the young people to make their films in collaboration with professionals and with professional equipment. The films must be live action, animation, fiction or creative documentary shot on digital cameras.

ELIGIBILITY

The organisation must have experience of working with young people aged 7 to 18, and a track record of producing more than one short film at a time.

DETAILS

The fund will provide up to 50% of the production budget with a ceiling of £36,000.

General Guidelines for both schemes

DEADLINE

There are regular deadlines throughout the year, which will be publicised two months before the deadline on the website.

ELIGIBILITY

Previous applicants may apply with a new proposal. Individuals are not eligible to apply. Organisations must have a legal constitution with a dedicated bank account.

APPLICATION

In addition to the application form, applicants must submit a contact sheet with: details, the film ideas, planning documents and budgets, details about the organisation, and a monitoring form.

ASSESSMENT

Each application is assessed principally on the idea, and filmmaking techniques. Projects must be accessible for young people. The geographical spread of applications may also come into play.

CONDITIONS

The organisation must supply First Light with appropriate documents and information to keep them informed, and monitor the progress of the project. In the event of the production being sold, First Light shall receive a proportion of the profits in relation to their investment, to be fed into future projects. They must also receive a screen credit and crediting in promotional material indicating their support of the project.

The Jerwood Charitable Trust

22 Fitzroy Square
London, W1T 6EN
Tel: 020 7388 6287
Email: info@jerwood.org
Web: www.jerwood.org.uk

The Jerwood Charitable Trust was founded in 1999 as a sister to the Jerwood Foundation set up 1977 in the name of John Jerwood. The charity offers funds to the performing and visual arts and education. It also supports conservation, the environment, medicine, science and engineering.

Funding

The charity is keen to support national institutions and smaller projects in need

KEN RUSSELL　　FROM STUDIO TO VIDEO

"The last studio film I did was Dog Boys which was a film for ShowTime. There was nothing of me in it - anyone could have made it. It would have looked exactly alike, the same. We had 21 days to shoot it, I went two days over schedule. Soon as it's done you send it to them, they send you three sheets of paper back the next day saying "change that, alter that, drop this, re-voice that person" and there's no one to talk to. In the old days, United Artists, you go in. there's two guys eating pastrami sandwiches and you can have a jolly good argument with them and usually you won it. They are all soft drinks salesmen anyway now, they know nothing about movies anyway. So it's to pay the rent.

"You obviously get a bit depressed at times but then something comes along and well you have to drag yourself up by your boot straps and get on and do something, so I bought myself a video camera.

"It started off as an economy thing but only because I'd seen how good it could get with these Danish films. I think film is fine - we all know what it looks like, but for me video especially for The Fall of the Louse of Usher is ideal because it heightens the colour somehow or other. You can do tremendous things with it as you're shooting, much more than a normal camera, and you can see exactly what you've got and you can change all sorts. There are about 30 possibilities -you can alter the exposure, give it a certain effect, whatever. Marvellous stuff. I found that I love it - I love the colour of it, I love the texture of it. Well it's obvious the film's going to be finished sooner or later. Just a question of when." *Stephen Applebaum* of seed funding. The smaller projects should aim to reward excellence in human endeavour, and the foundation is particularly keen to encourage high achievement in young people. It should be noted that film is not a priority in the funding budget and that the charity never support single projects, such as festivals or art/film productions. An example of a film award is the First Film Foundation's Jerwood first film prize that allows the selected applicant to develop a slate of short films.

The foundation does not grant awards to: individuals, capital costs, the running costs of an organisation, projects that fall under another funding organisation's remit, or locally-focussed projects. Initially, it only provides one-off funding, though continued support may be granted if the project is successful, and would obviously benefit from further support. The applicant may be required to seek match funding for the project, if the foundation feels it cannot be the sole sponsor. Applications may be made at any time for grants, which usually fall between £5,000 and £50,000. However, rather than the applicant applying for a certain amount, the foundation decides the amount that they would be prepared to contribute to the project to ensure its success.

Applicants should apply by letter, detailing the aims and objectives of the organisation and the proposed project. In addition to this, other items must be submitted such as: a budget, details of match funding,, details of the management and staff structure, the annual report, audited accounts and current accounts of the organisation. Applicants should not seek to discuss their application with the foundation before submission, as it receives such a large number or proposals.

The Wellcome Trust

The Wellcome Building
183 Euston Road
London, NW1 2BE
Tel: 020 7611 8888
Email: contact@wellcome.ac.uk
Web: www.wellcome.ac.uk

Established in 1936 under Sir Henry Wellcome's will, the Wellcome Trust is a charity funded through a private endowment. The aim is to support medical, social, cultural and scientific research that benefits humans and animals and encourages these fields to work together.

Sciart Awards

Part of the Engaging Science grants, these awards support research, development and production of arts-based projects that bring arts and science together. The aim is to develop and encourage public understanding of biomedical science and its ethics. Both of the awards below are open to any field of the arts, including film, TV and video.

Research & Development Awards

This annual fund, which closes in April, will support up to £15,000 to research and develop an idea. The research can be aimed towards "blue sky" research (anticipating how to achieve a certain outcome a long way down the line) or smaller projects, such as developing prototypes or pilots. Arts and science practitioners, mediators, academics and health workers are invited to apply for this award.

Production Awards

The Production Awards annual fund which closes in July, will fund up to £100,000 towards arts activities such as festivals, broadcast programmes, arts projects and films which aim to make a significant public impact. The application should come from organisations involved in arts, science and broadcast.

Chapter 6
INTERNATIONAL

Co-productions

By Adam P Davies with research by Caroline Hancock

Department for Culture, Media and Sport
2-4 Cockspur Street
London, SW1Y 5DH
Tel: 020 7211 6000
Email: film@culture.gov.uk
Web: www.culture.gov.uk

Council of Europe
Info Point, 67075 Strasbourg Cedex
France
Tel: +33 3 88 41 20 33
Fax: +33 3 88 41 27 45
Email: infopoint@coe.int
Web: www.coe.int

The producer of a film clearly needs to carry out several tasks in order to get his picture made. These include raising the finance, securing talent, engaging the crew, preparing budgets, sourcing locations, arranging post-production, and so on. There are times when it makes sense to pool resources with another producer, splitting these responsibilities in accordance with their respective expertise and resources. Where more than one producer makes a film in this way, it is known as a "co-production", and the producers are referred to as "co-producers". The co-producers (who may or may not be from the same country) will enter into a co-production agreement that will set out their respective obligations, together with their financial interest in the film.

However, the term "co-production" is often used specifically to refer to a film that is made under the umbrella of a particular treaty, or convention, entered into by the governments of two or more countries. It is this type of co-production, better referred to as an "official co-production", that is of most interest, as it is possible for producers to obtain certain financial benefits by making a film that qualifies under a particular treaty or convention.

"Official" Co-productions

There are two main types of official co-production; those made under the European Convention on Cinematic Co-production, imaginatively known as "Convention Co-productions", and those made under the bilateral treaties – "Treaty Co-productions". The UK currently has bilateral treaties with seven other countries: Germany (since 1975), Canada (since 1975), Norway (since 1983), Australia (since 1990), New Zealand (since 1993), France (since 1995), and Italy (since 1998).

The rules for qualifying as a Treaty Co-production, and the fiscal benefits available, differ in each case, sometimes quite considerably. The criteria for, and benefits of, a Convention Co-production are different again.

Local Benefits for National Films

Many governments are eager to promote their local film industry, and have therefore introduced incentives for producers to make films that qualify as a "National" film within their jurisdictions. A National film usually has to have a large proportion of the budget spent locally, and/or a predominantly local cast and crew. The benefits available to a National film range from simple "cash-back" from the government on completion of the picture, tax incentives for investors, exemption from paying certain taxes when engaging local crew or using local facilities, and so on. The beauty of the treaties (and the convention) is that they state that if a film qualifies as an official co-production, it will automatically qualify as a National film in each of the relevant countries. In other words, a film made under (say) the UK-Canada Co-production Treaty, would qualify both as a National British Film, and a National Canadian Film. Therefore, the rationale for making an official co-production (at least from a financial perspective) is to enable producers to become eligible for the financial benefits available in more than one country. The benefits in certain countries are not insubstantial, and it is not unheard of for a carefully structured picture to have 30% or more of its budget covered by this so-called "soft money".

It is important to note that a co-producer is generally only eligible to access the benefits in his/her own country in respect of the proportion of the budget raised in that country. So for example, benefits available through Canadian tax break schemes could not be applied to the UK element of the expenditure on an official UK-Canada co-production.

Competent Authorities

Each country has a "competent authority" appointed by its government, which has the role of granting official co-production status to films that comply with the regulations set down in the relevant Treaty. In the UK, the relevant authority is the Department of Culture, Media and Sport, and it is to this body that an application for co-production status must be made. A certified official UK co-production will qualify as a "British Film" under the Films Act 1985, allowing it to benefit from public funding, and tax legislation such as Sale and Leaseback.

Examples of Available Benefits

Governmental incentives do not last forever. Tax breaks come and go (perhaps the most poignant example of this being the sudden exclusion of television product from the UK sale & leaseback market by the British Chancellor in his 2002 Budget). However, below are summaries of some of the benefits available around the world at the time of publication. Naturally, producers should check their eligibility at any given time, and make sure that, where necessary, their films are completed in time in order to access the relevant benefit before it disappears (assuming its phasing out is actually announced in advance!). In each case, there are numerous eligibility criteria that will apply, often relating to such elements as the size of the budget, the nationality of cast/crew/producer/investor, ownership of copyright, extent of the investment, etc, and there is no substitute for taking proper advice before embarking on a production.

Australia

There are a number of tax breaks available in Australia. The so-called 10B and 10BA schemes provide Australian resident taxpayers with a 100% reduction in taxable income; equal to the amount they invest in the film(s) under the scheme. Alternatively, the "FLIC" (Film Licence Investment Company) scheme provides a 100% tax concession to investors in companies that are licensed to invest in a slate of television and film product. It is a pilot scheme, and there are currently only two such FLICs. They are permitted to raise and invest up to about A$40m (approx. £15.5m) over two years in projects that satisfy certain criteria. There is presently much lobbying going on to extend/repeat/enhance the scheme. Then there is also a newer "Refundable Tax Offset" scheme for larger films where more than A$15m (approx. £5.8m) is spent in Australia. This is effectively a tax rebate of 12.5% applicable to all "qualifying Australian production expenditure". There are also a few local film bodies, such as the Australian Film Commission and the Film Finance Corporation, which will provide funds for certain qualifying pictures.

Belgium

There is a new scheme being introduced in Belgium, although the numbers involved aren't exactly huge. Basically the scheme will allow a corporation tax set-off of up to E750,000 (approx. £520,000) if the investor's total tax liability exceeds E1.5m (approx. £1m). Tax relief is calculated at 150% of the investment, so an investment of E500,000 (approx. £345,000) would trigger the maximum relief.

Brazil

There are two options available to a Brazilian qualifying film. A law known locally as Article 1 provides an income tax rebate (max 3% of total income tax owed) to a Brazilian individual or company (or Brazilian Branch) for investment in an audiovisual work. Alternatively, Article 3 allows a certificated film to attract finance from foreign producers, distributors or intermediaries, who may deduct 70% from their taxes (charged at 25%), applicable to income or royalties from (Brazilian or foreign) film exploitation in Brazil. Apparently only one studio has actually used this incentive on a regular basis.

Canada

This is a very popular destination for those looking for co-production related benefits, as a substantial proportion of local expenditure (particularly labour tax costs) can be claimed back in the form of subsidies or tax credits. There are benefits available at both the federal and provincial level. The Federal Tax Credit is currently available to Canadian content productions, at the rate of 25% of qualified labour expenditure. The maximum permissible qualifying expenditure is 48% of the total budget, so this tax credit can potentially yield up to 12% of the budget. A slightly different system applies if the producer is not a Canadian resident. Specific provinces also have labour-based tax credit programmes, including British Columbia, Quebec, Nova Scotia, Manitoba, Saskatchewan, Newfoundland, and Ontario, with tax credit rates varying from 20% to 35%. These often require the individuals concerned to have been resident in the relevant province at the end of the financial year, prior to start of principal photography. Official co-productions will also be eligible for Telefilm Canada assistance, such as the Feature Film Fund and the Broadcast Program Development Fund.

France

Although, like Canada, France seems to have co-production treaties with almost every country that has a semblance of a film industry, its benefit regime is not nearly as attractive. The main tax-break scheme for production finance is the "SOFICA" system. Certain entities, known as SOFICA companies, are tax efficient vehicles for their investors, and will part-finance qualifying films by taking shares in the relevant production company (thereby always participating in the profits from the film).

Germany

The days when exuberant German media companies ran around offering upwards of 30% of a film's budget, in return for what seemed like little more than German-speaking rights, are long gone. Those companies that have managed to remain in business are now much more prudent about their investment strategies, although the legislative tax break utilised by them does still exist. There is, however, a large number of tax-based German "funds" that continue to make equity investments in qualifying pictures, although they usually impose a number of conditions relating to the size of the investment and/or overall budget, the location of production (and post-production), copyright ownership, etc. These funds come and go in cycles as money is raised from the German taxpayer and spent on production funding. In addition to these funds, the Filmforderungsanstalt (German film promotion agency) will in certain circumstances provides finance in the form of a grant.

Iceland

There is a simple refund (of 12%) on production costs spent in Iceland. If more than 80% of the budget is spent in Iceland, the producer can receive a refund equal to 12% of the entire budget (provided that the remainder of the budget is spent in an EEA country). The main caveat is that the production must be, "suited to the promotion of Icelandic culture and the nature of Iceland".

Ireland

Known affectionately throughout the industry as "section 481 finance (s481)" (replacing the old "section 35 finance"), the main Irish tax incentive is set to remain in force for 5 years from 6 April 2000. The scheme allows a large tax write-off for investors, who can cover up to 55% (or sometimes 66%) of the film's budget with s481 money, so long as it is spent on Irish elements. The investors usually require that approximately 80% of the amount invested is already covered by pre-sales and placed in escrow pending delivery. This comforts the banks, which actually lend the investors the bulk of their "investment". There are limits on the amounts that can be invested per film, and by any particular person or company, and the film itself must "make a significant contribution to the national economy of Ireland and/or act as an effective stimulus to the creation of an indigenous film industry". Further, a certain amount of production work must be carried out in Ireland.

The Netherlands

This scheme, which was used in financing Enigma, was originally intended for the shipbuilding industry. The "new improved" version came into force in July 2002. It only really relates to films with budgets over E15m, and allows a Dutch investor an income tax rebate against his/her investment. The benefit to the film's budget can be as high as 30%. There was initially some negative press and industry vibe about the ability to raise cash under the scheme, and the fairly cumbersome procedure involved in accessing it. A number of banks left the market in 2002, although the quasi-quango FINE (amongst others) is still fairly active. There is very little accurately written English-language documentation available, and so local advice must be sought.

Qualification Criteria for the Bilateral Treaties

Whereas the benefits available in each country range quite considerably, the qualification criteria under the various treaties - although not identical - do follow certain themes. The following is a summary of the typical requirements, imposed by the UK's co-production treaties, which a film must satisfy in order to be granted official co-production status. However, there are exceptions in nearly every case and, before applying for official co-production status, a producer should check carefully the terms of the relevant treaty under which s/he wishes the film to qualify. Links and order information for the treaties as well as details of the competent authorities and contacts for each country are at the end of this section.

Common Management and Control

The co-producers must be independent from each other, and may not be linked by common management (except to the extent that it is inherent in the making of the film itself).

Contractual Terms

The treaties require certain provisions to be included in the co-production agreement between the co-producers. These terms include, an explanation of the financial commitment (including dates) and recoupment position(s) of the respective co-producing companies, and must set out the contingency arrangement (ie what happens to the film and any money invested in it) in the event that the picture is not ultimately – or even provisionally - granted official co-production status. Generally, the income of each co-producer received from the exploitation of the film should be roughly proportional to that co-producer's financial contribution. Ownership of the negative (or, in the case of the Canadian Treaty, the copyright) must also be clearly specified, together with an acknowledgement that each co-producer has the right to access and copy the finished product. Producers should take proper advice when drafting the co-production contract, particularly in ensuring that these provisions are properly worded.

Financial and Creative Contribution

Normally, each country's producer must provide a minimum of 20% of the financial and creative contribution to the film. The minimum contribution stated is in fact 30% in the treaties with Germany and Australia, and the UK government has made moves to require the UK contribution in a UK-Canada co-production to exceed 40% in order to redress a perceived imbalance. The general rule is that the creative contribution must be approximately proportional to the financial contribution. Occasionally (as with the UK treaties with Italy and France), a substantial "finance only" contribution is permitted, where one co-producer may provide only finance (ie. no creative elements), without disqualifying the picture from official co-production status.

Location

The film must be made (including post-production) in the countries of the co-producer's origin. Generally, the majority of production must take place in the country from where the majority of the finance is provided. Location shooting in another country is usually permitted subject to the competent authorities' approval. Personnel involved in making the film who are nationals or residents of one co-producing country are granted easy access to the other co-producing country(ies), without the need to obtain work permits.

Qualifying Nationals

This is often the trickiest area, particularly when the project and/or lead cast originate from the United States. The basic rule is that all individuals taking part in the making of the film must be nationals or residents of one of the co-producer's countries (including a third co-producer's country, if any) or – except in the case of the German Treaty - a Member State of the European Union. However, "exceptional circumstances" (sometimes only if dictated by the script) will permit the competent authorities to approve certain talent (often only the leading roles), depending on which treaty is being utilised, from another state. This is incredibly important where an American director or lead artist is attached to the project. Also, where the authorities have approved location filming in another country, "necessary" local crew and/or crowd artists may be hired.

Musical Score

Generally, the music must be composed (and sometimes "directed" and performed) by nationals or residents of one of the co-producer's countries (including that of a third co-producer) or an EU Member State. The rules sometimes vary slightly for music that is not specifically commissioned for the picture.

Third Country Participation

A three-way co-production, with a producer from a third country, will usually be able to access the benefits of all three countries, if the third country has also entered into a co-production treaty with one of the other two. For example, as Canada has a co-production treaty with Algeria, a UK-Canada-Algeria co-production will be permitted under the UK-Canada Treaty, even though the UK has no treaty with Algeria. Of course, the film will only actually qualify if all the other criteria in the treaty are also satisfied.

The European Convention

The aim of the convention is to allow qualifying co-produced films the benefits that are available to national films in each convention country. Each co-producer can utilise whatever benefits are available in his/her own country. Again, the creative and financial contributions must be relatively proportional, and must exceed 20% (potentially 10% for multilateral co-productions) of the total budget. A financial-only contribution of between 10% and 25% is also permitted under certain conditions. Producers from one or more non-member states may be brought into a co-production agreement under the convention, provided that producers from at least three member states are party to the co-production agreement, and that the non-member producers contribute no more than 30% of total production costs.

Unlike the treaties, where individuals' nationality and/or residence are relevant for qualification purposes, the convention is only concerned with nationality. There is a "points" system ascribing values to various contributors (artists, creative department heads etc), and to qualify as a convention co-production, the film must have 15 of the 19 points. As the director, writer and lead artist are each "worth" three points, clearly only one of these may be from a non-convention country. If the film has a strong "European identity", it may still be possible to make it under the convention, as the 15/19 points rule may be waived slightly by the relevant competent authority(ies). Note that the convention is not currently in force in Belgium, Norway and Turkey (amongst others). The Council of Europe website (http://conventions.coe.int/Treaty/en/Treaties/Html/147.htm) has the convention in full, and also a list of the signatories (including dates when the convention came into force in each country).

The Convention or a Treaty?

BILATERAL CO-PRODUCTIONS

The general rule is that where there is a bilateral treaty between two convention countries, the film should be made under that treaty rather than under the convention, and the treaty rules will generally be applied. So, for example, the 30% minimum contribution under the UK-Germany treaty would still apply to a German-UK co-production. Where there is no relevant treaty between two convention countries, the film should be produced under the convention. In effect, the convention serves as a bilateral co-production treaty, where there is no actual bilateral agreement in force between the two countries. In these circumstances, the minimum contribution from the minority co-producer must be at least 20%.

MULTILATERAL CO-PRODUCTIONS

Where there is a treaty that would cover the film, it may be used (and the DCMS would prefer that it is) so long as it does not contravene the specific provisions of the Convention. Effectively, the film will be made "under the terms of the treaty". In other words, the 20% requirement in the UK-France Treaty would be overridden by the convention in a UK-France-Italy "three-way" Treaty co-production, and a 10% minimum would apply. Further, the various treaties usually require a minimum 20% financial commitment, whereas the convention allows for as little as 10% (reflecting the Eurimage position). As this is a direct contravention, the convention will override the treaties on the point, allowing a 10% minimum contribution. Where there is no treaty covering the co-production, the convention will of course apply, assuming the relevant countries are signatories. A non-convention co-producer may only be brought into a convention co-production, if it: brings less than 30% to the table, there are at least three other Convention country producers, and the points system is still satisfied.

The Application Process

Applying for official co-production status is a three-step process:

1 "Provisional" co-production status is granted by the competent authorities on the strength of an approved agreement between the co-producers (referred to here as the "provisional agreement").

2 Each co-producer, eligible to benefit from national film status in their country, then raises finance and makes the film.

3 Once the film is completed, a successful audit allows the competent authorities to grant the film official co-production status.

This simple breakdown hides the detail, which is vital to the success of co-production agreements. Broadly speaking, achieving official co-production status depends on meeting two main requirements: keeping to the terms indicated in the provisional agreement, and each co-producer meeting the conditions of the relevant treaty (or convention). It is vital that co-producers understand what is required of them and that they keep an eye on the detail throughout the process. The UK co-producer should make the preliminary application to the DCMS at least one month before production commences. Copies of documents such as the shooting script, budget, chain of title (etc) need to be provided, in addition to a copy of the co-production agreement. It is a good idea to get the DCMS "on-side" as soon as possible, and they will give detailed guidance on the various issues. The draft guidelines (which are due to become concrete "regulations" shortly) published in November 2002 on the DCMS website are also very useful.

The detailed nature of a co-production might deter some producers from employing it. In such cases, benefiting from the experience of an executive producer, or setting aside part of the budget to hire a firm that specialises in this area, should be considered.

The Final Audit

Once the film is completed, the competent authority will contact the co-producer, requesting an audit by an accountancy firm to establish if the film merits official co-production status. The accountants will assess how much money was sourced from the respective countries, and where this money was spent. The competent authority does allow some leeway in accepting changes to the co-producers final shares in the production, from the original proportions notified to the authority in the provisional agreement prior to production. However, it is advisable to keep the authority updated throughout the production period.

The intention of the audit is to provide evidence of the co-producers having met the requirements of official co-production status. It must be carried out after the film is "completed" (which does not necessarily mean "delivered"), either by an independent accountancy firm, which is recognised under section 25 of the Companies Act 1989, or an accountant recognised under section 34 of the Act. A film is classed as completed when it is ready to be shown to the general public.

As the achievement of official co-production status depends on the co-producers making certain financial and creative contributions, the budgets for each co-producer should be kept separately. The financial contributions are indicated by the finance each co-producer raises for the budget. The creative filmmaking contributions are indicated by the costs spent on labour, locations, facilities and resources in each territory. These contributions are compared to the total budget to establish if they meet the required percentages. Any contributions, or costs relating to parties of/from countries not covered by the relevant treaty, must also be budgeted separately, so the proportion of those figures, as part of the total budget, can be clearly examined.

In the final analysis, if the shares between co-producers work out to be different to those specified in the provisional agreement, the film can still be approved as an official co-production by the relevant competent authorities, as long as the minimum requirements are still met. The share of revenues and rights between co-producers must be amended to reflect any changes. The competent authorities may also approve a co-production where a co-producer's financial contribution has not been equal to its creative filmmaking contribution by re-aligning respective interests in the success of the film by re-apportioning the entitlement to any distribution advances.

Each co-producer is required to arrange an audit of their own accounts, and these audits brought together to be presented to all relevant competent authorities for examination. Rather than pay two firms to liase with each other over respective receipts, finance, payments, etc, it may be preferable to employ one accountancy firm to carry out the full production audit for both "sides".

Competent Authorities & Treaty Links

Australia

Jeremy Bean
Acting Director
The Australian Film Commission
Level 4, 150 William Street
Woolloomooloo
NSW 2011
GPO Box 3984
Sydney 2001
Australia
Tel: 00 612 9321 6444
Fax: 00 612 9357 3737
Web: www.afc.gov.au

Download the treaty from www.culture.gov.uk/PDF/uk-australia1990.PDF, or order a copy by phoning The Stationary Office Photocopying Department on 020 7873 8455 and quoting Cmd No 1758 Treaty Series No. 90 (1991) ISBN 0101175825

Canada

Deborah Drisdell
Director, International Relations
Téléfilm Canada
360 St. James Street
Suite 700
Montreal
Quebec, H2Y 4A9
Canada
Tel: 001 514 283 6363
Fax: 001 514 283 8212
Web: www.telefilm.gc.ca

Download the treaty from www.culture.gov.uk/PDF/uk-canada1991.PDF, or order a copy by phoning The Stationary Office Photocopying Department on 020 7873 8455 and quoting Cmd No 1807 Treaty Series No 9 (1992) ISBN 0101180721

France

Francois Hurard
Le Directeur de la production cinematographique
Centre National de la Cinematographie
12 rue de Lubeck
75784 Paris Cedex 16
France
Tel: 0033 1 44 34 36 26
Fax: 0033 1 44 34 36 97
Web: www.cnc.fr

Download the treaty from www.culture.gov.uk/PDF/uk-france1994.PDF, or order a copy by phoning The Stationary Office Photocopying Department on 020 7873 8455 and quoting Cmd No 2992 Treaty Series No .82 (1995) ISBN 0101299222

Germany

Herr Begovici
Bundesamt für Wirtschaft
Postfach 51 71
65726 Eschborn
Germany
Tel: 0049 6196 404 401
Fax: 0049 6196 404 422
Web: www.bawi.de

Download the treaty from
www.culture.gov.uk/PDF/uk-
germany1975.PDF, or order a copy
by phoning The Stationary Office
Photocopying Department on 020 7873
8455 and quoting Cmd No 6155 Treaty
Series No. 103 (1975) ISBN0101615507

Italy

Dr Francesco Ventura
Il Dirigente
Ministero per i Beni e le Attivita' Culturali
Ufficio II - Ripartizione I
Attivita Cinematagrafiche
Via della Ferraratella in Laterano n. 51
Roma
Italy
Tel: 00 39 06 773 2424
Fax: 00 39 06 773 2468
Web: www.beniculturali.it

Download the treaty from
www.culture.gov.uk/PDF/uk-italy1998.PDF,
or order a copy by phoning The Stationary
Office on 0870 600 5522 and quoting Cmd
No 4840 Treaty Series No. 105 (2000)

New Zealand

Mladen Ivancic
Deputy Chief Executive
New Zealand Film Commission
PO Box 11-546
Wellington
New Zealand
Tel: 00 64 4 382 7680
Fax: 00 64 4 384 9719
Web: www.nzfilm.co.nz

Download the treaty from
www.culture.gov.uk/PDF/uk-
newzealand1993.PDF, or order a copy
by phoning The Stationary Office
Photocopying Department on 020 7873
8455 and quoting Cmd No 2638 Treaty
Series No 39 (1994) ISBN 0101263821

Norway

Nina Okland
Head of Division
Royal Norwegian Ministry of Cultural Affairs
P.O. Box 8030 Dep.
N-0030 Oslo
Norway
Tel: 00 47 22 24 90 90
Fax: 00 47 22 24 95 50
Web: www.odin.dep.no/kd

Download the treaty from
www.culture.gov.uk/PDF/uk-
norway1982.PDF, or order a copy
by phoning The Stationary Office
Photocopying Department on 020 7873
8455 and quoting Cmd No 9007 Treaty
Series No 46 (1983) ISBN 0101900708

International Public Film Funds

Below is an overview of some of the film funds on offer around the globe. Qualifying international co-productions are usually able to take advantage of these national funds in each of the participating countries in addition to tax incentives.

Australia

Australian Film Commission

Sydney Office
Level 4, 150 William Street
Woolloomooloo NSW 2011
Australia
Tel: +61 2 9321 6444
Fax: +61 2 9357 3737
Email: info@afc.gov.au
Web: www.afc.gov.au

The Australian Film Commission provides nation-wide funds that international co-productions with Australian partners may be eligible to apply for. The commission's funding schemes cover development assistance for film, TV and interactive media, and production assistance for film, TV and interactive media.

Melbourne Film Office

Film Victoria
GPO Box 4361
Melbourne
Victoria 3001
Australia
Tel: +61 3 9660 3240
Fax: +61 3 9660 3201
Web: www.film.vic.gov.au

The film office serves the region of Victoria and provides two funds for productions that take place in the area: the Production Investment Attraction Fund (PIAF) and the Regional Victoria Film Location Attraction Fund (RLAF). Co-productions may access the first fund as long as a certain spend is achieved in the Region or local facilities are utilised. The second fund contributes to accommodation, living overheads and relocation costs for productions in Victoria.

Belgium

Flemish Audiovisual Fund (VAF)

Quai du Commerce 18/3
B-1000 Brussels
Belgium
Tel: +32 2 226 06 30
Fax: +32 2 219 19 36
Email: info@vaf.be
Web: www.vaf.be

The VAF supports film production in Flanders through funds that contribute to fiction, animation, experimental and animation films. At least 78% of the funding the VAF receives from the Flemish government goes towards film production including international co-productions with a Flemish producing partner. Other awards support scriptwriting, development and promotion.

Canada

Telefilm Canada

Head Office - Quebec Region
360 St. Jacques Street
Suite 700
Montréal
Quebec, H2Y 4A9
Canada
Tel: +1 514 283 6363
Fax: +1 514 283 8212
Email: info@telefilm.gc.ca
Web: www.telefilm.gc.ca

Telefilm Canada supports feature filmmaking in the country and is keen to invest in official international co-productions. Canada has a strong history in co-productions with over sixty treaties in existence, including the Anglo-Canadian Treaty. Funds are delivered through three streams: the Feature Film Fund – Development, Production and Marketing Programs, the Low Budget Independent Feature Film Assistance Program and the Screenwriting Assistance Program. The maximum investment for the Feature Film Fund Production fund is C$1.6m (approx. £691,000)

British Columbia Film

2225 West Broadway
Vancouver
British Columbia
V6K 2E4
Canada
Tel: +1 604 736 7997
Fax: +1 604 736 7290
Email: bcf@bcfilm.bc.ca
Web: www.bcfilm.bc.ca

British Columbia Film Fund is a society, funded mostly by the Ministry of Competition, Science and Enterprise of the provincial government. Co-productions with a partner from the region, and a film to be shot in British Columbia may benefit from the funding they provide for development and feature production. The Development Fund will support feature films, dramatic or animated television projects and documentaries with commitments from a broadcaster or distributor. The Feature Film production Fund will support low budget productions of less than C$1m (approx. £433,000), mid-range budget productions between C$1m and C$5m (approx. £2.2m), and higher budget productions of over C$5m. The maximum investment it will make is C$250,000 (approx. £108,000)

Societe de Developpement des Entreprises Culturelles (Sodec)

Head Office
36 rue Saint-Pierre
Quebec G1K 3Z6
Canada
Tel: +418 643-2581
Web: www.sodec.gouv.ca

Sodec is the Quebec Government's Ministry of Culture and Communications. In the case of film, it offers money for screenwriting, production, marketing and distribution and the support of young talent. The Production funding stream will invest up to C$1.4m (approx. £957,000) in feature productions, including Foreign-Canadian co-productions, as long as the film is shot in Quebec.

Denmark

Danish Film Institute

55 Gothersgade
DK-1123 Copenhagen K
Denmark
Tel: +45 33 74 34 00
Fax: +45 33 74 34 01
Email: dfi@dfi.dk
Web: www.dfi.dk

The Danish Film Fund provides three funding schemes to Danish producers: the feature film 60/40 scheme, the feature film consultant scheme and the shorts and documentaries consultant scheme. The 60/40 scheme will fund up to 60% of a feature's production costs, with this contributing to the Danish share only of a co-production. The Fund will support co-productions where the Danish producer is the minority partner up to DKK3m (approx. £280,000).

France

Centre National de la Cinématographie (CNC)

12 rue de Lübeck
75784 Paris cedex 16France
Tel: +33 1 44 34 34 40
Web: www.cnc.fr

The CNC is the principal film body and funding distributor in France. Fund schemes support distribution, cinema, and film development and production in France. International co-producers working with a French partner may access the production funds for fiction, animation, documentaries and television programmes, as long as the majority of filming takes place in France with French or European crew.

Rhône-Alpes Cinema

Villa Gillet - 25 rue Chazière
69004 Lyon
France
Tel : +33 4 72 98 08 98
Fax : +33 4 72 98 08 99
E-mail : contact.rac@Rhone-alpes-cinema.fr
Web: www.comfilm-rhone-alpes.fr

In addition to the national funds, some of the departments and regions of France offer film funding which international co-productions may be eligible to benefit from, if the film is shot in their region. One of these regions, the Rhones-Alpes Commission, invests between E146,000-E390,000 (approx. £100-£266,000) in each production.

Germany

Germany provides national and region film funding schemes, which foreign producers may access, even without a German co-producing partner for the regional funds. However, it may be advisable to benefit from a German co-producer's knowledge of his or her own system. For the regional funds, there are certain stipulations on the spend required in each area.

German Federal Film Board

FFA Filmförderungsanstalt
Große Präsidentenstraße 9
10178 Berlin
Germany
Tel: +49 030 27577 0
Fax: +49 030 27577 111
Web: www.ffa.de

For foreign producers to access the national funding available from the German Federal Film Board, they must be part of a German co-production, though the production need not take place in the country. The funds will contribute up to 50% of the German co-producer's costs with a ceiling of 2,040,816 Euros (approx. £1.4m).

FilmFörderung Hamburg

Friedensallee 14-16
D - 22765 Hamburg
Germany
Tel: (040) 398 37 - 0
Fax: (040) 398 37 – 10
Web: http://www.ffhh.de/

FilmFörderung Hamburg, who part financed Bend It Like Beckham, is a company that supports film and TV production in Hamburg, through funding, film commission, services and events. It has an annual budget of E9.5m (approx. £6.4m) which is financed by the City of Hamburg and the broadcasters, NDR and ZDF.

DEVELOPMENT AND PRODUCTION FUNDING

Financial support is available to film and TV production from the initial development to the exhibition. There is no restriction on genre, budget or length, nor on the country of origin of the production company, though filming must take place in Hamburg. Two committees judge the applications; committee 1 is responsible for high budgets, and committee 2 is responsible for low budgets. Funding will cover screenplays, project development, production, special projects, distribution, sales, theatrical release and presentation.

SCREENPLAY SUPPORT

This fund supports the writing of a screenplay for feature films, or the writing of a project description for documentary films. Applicants may apply for up to E50,000 (approx. £33,500). In addition to the application form, applicants must submit a treatment and sample dialogue for a screenplay, or an outline of the project, for documentary.

DARREN WARD   TICKETS TO HELL

An encounter at Fright Fest and an interview with a German horror magazine helped Southampton filmmaker Darren Ward raise completion finance for his part-shot feature film and get three previous shorts released in seven countries on video & DVD.

"I initially made three short films: Paura il Diavolo in 1992 (42 mins), Blue Fear in 1993 (70 Mins) and Bitter Vengeance in 1994 (17 Mins).

"Bitter Vengeance is a short action movie made specifically for the 1994 British Amateur Video Awards. The film did well and received a 'Highly commended' judges award narrowly missing out on an award. One of the criteria of 'BAVA', was that the film had to have a running time of no longer than 17mins, and I personally wanted to see more of the characters I had created in 'Bitter Vengeance'. So in early 1995 I started writing scenes that I could add to the existing film and simply extend the running time. One thing led to another and I finally decided to remake 'Bitter Vengeance' into a feature as Sudden Fury rather than just adding footage.

"The film began its long production in April 1995. I had done several radio and local newspaper interviews, and that's where most of the actors eventually came from. The movie could only be shot on weekends and holidays as the cast and most of the crew had full time jobs. The budget simply wasn't there to cover the cast/crews time off work. After a period of time in early 1996 I ran out of money and the production ground to a halt for a few months.

"It was at this time I was at Fright Fest in London where I met David Warbeck. I had grown up watching David's films especially the Italian horror films of the early 80's. I jumped at the chance and presented my business card under his nose, much to his surprise. After a long chat David agreed to meet up with me the following week. I presented him some of the rough-cuts for scenes I had shot the previous months and he was very excited about playing the role of the bad guy Pike (in 99% of his roles David played the hero). With David on board, interest in the film started to pick up. I was almost immediately approached to do an interview in a German horror/sci-fi magazine named 'Doom'.

"A few weeks later I received a phone call from Incredibly Strange Video in Berlin, who had seen the interview piece I had done and were very interested in funding the remainder of the film. We agreed on a contract and I received the money needed to finish Sudden Fury. Whilst I was still working on that, Incredibly Strange Video bought the rights to my three shorts and released them onto video re-titled as 'Darren Wards Three tickets to hell'. The film was finished in August 1997. The British premiere was in March 1998 at 'Harbour Lights, Southampton. This was followed by festivals around Europe and to date the film has been released in seven countries on video and DVD." *CH*

PROJECT DEVELOPMENT SUPPORT

This fund supports the development of cinema or television film projects. Producers may apply, as long as the production is planned to be in Hamburg. Applicants may apply for up to 80% of the costs, with a ceiling of E110,000 (approx. £74,000). In addition to the application form, applicants must submit a screenplay for feature films, or a description of the project for television films, as well as a budget.

Support for production of films with budgets exceeding E800,000 (approx. £535,000)

Producers are eligible to apply for up to 50% of production costs. Exceptions may be made to provide up to 70% of the production costs for low budget films, or films of exceptional artistic value.

Support for production of films with production budgets up to E800,000

This scheme will fund television productions with an important cultural significance, as well as films for cinema. Applicants may apply for up to 50% of the production costs. Exceptions may be made to provide up to 80% of the production costs for films that may be difficult to sell. In general, partnership funding is required, however, exceptions may be made to this rule.

Ireland

The Irish Film Board / Bord Scannán na hÉireann

Rockfort House
St Augustine Street
Galway
Ireland
Tel: +353 91 561398
Fax: +353 91 561405
Email: info@filmboard.ie
Web: www.filmboard.ie

The Irish Film Board offers funding to Irish features and short films. The funding priority is to support Irish filmmakers, but a foreign film project could benefit through a partnership with Irish producers on a co-production. The UK has no co-production treaty with Ireland so it would have to be agreed under the terms of the European Cinematograph Convention.

Films that apply for funding are assessed for their Irishness through a points system, which examines the Irish elements of the production. It is usually expected that key creative personnel working on the project are Irish, and that a proportion of the film be shot in Ireland. The funding is distributed as development or production finance for feature length films of micro budgets, low budgets and higher budgets, for documentaries, and for animation. Short films can benefit from a rage of schemes including: Short Cuts, Oscailt, Frameworks, Irish Flash and Short Shorts.

Norway

Norwegian Film Fund

P.O.Box 752
Sentrum
NO-0106 Oslo
Norway
Tel: +47 22 47 80 40
Fax: +47 22 47 80 41
Email mail@filmfondet.no
Web: www.filmfondet.no

The fund offers six streams of support for Norwegian filmmakers: feature films and Norwegian majority co-productions, Norwegian minority co-productions, short films, commercially focussed films, box office bonuses (which offers support in proportion to ticket sales), and development for production companies. There is a ceiling of NOK30m (approx. £2.6m) on single investments.

Pan European Funds

Culture 2000

Cultural Contact Point UK
EUCLID
46-48 Mount Pleasant
Liverpool, L3 5SD
Tel: 0151 709 25 64
Fax: 0151 709 86 47
Email: info@euclid.co.uk
www.euclid.co.uk
www.culture2000.info

The aim behind the Culture 2000 programme is to promote the culture, heritage and diversity of Europe; encourage integration between European countries and support practice and participation in arts and culture. A total budget of E167m has been made available for the period of the programme between 2000 and 2004, now extended to 2006, and is distributed through an annual funding call. It is administered by the European Commission and managed in each country through the relevant cultural contact point. In the UK, this is EUCLID.

Culture 2000 Call for proposals 2004

Cultural Heritage is the priority for projects taking place in 2004. However, this does not exclude other arts and culture projects from applying.

DEADLINE

The call for proposals for 2004 is due to be announced in early Spring 2003. The deadline for applications is likely to be in September/October. To be kept up-to-date on developments, EUCLID provides the free Alert e-mail newsletter (for subscriptions go to www.euclid.info/opportunities/).

ELIGIBILITY

Applications must come from at least three organisations involved in the arts or heritage from at least three eligible countries (15 EU member states, 3 EFTA countries and 12 accession countries of central & eastern Europe) and for the benefit of at least three European countries.

DETAILS

The available contribution is up to 50% of the project costs or between E100,000 (approx. £68,000), and E300,000 (approx. £205,000) for one year long projects, or up to 60% of the project costs to a maximum of E300,000 (approx. £205,000) per year for two three-year long projects.

APPLICATIONS

In addition to the application form, applicants must submit details of their organisation, including finances and structure, details of personnel involved including CVs, and details of the project including budget and costs.

ASSESSMENT

The general assessment criteria for every call are: quality, innovation and creativity, the need for funding, and addressing relevant concerns and interests of the cultural arena. Projects should also take into account: the needs and interests of the citizens of Europe, new technology, media and creativity, and tradition and innovation. Each call has added priorities and criteria, which are detailed when each call is published.

CONDITIONS

Culture 2000 and the EC must be credited in any promotional material for the project.

join the uk's premier membership led
organisation for the film industry

BRITISH
ACADEMY
OF FILM AND
TELEVISION
ARTS

visit www.bafta.org   or   email membership@bafta.org

Eurimages

Eurimages
Council of Europe
F-67075 Strasbourg Cedex
France
Tel: 33 (0) 3 88 41 26 40
Fax: 33 (0) 3 88 41 27 60
Email: eurimages@coe.int
Web: www.coe.int/eurimages

Eurimages, a fund established in 1988 by the Cultural division of the Council of Europe to support European cinema, is backed by 28 member states. The UK is not a member of Eurimages, so is only eligible to benefit from the fund if invited to join a co-production project by a member of Eurimages, and the contribution is limited.

The co-production fund is intended to support European co-productions by investing a proportion of a film's budget. It is for feature films, animation or documentaries intended for theatrical release, which are no shorter than 70 minutes. The fund is delivered through two schemes:

Films with real circulation potential

The maximum fund available for films with budgets lower than E5.4m (approx. £3.7m), is E610,000 (approx. £417,000). The maximum fund available for films with budgets of higher than E5.4m is E763,000 (approx. £521,000). Applications will be assessed firstly against the commercial potential, and secondly the creative and artistic value of the film. Taken into account will be: sales estimates, commitments from distributors, confirmed finance, and the track record of the producers, the director and the artistic and technical teams.

Films reflecting the cultural diversity of European Cinema

The maximum fund available for films with budgets lower than E3m (approx. £2m),

is E380,000 (approx. £260,000). The maximum fund available for films with budgets of higher than E3m is E460,000 (approx. £314,000). Applications will be assessed firstly against the artistic and cultural value of the film, and secondly whether the co-production involves parties new to co-production, or who have not worked together before. The language of the film will also be under consideration, favouring films shot in the language of one of the co-producing territories.

Guidelines for both schemes

DEADLINES

The remaining deadlines at time of publication for 2003 applications are 22nd August and 17th October.

ELIGIBILITY

Member states of Eurimages that co-produce through a co-production agreement, based on the European Convention, or the co-producing countries' bilateral agreements, have automatic access to the Eurimages fund. However, the requirements of the European Conventions will apply should there be any differences to a bilateral agreement between parties.

The co-producers must contribute to the production costs. For members of Eurimages, the minimum contribution for a co-producer in a multilateral co-production agreement is 10% of the total production cost, and 20% of the total production cost for a bilateral co-production. However, if the budget for a film applying for this fund exceeds E5.4m, the minimum contribution from a co-producer is 10% and the maximum is 90%.

The total contribution for co-producers who are not members of Eurimages must not exceed 30% for a multilateral co-production, or 20% for a bilateral co-production. This applies to UK co-producers.

DETAILS

The funding is paid in three instalments to the co-producers relating to their share of the total production costs. It is paid as an advance on receipts, which means it is repayable from the net receipts of the co-producers.

APPLICATION PROCESS

The co-producers must contact their national representatives initially so the project can be placed on the Eurimages agenda. All the co-producers must agree to the project in writing, which must be submitted along with the application form by one of the co-producers to the Executive Secretary of Eurimages. The applications must be printed in English or French.

MEDIA Plus

UK MEDIA Desk
Agnieszka Moody
Fourth Floor
66-68 Margaret Street
London, W1W 8SR
T: 020 7323 9733
F: 020 7323 9747
E: england@mediadesk.co.uk
W: www.mediadesk.co.uk/england

MEDIA Antenna Scotland
Emma Valentine
249 West George Street
Glasgow, G2 4QE
T: 0141 302 1776/7
F: 0141 302 1778
E: scotland@mediadesk.co.uk
W: www.mediadesk.co.uk/scotland

MEDIA Services Northern Ireland
Cian Smyth
c/o Northern Ireland Film Commission
Third Floor, Alfred House
21 Alfred Street
Belfast , BT2 8ED
T: 02890 232 444
F: 02890 239 918
E: media@niftc.co.uk
W: www.mediadesk.co.uk/northernireland

MEDIA Antenna Wales
Gwion Owain
c/o SGRIN, 10 Mount Stuart Square
Cardiff Bay
Cardiff, CF10 5EE
Tel: 02920 333 304
Fax: 02920 333 320
Email: wales@mediadesk.co.uk
Web: www.mediadesk.co.uk/wales

This is the third phase of the MEDIA Programme, part of the European Union's audiovisual policy to support and develop European cinema and audiovisual media. The programme aims to develop training programmes, and to some extent the production and distribution of works, and the preservation of audiovisual and cinema heritage. The MEDIA Plus programme began in 2001 and runs until the end of 2005. It is administered through MEDIA Desks appointed in each country taking part in the programme, and the schemes and funds are the same in each participating country. The funding on offer supports distributors, training providers and project development for producers. Below shows the current call for available development funding, which will close on 16 June 2003. The MEDIA Programme intends to publish the next development funding call around November 2003 to be open for a six month period.

Single Animation Projects

The grant will fund animation projects that run no less than 25 minutes which are aimed for theatrical release or television broadcast. Specific items this scheme will cover are graphics research and pilot production.

ELIGIBILITY

The production company must have produced at least one twenty-five minute animation production or two animated shorts, prior to their application. This must have received national distribution for first time applicants, and international distribution for previous applicants.

DETAILS

Amounts of E10,000, (£6830 approx.) E20,000 (£13,650 approx.), E30,000 (£20,490 approx.), E40,000 (£27,330 approx.) and E50,000 (£34,160 approx.) can be applied for. Feature length animation intended for theatrical release may apply for E80,000 (£54,660 approx.)

APPLICATIONS

In addition to the application form, applicants must submit items such as: a producer's/director's statement of intent, a treatment, sample dialogue, a script, illustrations, production costs, CVs, details of crew and key personnel.

Single Documentary Projects

The grant will fund creative documentaries that run no less than twenty-five minutes which are aimed for theatrical release or television broadcast. Specific items this scheme will cover include realisation of a video treatment.

ELIGIBILITY

The production company must have produced at least one twenty-five minute creative documentary or fifty minute fiction production previous to their application. This must have received national distribution for first time applicants, and international distribution for previous applicants.

DETAILS

Amounts of E10,000 (£6830 approx.), E15,000 (£10,249 approx.), E20,000 (£13,650 approx.), and E30,000 (£20,490 approx.) can be applied for.

APPLICATIONS

In addition to the application form, applicants must submit items such as: a statement of intent, a treatment, CVs and details of crew and key personnel.

Single Fiction Projects

The grant will fund fiction projects that run no less than 50 minutes which are aimed for theatrical release or television broadcast.

ELIGIBILITY

The production company must have produced at least one fifty minute fiction or twenty-five minute creative documentary production previous to their application. This must have received national distribution for first time applicants, and international distribution for previous applicants.

DETAILS

Amounts of E10,000 (£6830 approx.), E20,000 (£13,650 approx.), E30,000 (£20,490 approx.), E40,000 (£27,330 approx.) and E50,000 (£34,160 approx.) can be applied for.

APPLICATIONS

In addition to the application form, applicants must submit items such as: a statement of intent, a treatment, sample dialogue, a script, CVs and details of crew and key personnel.

Single Multimedia Projects

The grant will fund multimedia projects in various platforms including interactive audio-visual projects, CD-ROM, DVD-ROM, or web sites. Projects might, for example, be animation for online distribution, computer games, innovative interactive entertainment, interactive programmes as part of a package of VHS or CD-Rom box sets. Specific items this scheme will cover are creation of programme content, creation of basic audio and video graphic elements, software programming, and production of a demo.

ELIGIBILITY

The production company must have produced at least one multimedia or animation project in at least two languages with distribution or broadcast online in at least one country outside the country of origin.

DETAILS

Amounts of E10,000 (£6830 approx.), E20,000 (£13,650 approx.), E30,000 (£20,490 approx.), and E50,000 (£34,160 approx.) can be applied for.

APPLICATIONS

In addition to the application form, applicants must submit items such as: a statement of intent, examples of video and graphic work, a flowchart, estimated costs, CVs and details of crew and key personnel.

Slate of Projects

There are two funding streams available, Slate 1 and Slate 2, for projects in the fields of fiction, documentary, animation and multimedia. Projects should be aimed for theatrical release, television broadcast and web broadcast. This stream will cover costs for the specific items listed in each of the single development streams above.

ELIGIBILITY

For Slate 1 funds the production company must have produced in the previous 3 years one audio-visual work with distribution or broadcast in at least one country outside the country of origin.

For Slate 2 funds the production company must have produced in the previous 3 years (or 5 years for fiction and animation) two audio-visual works with distribution or broadcast in at least one country outside the country of origin.

DETAILS

Slate 1 will provide funding for 3 to 9 projects for the sums of E60,000 (£41,000 approx.) E70,000 (£47,840 approx.), E80,000 (£54,670 approx.) and E90,000 (£61,512 approx.). Slate 2 will provide funding for 3 to 15 projects for the sums of E100,000 (£68,345 approx.), E110,000 (£75,180 approx.), and E125,000 (£85,432 approx.)

APPLICATIONS

In addition to the application form, applicants must submit items such as CVs and a company registration certificate. Slate 1 funding must include between three and nine projects. Slate 2 funding must include between five and fifteen projects.

General Guidelines (common to all funding streams)

Funding for all development projects will cover development costs, such as: acquisition of rights, research, script-writing fees up to final draft, storyboards, cast and crew identification, preparation of budget, financing plan and schedule, key partner identification, and marketing plans. There are additional eligible costs detailed under each stream.

DEADLINE

All applications for this year's call are accepted up to 16 June 2003.

ELIGIBILITY

Independent production companies based within the EU or EEA and run by nationals of the EU or EEA are eligible to apply.

DETAILS

Match funding of at least 50% is required.

APPLICATIONS

In addition to the materials required for each stream, other submission items are common to all applications, such as, amongst others: agreements with co-producers and distributors, details of ownership of rights, certificate of company incorporation, and bank statements.

ASSESSMENT

Each application will be assessed against the following criteria: quality and originality of concept, project development strategy, finance plan and production potential, and the exploitation potential. The utilisation of new technologies in creation, production and distribution is also encouraged.

WANTON MUSE

LITTLE ASHES

Wanton Muse is a young British production outfit that were kick-started with development funding from Media II for Little Ashes, a feature about the relationship between Salvador Dali and Lorca. Three years later and the muses - Philippa Goslett (above, right), Moira Campbell (above, left) and Pikka Brassey - have an international A-List director attached and shooting scheduled for Autumn 2003.

Philippa "We were entering a few ideas for a story competition, I think we had to enter four and we only had three, so I put down this idea that had been brewing in the back of my mind for a while. I've always been extremely interested in Federico Garcia Lorca, but the more I researched him, the more interested I became in his relationship with Salvador Dali and how that transformed both their lives. So we entered a four page outline of the story into the competition and it got selected. And then I had to write it! I'd never written anything before, so that was rather daunting."

Moira "But the competition provided a script editor who was wonderful. Then that draft got funding from Media II. At that time we were one of three companies that got funding and the other two were really well established - they normally go on track record so it was real coup for us. It was about E10,000, £6k. We probably should have applied for more because we would have got it, but at the time that seemed absolutely fine!"

Pikka "Before we went to Cannes first time round we rang a lot of European production companies to set up meetings. Interestingly, the first company we met was Egmond who had produced Antonia's Line and developed *The Luzhin Defense*, two of Marleen Gorris' projects."

Moira "So they gave the script to Marleen - we'd heard before that she didn't want to direct it, but in fact she'd not even seen the script - anyway we went over to meet her and that was that. She was just fantastic and we shared the same passion for it - it's very nice when that happens."

Philippa "We've been lucky with *Little Ashes* because we had script editing on the first draft through Euroscript. Then we had Marleen giving her input and finally the Moonstone Writer's Lab, which was an incredible experience and turned the project around."

Moira "So after going through two or three co-producers, I think we've finally found the right ones. We're negotiating with them for 50% at the moment. Then we're getting a chunk from Spain, through the Catalan film fund, and we're currently talking to interested parties about the remainder. We're scheduled to start shooting in August 2003 in Barcelona. The main cast are in place and it's getting rather exciting."

Phillipa "We've been extremely lucky in three people in particular: our line producer, Paul Sarony, our lawyer, Laurence Brown and above all our casting director, Sharon Howard Field who seems to have single-handedly packaged the project. They're the backbone of the production and it's great to have their expertise."

THE LESSONS LEARNT

Pikka "Don't send a screenplay out until it's at its strongest stage. I think another common mistake people make is to tire the contacts they make, or approach people the wrong way - they think they have to pitch to everyone all the time. I think that when making contacts you need to be as natural as possible, not harassing them with phone calls."

Moira "Don't be afraid if you want to start on your own. You need to be confident in yourself and in your talents. You have what it takes!"

Philippa "Also, prepare yourselves for a long process. When we started out everyone said it would take several years to get this film made and we thought, oh yes, but we'll do it in six months. Now it's been, what, three years? But don't lose faith, and surround yourself with people you trust and who share your passion for what you're doing." *TF*

(MEDIA Plus cntd.)

CONDITIONS

Once the project goes into production, the applicant must re-invest the same sum received in support from MEDIA into a new development project. In the case of slate development funding being issued, once one project on the development slate goes into production, the applicant must re-invest the same sum received in support from MEDIA into the next project on the development slate. MEDIA must be kept up-to-date and allowed access to relevant financial and management information.

Other Organisations
Japan Foundation

The Japan Foundation London Office
17 Old Park Lane
London, W1K 1QT
Tel: 020 7499 4726
Fax: 020 7495 1133
Email: info@japanfoundation.org.uk
Web: www.jpf.go.jp

The Japan Foundation was established by the Japanese Government thirty years ago to promote Japanese culture abroad, and to build on Japan's international relations. It has offices worldwide and primarily supports schemes that encourage cultural exchange between nations.

Film-Production Support Program

This scheme aims to encourage original film, TV and audio-visual productions, which help to increase understanding of Japanese culture abroad, and that have a good chance of achieving broadcast or public release.

DEADLINE

There is an annual deadline in December.

ELIGIBILITY

Individuals and companies experienced in filmmaking are eligible to apply. Feature films, TV programmes, video works, CD Roms and other audio-visual works may be funded in any language and the content must relate to Japan.

DETAILS

The maximum grant available is 50% of the production costs with a ceiling of ¥5m (approx. £26,250). The grant will only be paid once the production is completed and will not go towards research and development costs.

APPLICATIONS

It is advised for applicants to contact their national Japan Foundation Office to discuss the project. In addition to the application form, applicants must submit: a summary of the project and detailed synopsis, previous work, background information, budget and finance plans, partnership funding, schedule, script, letter of recommendation from a distributor, and other items. Applications must be sent by post or courier.

ASSESSMENT

Applications will be assessed against the following criteria: the ability of the applicant to deliver the project; applicant's track record; the need for the grant; realistic planning; potential for success; potential for public screening; no religious or political connotations; originality; and the stage of the project (those in production or post-production are favoured).

CONDITIONS

The applicant will not receive the grant until the project is completed and a copy given to the Foundation. The Foundation must receive a screen credit and may publicise their involvement in the project. They do not require the grant to be repaid at any time.

Roy W. Dean Grants

From The Heart Productions
1455 Mandalay Beach Road
Oxnard
California 93035-2845, USA
Email: CaroleEDean@worldnet.att.net
Web: www.fromtheheartproductions.com

Film Grant for New Zealand award applications:
Carole Dean,
The Wye Cottage,
Rd 1 Highway 63 # 4613,
Blenheim
New Zealand 007321

The Roy W. Dean Grant Foundation was established in 1992 primarily to support documentary filmmakers. The foundation encourages the film community to give resources and services to each award winner, enabling them to produce their film ideas.

Los Angeles Film Grant & Los Angeles Video Grant

Winning filmmakers of each of these awards have the opportunity to benefit from a range of free products and services to allow them to film their proposal in Los Angeles. The prizes are worth in excess of $40,000 (around £25,000) and include: musical score, camera rental, editing, titles and opticals, production management, production and technical advice, film processing, marketing strategy, equipment, screenwriting software, and various discounts. The deadline is in July.

New York City Film Grant

A range of products and services are made available to the winner of this award, enabling them to film their proposal in New York. The award is worth in excess of $65,000 (over £41,000) and includes: editing time, musical score, film stock, titles, equipment, tap transfers, sound and mixing sessions, animation, storyboarding and digital compositing, internet promotion, fundraising consultation and screenwriting software. Four runners up will also receive prizes worth $750 (around £470) in film stock and access to production facilities.

Editing Grant

The recipient of this award is given the opportunity to do an off-line edit of completed film footage. The prize includes: a return ticket to New Zealand, four weeks residency in a furnished cottage on the South Island, $120NZ (around £40) a week to live on and access to a car and phone card. The recipient must have a dub of the footage with original time-code on mini-DV and will work with a local filmmaker and local facilities. The deadline is in September.

Writing/Research Grant

The recipient of this award is given the opportunity in March or September to work on their writing and research for features, short films and documentaries for four to six weeks in a cottage on the South Island of New Zealand. The prize also includes: return ticket, access to a computer, money for expenses, a phone card, access to a car, and screenwriting software.

Film Grant for New Zealand

Documentary filmmakers chosen to receive this award are given access to goods and services that enable them to film a documentary in New Zealand. The prize includes: film stock, film processing, camera hire, equipment, editing, music, tape transfers, a web site and legal advice. The deadline is in February

General Guidelines

DETAILS

Finished films will be screened on Discovery, Starz, PBS, History and other networks.

ELIGIBILITY

Filmmakers, students, independent producers and independent production companies are eligible to apply for these documentary awards. There is no restriction on where applicants are based, but the awards are given in the relevant location (New York, Los Angeles or New Zealand).

APPLICATIONS

Applicants for each award must submit a completed application form, a fee of $38 or $28 for students, plus a proposal for the project and examples of past work.

ASSESSMENT

The awards are given to new film and video documentary projects that are unique and benefit society, and works in progress. There is no restriction on length.

CONDITIONS

The films must be shot in the location the prize is offered, and filmmakers may have to credit the award sponsors.

Sundance Documentary Fund

Sundance Documentary Fund
8857 W. Olympic Blvd.
Beverly Hills CA 90211
USA
Email: sdf@sundance.org
Web: www.sunadance.org

The Institute was founded in 1981 by Robert Redford to provide training, support and development opportunities for emerging screenwriters, directors and other disciplines of the film and theatre arts. The Sundance

Film Festival for independent filmmakers is held annually in January.

Documentary Development and Work in Progress Funds

The Documentary Fund has evolved from Sundance's Soros Documentary Fund, which has now closed. The fund aims to support emerging independent filmmakers, to produce documentaries on challenging contemporary issues related to human rights and social injustice. It is a very competitive scheme and will fund about thirty projects each year selected from hundreds of proposals. There are two types of funding available for development of projects and works in progress.

DEADLINE

There is no deadline as the fund works on a rolling basis.

ELIGIBILITY

Applicants can be based anywhere in the world. Projects should range from one hour long to feature length, making them suitable for television broadcast or theatrical release.

DETAILS

The Development Fund will support projects in the research or pre-production stage with funding of up to $15,000 (about £9500). Once projects are in production they are eligible to receive funding from the work in progress scheme but the producers must re-apply. The Work in progress Fund will support projects that are in production or in post-production with funding of up to $50,000 (about £31,700). The likely average funding amount is $25,000 (about £15,800).

APPLICATIONS

Applicants for both funds must submit a treatment or synopsis including: filmographies of the key personnel, a budget in US dollars including details of the secured finance, an example of prior work (completed) from the director, or if not available, an example of a creative work, and an application checklist confirming all these items have been enclosed. If no funding has been secured the applicant must include a plan to raise further finance. Applicants for the work in progress fund must also submit a rough cut of at least 20 – 30 minutes (no rushes or unedited cuts) on VHS.

ASSESSMENT

The applications will be assessed for the quality of the examples of work, the strength of the proposal, the potential for international distribution and the significance of the documentary's issue.

Chapter 7
SUPPORT & ADVICE

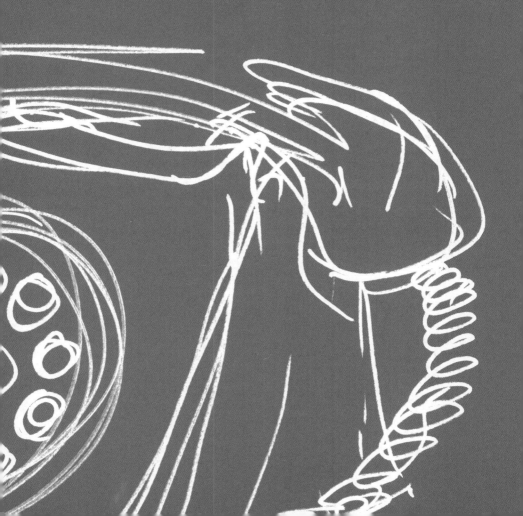

Business Support

Starting Out

Before almost any financier will give you a cheque, you need to be a registered company with a dedicated business bank account. Incorporating is a relatively straightforward process, but the associated workload should not be underestimated. Limited companies offer their directors limited liability in case the company goes bankrupt – that is, when the company is set up, each of its directors guarantee a minimum amount of capital that they will provide to cover the company if it is wound up with outstanding debts.

But in return for this protection, a limited company has a number of obligations: you need to submit annual accounts to Companies House as well as an annual return; and submit accounts and a tax return to the Inland Revenue. If your turnover is above £350,000 the company accounts must be audited. If you as a director pay yourself – or anyone else who isn't a freelancer - you will need to be registered as an employer with the Inland Revenue, which means deducting National Insurance and tax from wages via Pay As You Earn (PAYE). Furthermore, once your annual turnover passes £55,000, or before if you wish to start claiming back VAT receipts, you will need to register with HM Customs & Excise for VAT, submitting quarterly returns.

Ideally you will have an accountant to look after these responsibilities, but many new companies attempt to do much of the bookkeeping and filing themselves, which is a sizeable administrative workload, particularly if you're learning as you go along. There is the constant pressure that failure to deliver accurate accounts and forms at the right time in the right state can lead to an inspection, a fine, or even a prison sentence.

So, before forming a company (or a partnership), it is worth ensuring that you'll be able to meet your obligations. A jumping-off point that outlines these requirements is the government's starting up in business site - www.ukonline.gov.uk/YourLife/StartingUpBusiness/YLIndex/ and the Inland Revenue's starting up in business booklet – download from www.inlandrevenue.gov.uk/startingup/pages.pdf.

You can also arrange a meeting with a Business Link advisor (see below) to discuss your plans.

DIY Incorporation

A solicitor will charge around £100 to set-up a limited company; following the guide below you can do it yourself for just over £30. That said, this isn't legal advice, and if you have any doubts you should contact a solicitor, accountant or Companies House.

1   Check that the name of your company is available by ringing Company's House on 0870 3333636 or searching their website at www.companieshouse.gov.uk. Decide upon company directors, registered offices and appoint a company secretary.

2   Download form 10 and form 12 from the Companies' House website. Download form 10cs if you have more than two directors. Download or order the relevant guidance notes which includes Company Formation - code GBF1, Company Names - code GBF2, Business Names - code GBF3, Director's and Secretaries Guide - code GBA1

3   Fill in the forms on your computer and print out. Get the company directors and secretary to sign form 10 (and 10cs if necessary).

4   Buy a copy of Memorandums and Articles for company formation, for about £6 from a legal stationer such as Oyez. Oyez is based in London, but can mail the Articles if you purchase them via 0870 7377370 or at www.formslink.co.uk.

5   Fill in the Memorandums and Articles and get all directors and the company

secretary to sign it with a witness (the witness can be anyone).

6 Take form 12 to a solicitor and sign it in front of them. Get their signature on the form. Most solicitors charge £5 per signature. Photocopy each form for your records.

7 Post form 10, form 10cs (if used), form 12 and the Memorandum and Articles, with a cheque for £20 to Companies House. This is supposed to take 5-6 working days to process upon receipt.

Business Link

Tel: 0845 600 9006
Web: www.businesslink.org

There are regional Business Links across the UK that can be accessed through the main web site or phone line. New businesses and those thinking of starting up can contact Business Link for an introductory meeting, as well as using their website as a starting point for further information about running their own company.

Business Link is an advice service that works with the Government Offices and the Regional Development Agencies, and is operated by the Small Business Service at the DTI to provide information on available grants and loans and government schemes and policies. Business Link also offers support, guidance and advice in relevant areas such as starting a business; finance and money; people, sales and marketing; e-commerce and IT; management and operations and business improvement, amongst others.

Government Offices

EAST OF ENGLAND

GO-East
Victory House, Vision Park
Histon, CB4 9ZR
Tel: 01223 202000
Fax: 01223 202020
Email: enquiries.go-east@go-regions.gsi.gov.uk
Web: www.go-east.gov.uk

EAST MIDLANDS

Government Office for the East Midlands
The Belgrave Centre
Stanley Place, Talbot Street
Nottingham, NG1 5GG
Tel: 0115 971 2759
Fax: 0115 971 2404
Email: enquiries.goem@go-regions.gsi.gov.uk
Web: www.go-em.gov.uk

LONDON

Riverwalk House
157-161 Millbank
London, SW1P 4RR
Tel: 020 7217 3328
Fax: 020 7217 3450
Email: enquiries.gol@go-regions.gov.uk
Web: www.go-london.gov.uk

NORTH EAST

Wellbar House, Gallowgate
Newcastle upon Tyne, NE1 4TD
Tel: 0191 201 3300
Fax: 0191 202 3830
Email: general.enquiries.gone@go-regions.gsi.gov.uk
Web: www.go-ne.gov.uk

NORTH WEST

Sunley Tower, Piccadilly Plaza
Manchester, M1 4BE
Tel: 0161 952 4000
Fax: 0161 952 4099
Email: gward.gonw@go-regions.gsi.gov.uk
Web: www.go-nw.gov.uk

Cunard Building
Pier head, Water Street
Liverpool, L3 1QB
Tel: 0151 224 6300
Fax: 0151 224 6470
Email: gward.gonw@go-regions.gsi.gov.uk
Web: www.go-nw.gov.uk

SOUTH EAST

Bridge House
1 Walnut Tree Close
Guildford, GU1 4GA
Tel: 01483 882255
Email: gose.info.gose@go-regions.gov.uk
Web: www.go-se.gov.uk

SOUTH WEST

2 Rivergate
Temple Quay
Bristol, BS1 6ED
Tel: 0117 900 1700
Fax: 0117 900 1900
Email: contactus@go-regions.gsi.gov.uk
Web: www.go-sw.gov.uk

Mast House
Shepherds Wharf
24 Sutton Road
Plymouth , PL4 0HJ
Tel: 01752 635000
Fax: 01752 227647
Email: goswdc@eurobell.co.uk
Web: www.go-se.gov.uk

Castle House
Pydar Street
Truro, TR1 2UD
Tel: 01872 264500
Fax: 01872 264503
Web: www.go-se.gov.uk

WEST MIDLANDS

Government Office for the West Midlands
77 Paradise Circus Queensway
Birmingham , B1 2DT
Tel: 0121 212 5050
Fax: 0121 212 1010
Email: enquiries.gowm@go-regions.gov.uk
Web: www.go-wm.gov.uk

The Government Offices are the regional
contact and information points between
business and the government, particularly
the Department of Trade and Industry.
They are responsible for delivering
government policy and providing a source
of information on government and EU
business grants and legislation. The
Enterprise Grant Scheme (see page 172),
which provides financial support for small
and medium sized enterprises in eligible
areas of the UK, is administered by the
Government Offices. They also advise on
the Regional Selective Assistance scheme,
which provides financial assistance for
projects in Assisted Areas. Information

about the EU Structural Funds, which assist
areas in need of economic development,
and how these funds are fed into projects
that benefit business, is available on each
regional Government Office web site.

The Prince's Trust

HEAD OFFICE

The Prince's Trust
18 Park Square East
London NW1 4LH
Tel: 020 7543 1234
Fax: 020 7543 1200

SCOTLAND

1st Floor, The Guildhall
57 Queen Street
Glasgow G1 3EN
Tel: 0141 204 4409
Fax: 0141 221 8221

NORTHERN IRELAND

Block 5, Jennymount Court
North Derby Street
Belfast, BT15 3HN
Tel: 028 9074 5454
Fax 028 9074 8416
Email: ptnire@princes-trust.org.uk

WALES

Baltic House, Mount Stuart Square
Cardiff CF10 5FH
Tel: 029 2043 7000
Fax 029 2043 7001
Email: nicola.robins@princes-trust.org.uk

LONDON

3rd Floor, Tribute House, 120 Moorgate
London EC2M 6TS
Tel: 020 7382 5100
Fax: 020 7382 5199
Email: buselon@princes-trust.org.uk

EAST OF ENGLAND

3a Princes Street
Suffolk IP1 1PN
Tel: 01473 228844

Fax: 01473 228845

EAST MIDLANDS

Mansion House, 41 Guildhall Lane
Leicester LE1 5FQ
Tel: 0116 253 7824
Fax: 0116 253 7866
Email: busderb@princes-trust.org.uk

NORTH EAST

Tynegate Business Centre
5th Floor, Aidan House
Sunderland Road, Gateshead,

Tyne and Wear, NE8 3HU
Tel: 0191 4788488
Fax: 0191 4788487
Email: davidbea@princes-trust.org.uk

NORTH WEST

Northbridge House
Elm Street Business Park
Burnley, Lancashire BB10 1PD
Tel: 01282 714161
Fax: 01925 442074

SOUTH EAST

Headway House, Crosby Way
Farnham, Surrey GU9 7XG
Tel: 01252 891330 or
Email: offfarnh@princes-trust.org.uk

SOUTH WEST

Westmoreland House, Westmoreland Street
Bath BA2 3HE
Tel: 01225 489 930
Fax: 01225 489 931
Email: westerncounties@princes-trust.org.uk

WEST MIDLANDS

Lye Business Centre
Enterprise Drive, Hayes Lane
Lye, Stourbridge, West Midlands DY9 8QH
Tel: 01384 892100
Fax: 01384 895381
Email: busbirm@princes-trust.org.uk

YORKSHIRE AND THE HUMBER

1st Floor , King Charles II House
Headlands Road, Pontefract, WF8 1DD
Tel: 01977 698 000
Fax: 01977 698 001
Email: busyork@princes-trust.org.uk

The Prince's Trust is a UK charity that has been helping young people overcome barriers and get their lives working since 1976. Through practical support including training, mentoring and financial assistance, The Prince's Trust helps 14-30 year olds realise their potential and transform their lives. The Trust focuses its efforts on those who've struggled at school, have been in care, are long-term unemployed or who have been in trouble with the law. Details on the programmes run by the Prince's Trust can be found in Chapter 5.

Regional Development Agencies

Advantage West Midlands (AWM)
3 Priestly Wharf
Holt Street
Aston Science Park
Birmingham, B7 4BN
Tel: 0121 380 5480

East of England Development Agency (EEDA)
The Business Centre
Station Road
Histon
Cambridge, CB4 9LQ
Tel: 01223 484 519

East Midlands Development Agency (EMDA)
Apex Court
Citylink
Nottingham, NG2 4LA
Tel: 0115 988 8305

London Development Agency (LDA)
Devon House
58-60 St. Katharines Way
London, E1W 1JX
Tel: 020 7954 4688
North West Development Agency (NWDA)

Renaissance House
PO Box 37
Centre Park
Warrington, WA1 1XB
Tel: 01925 400 216

One North East (ONE)
Hadrian House
Higham Place
Newcastle Upon Tyne, NE1 8AF
Tel: 0191 233 9204

South East of England Development Agency (SEEDA)
Cross Lanes
Guildford, GU1 1YA
Tel: 01483 500 731

South West of England Regional Development Agency
(SWERDA)
North Quay House
Sutton Harbour
Plymouth, PL4 0RA
Tel: 01752 635042

Yorkshire Forward (YF)
RSA Team
Victoria House
2 Victoria Place
Leeds, LS11 5AE
Tel: 0113 233 8283

In 1998, the government introduced the Regional Development Act, with the intention of setting up Regional Development Agencies across England. Key priorities focus on: economic development and regeneration, business efficiency, investment and competitiveness, employment, skills development, and sustainable development across the UK in rural and non-rural areas. The RDA's work with the Government Offices and Business Link, as well as regional film agencies, advising on suitable regional projects and schemes. They organise events and develop programmes with significance for their region.

Cultural Industries Development Agency (CIDA)

Business Development Centre
7-15 Greatorex Street
London, E1 5NF
Tel: 020 7247 4720
Fax: 020 7247 7852
Email info@cida.co.uk
Web: www.cida.co.uk

This agency supports the cultural industries in Tower Hamlets, Hackney and Newham across East London. Once registered, a company can benefit from: business, marketing and development support services, information services, creative industry networks, education, training and skills development, advertising opportunities, and small grants. In addition the organisation focuses on: social inclusion, capacity building, inward investment, and fundraising activities.

Film Commissions

British Film Commission

10 Little Portland Street
London, W1W 7JG
Tel: 020 7861 7860
Fax: 020 7861 7864
Email: info@bfc.co.uk
Web: www.bfc.co.uk

The British Film Commission (BFC) is a division of the Film Council, responsible for promoting the UK internationally, as a base for filmmaking to attract inward investment. It provides information about locations, services, facilities and personnel, and lobbies on important regulatory issues that affect film and television production in the UK. The BFC works in collaboration with other commissions. These include: the British Film Office in Los Angeles, which specifically promotes the UK to Hollywood, the three national commissions for Scotland, Ireland and Wales, and the regional film commissions, responsible for ensuring the attraction of their region to national and international productions.

ENGLAND

Bath Film Office

Trimbridge House
Trim Street
Bath, BA1 2DP
Tel: 012 2547 7711
Fax: 012 2547 7279
Email: maggie_ainley@bathnes.gov.uk
Web: www.visitbath.co.uk

Covering: Bath and North East Somerset

East Midlands Screen Commission

35-37 St Mary's Gate
Nottingham, NG1 3AL
Tel: 0115 934 9090
Fax: 0115 9500988
Email: emsc@emsc.org.uk
Web: www.emsc.org.uk
Covering: Derbyshire, Leicestershire, Lincolnshire, Northamptonshire & Rutland

North West Vision

109 Mount Pleasant
Liverpool, L3 5TF
Tel: 0151 708 8099
Fax: 0151 708 9859
Email: lornaw@northwestvision.co.uk
Web: www.northwestvision.co.uk

Covering: Cheshire, Greater Manchester, Lancashire, Merseyside

Northern Film & Media

Central Square, Forth Street
Newcastle Upon Tyne, NE1 3PJ
Tel: 019 1269 9212
Fax: 019 1269 9213
Email: nsc@northernmedia.org
Web: www.northernmedia.org

Covering: Cumbria, Durham, Teeside, Tyne & Wear, Northumberland

Screen East

Anglia Television
Anglia House
Norwich, NR1 3JG
Tel: 016 0376 7077
Fax: 016 0376 7191
Email: chris@screeneast.co.uk
Web: www.screeneast.co.uk

Covering: Bedfordshire, Essex, Cambridgeshire, Hertfordshire, Norfolk, Suffolk

Screen South

The Metropole Galleries
The Leas
Folkestone, CT20 2LS
Tel: 01303 298 222
Fax: 01303 298 227
Email: lara.lowe@screensouth.org
Web: www.screensouth.org

Covering: Berkshire, Buckinghamshire, City of Oxford, Hampshire, Isle of Wight, Kent, Surrey, Sussex, Channel

Screen West Midlands

3rd Floor, Broad Street House
212 Broad Street
Birmingham, B15 1AY
Tel: 012 1643 9309
Fax: 012 1643 9064
Email: info@screenwm.co.uk
Web: www.screenwm.co.uk

Covering: Herefordshire, Oxfordshire, Shropshire, Warwickshire, Staffordshire, West Midlands, Worcestershire

South West Screen

St Bartholomew's Court
Lewins Mead
Bristol, BS1 5BT
Tel: 0117 952 9977
Fax: 0117 952 9988
Email: info@swscreen.co.uk
Web: www.swscreen.co.uk

Covering: Cornwall, Devon, Dorset, South Somerset

Liverpool Film Office

Pioneer Buildings
65-67 Dale Street
Liverpool, L2 2NS
Tel: 015 1291 9191
Fax: 015 1291 9199
Email: lfo@liverpool.gov.uk
Web: www.filmliverpool.com

Covering: Liverpool, Merseyside

London Film Commission

20 Euston Centre
Regents Place
London, NW1 3JH
Tel: 020 7387 8787
Fax: 020 7387 8788
Email: lfc@london-film.co.uk
Web: www.london-film.co.uk

Covering: Greater London. Now part of
Film London

Screen Yorkshire

40 Hanover Square
Leeds, LS3 18Q
Tel: 0113 294 4410
Fax: 0113 294 4989
Email: info@screenyorkshire.co.uk

Covering: Yorkshire & Humberside

SCOTLAND

Scottish Screen

2nd Floor
249 West George Street
Glasgow, G2 4QE
Tel: 014 1 302 1700
Fax: 014 1 302 1711
Email: kevin.cowle@scottishscreen.com
Web: www.scottishscreen.com

Scottish Screen is the main screen body
for Scotland. As a film commission it is
responsible for attracting international
production to Scotland by providing
location and crew databases, production
information, and the latest related news.

Edinburgh Film Focus

Castlecliff
25 Johnston Terrace
Edinburgh, EH1 2NH
Tel: 013 1622 7337
Fax: 013 1622 7338
Email: edinfilm@ednet.co.uk
Web: www.edinfilm.com

Covering: Edinburgh, Lothians, Scottish
Borders

Glasgow Film Office

City Chambers
Glasgow, G2 1DU
Tel: 014 1287 0424
Fax: 014 1287 0311
Email: film.office@ced.glasgow.gov.uk
Web: www.glasgowfilm.org.uk

Covering: Glasgow

Scottish Highlands and Islands Film Commission

Cultural & Leisure Services
The Highland Council
Inverness Castle
Castle Hill
Inverness, IV2 3EG
Tel: 014 6371 0221
Fax: 014 6371 0848
Email: trish@scotfilm.org
Web: www.scotfilm.org

Covering: Scottish Highlands & Islands

South West Scotland Film Commission

Gracefield Arts Centre
28 Edinburgh Road
Dumfries, DG1 1NW
Tel: 013 8726 3666
Fax: 013 8726 3666
Email: screencom@dumgal.gov.uk

Covering: Dumfries, Galloway

Tayside Film Commission

152 Nethergate
Dundee, DD1 4DY
Scotland
Tel: 01382 432321
Fax: 01382 432252
Email: julie.craik@dundeecity.gov.uk

WALES

Wales Screen Commission

The Media Centre
Culverhouse Cross
Cardiff, CF5 6XJ
Tel: 029 2059 0240
Fax: 029 2059 0511
Email: southwalesfilm@compuserve.com
Web: www.sgrin.co.uk

The Wales Screen Commission, a
partnership with SGRIN (the film funding
body for Wales), the Welsh Development
Agency, and Education and Learning Wales,
work with the regional screen commissions
to promote Wales as a location and base for
international productions.

Mid Wales Screen Commission

Unit 6G, Science Park
Cefn Llan
Aberystwyth
Ceredigion, SY23 3AH
Tel: 019 7061 7995
Fax: 019 7061 7 942
Email: enquiries@midwalesfilm.com
Web: www.midwalesfilm.com

Covering: Mid Wales: Cardiganshire, Powys

North Wales Screen Commission

Mentec, Deiniol Road
Bangor
Gwynedd, LL57 2UP
Tel: 012 4835 3769
Fax: 012 4835 2497
Email: film@gwynedd.gov.uk
Web: www.filmnorthwales.com

Covering: North Wales

South East Wales Screen Commission

c/o Sgrin
The Bank
10 Mount Stuart Square
Cardiff, CF1 6EE
Tel: 02920 435385
Fax: 02920 435380
Email: penny@walesscreencommission.co.uk
Web: www.sgrin.co.uk

Covering: South East Wales

South West Wales Screen Commission

Media Technium, Gelli Aur
Carmarthen, SA32 8LR
Tel: 01558 668573
Fax: 01558 669003
Email: illtud@walesscreencommission.co.uk
Web: www.sgrin.co.uk

Covering: South West Wales

NORTHERN IRELAND

Northern Ireland Film & TV Commission

21 Ormeau Avenue
Belfast, BT2 8HD
Tel: 028 9023 2444
Fax: 028 9023 9918
Email: nifc@nifc.co.uk
Web: www.nifc.co.uk

The NIFTC is the main screen body for
Northern Ireland. It provides funding for
Northern Ireland including production and
training programmes, and acts as a screen
commission by providing information
on locations, crews and resources and
promoting this to the international film
industry.

ISLE OF MAN

Isle of Man Film Commission

First Floor
Hamilton House
Peel Road
Douglas
Isle of Man, IM1 5EP
Tel: 01624 685 864
Fax: 01624 685 454
Email: kim.fletcher@iomfilm.dti.gov.im
Web: www.gov.im/dti/isleofmanfilm

The Isle of Man Department for Trade and
Industry operates the Film Commission,
which aims to attract international
production to the island. It promotes the
locations available and offers an attractive
Film & Television Fund for films that fit
their guidelines, such as filming on the
island and utilising local services and
resources.

Government Agencies

Department of Culture, Media and Sport (DCMS)

2-4 Cockspur Street
London, SW1Y 5DH
Tel: 020 7211 6000
Fax: 020 7711 6249
Email: enquiries@culture.gov.uk
Web: www.culture.gov.uk

The DCMS is responsible for improving
and promoting access to culture, media
and sport, with key priorities on social
inclusion, cultural regeneration and support
for the creative industries. It is directly
responsible for granting British films with
their official status, according to the Films
Act 1985, and is the appointed competent
authority for British co-productions. The
Film Policy Review Group published a
report for the DCMS in 1998 about the
British film industry called, "A Bigger
Picture", identifying key areas in need of
improvement and informing film policy. It
resulted in: the creation of the Film Council,
the British Film Office (in Los Angeles),
the Film Education Working Group and
the Skills Investment Fund. The DCMS
also works with other film-related bodies,
such as the National Film and Television
School (which it funds), the British Film
Commission, and the British Film Institute.

Department of Trade and Industry

Department Of Trade and Industry (DTI)
1 Victoria Street
London, SW1H OET
Tel: 020 7215 5000
Web: www.dti.gov.uk

The DTI is responsible for policy-making,
promoting, and supporting business and
industry in the UK. A particular priority
is to encourage small and medium–sized
enterprises through the Small Business
Service (SBS). The SBS has set up initiatives
such as: the Regional Venture Capital
Fund, the Enterprise Grant Scheme, the
Small Business Loan Service and Regional
Selective Assistance. They also provide:
information, advice and guidelines on
business practice, training, key business-
related topics and schemes.

Inland Revenue

Film Industry Unit
Inland revenue
Tyne Bridge Tower
Gateshead
Tyne & Wear, NE8 2DT
Tel: 0191 490 3662
Fax: 0191 490 3851
Web: www.inlandrevnue.gov.uk

There are also general enquiry centres
located throughout the UK, details of which
are available at the website or by calling
020 7667 4001.

The Inland Revenue is responsible to
the Treasury for the administration of
tax-related matters, and acts a source of

information for the public. Film-related tax and investment issues form part of its remit.

Office of National Statistics

The Library
Office for National Statistics
1 Drummond Gate
London, SW1V 2QQ

The Library
Office for National Statistics
Cardiff Road
Newport, NP10 8XG
Tel: 0845 601 3034
Fax: 01633 652747
Email: info@statistics.gov.uk
Web: www.statistics.gov.uk

This government office provides access to statistics on the national economy, society and population with an extensive searchable database of statistics and related articles.

Patent Office

The Patent Office
Concept House
Cardiff Road
Newport
South Wales, NP10 8QQ
DX 722 542
Tel: 0845 9 500 505
Fax: 01633 813600
Email: enquiries@patent.gov.uk
Web: www.patent.gov.uk

This is the office where patents and trademarks are registered. They also provide information to the public and clients through their web site, publications, free leaflets and their consultation service.

International Organisations

Academy of Motion Picture Arts and Sciences (AMPAS)

Academy Foundation
8949 Wilshire Boulevard
Beverly Hills
CA 90211-1972, USA
Tel: +1 310-247-3000
Fax: +1 310-859-9351
Email: ampas@oscars.org
Web: www.oscars.org

An organisation of people working across the film industry, including producers, writers, actors, directors and technicians. As well as providing industry support, AMPAS awards the Oscars annually.

Association of Film Commissioners International

314 N. Main, Suite 307
Helena, MT 59601, USA
Tel: +1 406 495 8040
Fax: +1 406 495 8039
Email: info@afci.org
Web: www.afci.org
This is the professional organisation linking a network of over 300 world-wide film commissions. Links to all members and their contact details are available on the web site.

Cineuropa

Cineuropa
c/o Italia Cinema S.r.l.
Via Aureliana 63 - 00187
Roma, Italy
Tel: +39 06 42005798
Fax: +39 06 42003530
Email: info@cineuropa.org
Web: www.cineuropa.org

The EU MEDIA Programme and a range of film-related organisations support this initiative of Italia Cinema. It provides an online information resource for the European film industry, with news, features, various databases for scripts, films, festivals, training, industry professionals and funding and legal advice.

European Coordination of Film Festivals

64 rue Philippe le Bon
B-1000 Brussels, Belgium
Tel: +32 2 280 1376
Fax: +32 2 230 9141
E-mail: yblairon@eurofilmfest.org
Web: www.eurofilmfest.org

Over 200 members make up this network of European audio-visual festivals. The association aims to support its members through exchange and co-operation in transnational partnerships and collective promotion.

European Film Academy

Kurfürstendamm 25
10719 Berlin
Germany
Tel: +49 (30) 887 167-0
Fax: +49 (30) 887 167-77
Email: efa@europeanfilmacademy.org
Web: www.europeanfilmacademy.org
The European Film Academy organises annual events for its members to support and promote European film production. The most notable of these is the European Film Awards, presented each year in December. Members are invited to nominate films for the different categories, and then asked to vote on the selected short list.

The Academy is in part funded by membership fees, which range from 110 Euros for voting members (individuals), and 11,100 Euros for patrons (companies).

Independent Feature Project (IFP)

NEW YORK OFFICE
104 West 29th Street
12th Floor, New York
NY 10001-5310, USA
Tel: +1 212 465-8200
Fax: +1 212 465-8525
ifpny@ifp.org

LOS ANGELES OFFICE
8750 Wilshire Boulevard
Second Floor
Beverly Hills CA. 90211 , USA
Phone: +1 310 432-1200
Fax: +1 310 432-1203

IFP is a non-profit organisation that provides resources, information, and avenues of communication to its US independent filmmaker membership. It aims to strengthen the connections between business and filmmaker communities; expand and educate the audience for independent film; and encourage diversity and quality in independent production. The body has six offices across the US and publishes Filmmaker magazine.

Mediasalles

Via Soperga 2
20127 Milano, Italy
Tel: +39 02 66 98 44 05
Fax: +39 02 66 91 574
Email: infocinema@mediasalles.it
Web: www.mediasalles.it
This is a joint initiative between the EU MEDIA Programme and the Italian Government, to support, encourage and promote theatrical distribution for European productions. The service includes the European Cinema Online Database, containing information on films, production, distribution, world sales, theatres and exhibition companies.

Zeotrope Virtual Studio

www.zoetrope.com

This initiative was founded in 1998 by Francis Ford Copolla as a web site for his magazine Zoetrope: All-Story, where writers could submit short stories. By the year 2000 the idea had grown to create the Virtual Studio, a network and resource for creatives involved in the film industry. To be able to access the full site, visitors must become members (for free). This allows them to upload their work for criticism by other members and to benefit from the networks, information and tools available. These include a forum for producers that can assist them in getting projects off the ground and in finding new talent from the directory of members and their work.

BARRY HUTCHINSON   ZOMBIE LOVE STORIES

Barry Hutchinson spent just £15,000 on his first DV feature and ended up with a US sales agent for the project and an option from a New York producer for his follow-up.

"I wrote a script that we could shoot as cheaply as possible. First of all we were going to make it about vampires, but then vampires usually fly, or turn into mist or stuff, whereas zombies just tend to walk about a bit fairly slowly, so zombies it was.

"We raised the money mostly through private investors. My Dad had just taken early retirement, so between him and my Mum, they chucked in £4000 from redundancy money and savings (which I'll never hear the bloody end of). A couple of local businesses forked out some cash, too, and the rest came as an advance from our sales agent and from the Scottish Youth Prince's Business Trust.

"The cast was made up for the most part by actor friends, though we did recruit one leading actress through a hasty ad in Shooting People, after the original actress had to pull out about a fortnight before shooting started. Because I'd deliberately written it round locations I knew we had access to for free, and because everyone worked for nothing, we pulled the whole thing in for under £15,000. The cast stayed in my house, apart from on their last night of shooting, when we put them up in a hotel as a little thank you. It was a cheap hotel, mind, we didn't go overboard or anything.

"Amazingly, though, as soon as it became local knowledge that we were shooting this thing, loads of people called up to offer assistance. Not just people keen to get into films, either. We had the guy who was the armourer for *Cuthroat Island*, *The Mummy* and for *Braveheart* phone us up and offer his services for free! And another guy who was a stuntman on *999* phoned up and said if we needed anyone to fall off anything high without dying, he was the man for the job. Everyone was keen to help. A local fishing and hunting shop loaned us a sword and some blank-firing handguns, a local chip shop gave us free fish suppers, and we were given free access to all our locations, too.

"Distribution was one of our biggest worries right from the start, and we had actually intended to go the self-distribution route, doing all the copying and packaging ourselves and trying to get the tape into Blockbuster or somewhere. Luckily, this didn't happen. The sales agent actually gave us an advance based on the script - I posted it on Francis Ford Coppola's American Zoetrope site, where it was read by Chris Bancel in New York. Chris said when he first read the title on Zoetrope he laughed, then he read the script and he laughed some more, so he optioned it. I had a contract in my hands about a fortnight later." *JM*

UK Screen Organisations & Associations

British Academy of Film & Television Arts (BAFTA)

195 Piccadilly
London, W1J 9LN
Tel: 020 7734 0022
Fax: 020 7734 1792
Web: www.bafta.org

BAFTA organises many events for its members from the film, television, interactive and children's entertainment industries. The most notable is the British Academy Film Awards presented each year in February. Members are invited to nominate films for the different categories; the shortlist is then voted on either by the voting members or a selected jury.

Members must have at least three years experience in the industry contributing significantly within it. A current member with experience of the individual's work must also act as a referee.

British Board of Film Classification (BBFC)

3 Soho Square
London, W1D 3HD
Tel: 020 7440 1570
Fax: 020 7287 0141
Web: www.bbfc.co.uk

The BBFC are responsible for viewing, and classifying, all films intended for theatrical and video/DVD release in the UK, under the Cinemas Act 1985, or the Video Recordings Act 1984, respectively. They may also ban a film or censor certain parts of it. The organisation is independent, funded by fees from those submitting films for classification. Classification is a two-tier process, with senior examiners responsible for ratifying the suggestions of examiners who come from a range of backgrounds.

British Council

Film & Television Department
11 Portland Place
London, W1B 1EJ
Tel: 020 7389 3065
Fax: 020 7389 3041
Email: films@brtishcouncil.org
Web: www.britishcouncil.org and www.britfilms.com

The British Council is a non-departmental public body. It works independently from the government, but retains close links to the Foreign and Commonwealth Office. It is responsible for international educational and cultural relations, and supports the British Film Industry, by promoting British films through key national events and festivals.

It does this in a number of ways, including: the provision of grants for filmmakers to travel to overseas events, co-financing screenings to showcase British films (such as the First Film Foundation's New Directions scheme), and ensuring and supporting British representation and participation at festivals and events around the globe. Short filmmakers can benefit from the film festival submission scheme, which selects high quality, short British films to be entered into international festivals on behalf of the filmmaker. Films must be sent on VHS to the British Council along with the submission form for selection.

The British Council also runs a web site, www.britfilms.com, dedicated specifically to the film industry. It provides an information resource for UK and overseas filmmakers and industry professionals, about British films, training, festivals, and how to make films in the UK.

British Film Institute (BFI)

21 Stephen Street
London, W1T 1LN
Tel: 020 7255 1444
Fax: 020 7436 7950
Web: www.bfi.org.uk

The BFI is funded mainly by the
Film Council to raise awareness and
understanding of film in the UK. It works
in three distinct areas: informing and
educating the general public, providing
access to its collections of prints, books and
related film materials, and supporting the
exhibition of films to a wide audience. The
BFI is responsible for: the BFI National
Library, the National Film & Television
Archive, the National Film Theatre, the
London IMAX Cinema, the Museum of the
Moving Image, Sight & Sound magazine,
and other publications, and various
education programmes.

Broadcasting Entertainment Cinematograph and Theatre Union (BECTU)

373-377 Clapham Road
London, SW9 9BT
Tel: 020 7346 0900
Fax: 020 7346 0901
Email: info@bectu.org.uk
Web: www.bectu.org.uk

BECTU represents the interests of its
members, who comprise of permanently
employed, freelance and contract workers
within the screen, theatre, entertainment,
leisure, media and related industries in the
UK. Members benefit from pay and safety
negotiations with employers, a monthly
newsletter, personal advice, and a range of
free and discount services.

BECTU is funded by annual membership
fees, which range depending on the
membership type. Full membership can
cost 1% of the individual's earnings with
a ceiling of £400. Changes to this exist
for payments by standing order, and

introductory rates apply for new members
in their first year, of either £120 for
professionals or £30 for recent graduates.

British Kinematograph, Sound and Television Society (BKSTS)

Ealing Studios
Ealing Green
London, W5 5EP
Tel: 020 8584 5220
Fax: 020 8584 5230
Email: info@bksts.com
Web: www.bksts.com

The BKSTS supports individuals involved in
the creative or technological production of
the moving image, by offering its members
events, lectures, training, courses and
information. Members range from students
to retired practitioners. The BKSTS is
funded by sponsors and annual member fees,
which range from £24 to £88, depending on
the stage the member has reached in their
career.

Directors Guild of Great Britain (DGGB)

Acorn House
314-320 Gray's Inn Road
London, WC1X 8DP
Tel: 020 7278 4343
Fax: 020 7278 4742
Email: guild@dggb.co.uk
Web: www.dggb.co.uk

The DGGB is a trade union for directors
in screen media, theatre, radio and opera.
Members benefit from a range of training,
events, information, publications and
services. The Director's Guild also lobbies
important issues on behalf of its members.

The DGGB is funded by annual membership
fees, which vary from £15 to £900.
Established directors may apply for full
membership, with their fee calculated as a
proportion of the previous year's income.
There is also membership available for
students, training providers and associates,

without the qualifications for a full membership.

Equity

London Office
Guild House
Upper St Martins Lane
London, WC2H 9EG
Tel: 020 7379 6000
Fax: 020 7379 7001
Web: www.equity.org.uk

This trade union represents the rights of artists from the fields of arts and entertainment. Members receive an equity card, indicating their professional status, and can benefit from help and advice, a pension fund, and minimum pay and conditions negotiated for Equity members.

Membership rates vary depending on whether the member is a young person (£20/year plus joining fee of £25), a student (£10), a long serving member (free), or full member (1% of annual earnings for those on a certain salary minimum and a joining fee of £25). To receive membership, applicants must already be working professionally in the industry.

The Guild of British Camera Technicians (GBCT)

C/o Panavision UK
Metropolitan Centre
Bristol Road
Greenford, UB6 8GD
Tel: 020 8813 1999
Email: admin@gbct.org
Web: www.gbct.org

The GBCT is a member association for individuals who work with motion picture cameras. This includes: directors of photography, camera operators, camera assistants, grips, gaffers, script supervisors, and stills photographers. Members benefit from training, products and services and a crew directory used by industry employers.

The guild is funded by annual membership fees of £120 each, and joining fees of £50. Individuals must be nominated by four current members that have experience of the individual's work.

New Producer's Alliance (NPA)

9 Bourlet Close
London, W1W 7BP
Tel: 020 77580 2480
Fax: 020 77580 2484
Email: queries@npa.org.uk
Web: www.npa.org.uk

The NPA is a charitable organisation set up to support independent new producers in the UK. Members benefit from a range of training, events, information and free and discount services, including legal and financial telephone hot lines, and an online member's directory. NPA also lobbies important issues on behalf of its members.

The NPA is funded by sponsors and minimal annual membership fees, which range from £50 to £650. Individuals and organisations within the industry are eligible to join, and members vary from students to established companies.

Producer's Alliance for Film and Television (PACT)

ENGLAND

45 Mortimer Street
London, W1W 8HJ
Tel: 020 7331 6000
Fax: 020 7331 6100

SCOTLAND

249 West George Street
Glasgow, G2 4QE
Tel: 0141 222 4880
Fax: 0141 222 4881
Web: www.pact.co.uk

PACT is a trade association for the independent film, television and media industries, representing the interests of its members to broadcasters, the government and the EU. Members range from production companies, financial companies, distribution companies and other related commercial services that can benefit from a range of resources, training, services, events, publications, and information.

PACT is funded by annual membership fees and you must be a limited company to apply. The fees vary from £705 per annum to £2115 per annum, depending on the company's annual turnover and field within the industry. Members will also be charged a levy of either 0.5% or 0.25% of their production budgets, which fund the Producer's Rights Agency; an associate company of PACT that negotiates agreements with the unions and rights organisations that producer's must deal with.

The Production Guild of Great Britain (PGGB)

Pinewood Studios
Iver Heath
Buckinghamshire, SL0 0NH
Tel: 01753 651767
Fax: 01753 652803
Email: lynne@productionguild.com
Web: www.productionguild.com

The Production Guild is a membership association for senior management individuals in film and television. Membership guarantees that an individual has achieved a certain level of experience and expertise in their field, encouraging employers to use the guild as a resource for personnel. The guild also offers some services to its members and lobbies important issues on behalf of the members.

The PGGB is funded by annual membership fees, which range from £50 to £250, with an additional application fee. The fee depends on the grade of membership.

Professional Lighting and Sound Association (PLASA)

38 St Leonards Road
Eastbourne, BN21 3UT
Tel: 01323 410335
Fax: 01323 646905
Email: membership@plasa.org
Web: www.plasa.org

PLASA is a trade association for companies all over the globe, which trade with light, sound and audio-visual technologies. Member companies are from entertainment, presentation, architectural and communication industries. Members benefit from services, information and discounts, and clients of a PLASA member, are guaranteed a certain standard of practice, required from members of the association.

The association is funded by annual membership fees, which range from £50, for an individual's membership, to £450 plus a £100 joining fee for full company membership.

Rocliffe New Writing Forum

Rocliffe Ltd
PO Box 37344,
London, N1 8YB
Tel: 07801 650 602
Email: info@rocliffe.com
Web: www.rocliffe.com

Rocliffe New Writing Forum was created in 2000 as a platform for new writing and a networking event. The formula is simple yet original - 5-8 minutes of four different scripts, rehearsed for 30-40 minutes with a director, the writer, and actors who are cast on the night. The scene is then performed to an audience of actors, writers, directors and producers, who then give the writer feedback on his or her work. After each scene the cast become the audience and another scene is performed to the audience. Each forum has a guest co-chair from the industry giving feedback from a commercial perspective about the work performed.

Past co-chairs have included Nik Powell, Michael Kuhn, Martha Coleman from Icon, Ed King from Rocket Pictures, Simon Heath from World Productions and Rachael Prior from WT2.

The Rocliffe New Film Forum is a platform for the short film making process exploring the production values, funding, casting, script development and budget considerations. This event focuses on how short films are made and financed. Rocliffe has as its patrons BAFTA, Alan and Shirley Plater, Producer Nik Powell and Variety.

Screenwriters Workshop

Suffolk House, Whitfield Place,
off Whitfield Street, London W1T 5JA
Tel: 0207 387 5511
Email: screenoffice@tiscali.net
www.lsw.org.uk

The Screenwriters Workshop was set up in 1983 by writers to help other writers learn how to rite for film and television. All current tutors are themselves writers with credits and commissions and therefore have a working knowledge of how to present treatments and scripts to the industry.

The Screenwriters Workshop runs courses, workshops, events, a report service and script consultancies for writers and producers who wish to learn about screenwriting and develop a treatment or script to industry standard. The Screenwriters Workshop has a close working relationship with the New Producers Alliance. One of it schemes is MATCH, which pairs a writer with a producer at an early stage of development.

The Script Factory

Welbeck House, 66 –67 Wells Street
London W1T 3PY
Tel: 020 7323 1414
Email: general@scriptfactory.co.uk
Web: www.scriptfactory.co.uk

The Script Factory provides new film-making talent with a range of innovative events and services, their stated mission is to 'Make Words Make Pictures'. The current range of services includes:

SCENE
A Festival of live screenwriting events staged in partnership with premier film festivals in the UK and internationally since 2000 in London, Edinburgh, Berlin, Rio and Göteborg with countless leading filmmakers such as Richard Curtis, Robert Altman, Lynne Ramsay, Spike Lee and Lone Sherfig.

MASTERCLASSES
Masterclasses, with preview screenings, take place in London and across the UK, and feature major filmmakers onstage in public sessions talking about the craft of film-making. A major element of the Masterclass programme is co-funded by the UK Film Council enabling the creation of The Script Factory Writers' Group, a selected group of screenwriters who have unprecedented access to the classes, receive transcripts, and are promoted to industry players looking for writing talent.

TRAINING
Co-funded by the UK Film Council, the Script Factory training programme includes:

Script Factory short courses for producers and developers including Introduction to Script Reading; Industry Reader & Development Training; Development Executive Modules. Also, soon to launch is an MA/PgDip in Script Development – the first one in the UK.

Script Factory Programmes for Writers including Writers' Passage – 12 month structured development course for selected screenwriters; First Draft to First Chance – Development course for screenwriters; Fade In – Introductory course for screenwriters

OTHER SERVICES
- Open script submission policy, for consideration for a public or private performed reading, as a development tool and platform to promote new talent to the industry

- A script report service offering constructive written feedback on scripts and treatments

- Script registration

- UK Screenwriters Network & Script Pitch list – the two Shooting People daily email digest of news and views are moderated by The Script Factory

- Selected in-house development for new writers and product placement in the industry

- Facilities hire – spacious, funky rooms and resources for up to 35 people

- General help and assistance by post, phone and email for anyone seeking advice on film industry issues.

- For currents dates/prices, events and additions to the range of services the The Script Factory offers, check the website: www.scriptfactory.co.uk

The Writer's Guild of Great Britain

The Writer's Guild of Great Britain (WGGB)
15 Britannia Street
London, WC1X 9JN
Tel: 020 7833 0777
Fax: 020 7833 4777
Tel: admin@writersguild.org.uk
Web: www.writersguild.org.uk

The Writer's Guild is a trade union representing the rights of writers in the screen industries, theatre and books. Members benefit from services including pensions, events, lobbying and connection with a network of other writers.

The guild is funded by annual membership fees, which range from £75 to £225. Full members will also be asked to pay the guild 1% of their annual earnings over £12,500 with a ceiling of £1250. Members will be eligible to join the Writer's Guild of America if they work in the USA, without needing to pay the $2500 membership fee.

Short Films

BritShorts

BritShorts Limited
25 Beak Street
London, W1F 9RT
Tel: 020 7734 2277
Fax: 020 7734 2242
Email: contactus@britshorts.com
Web: www.britshorts.com

BritShorts is a short film producer, distributor and sales agent. They screen British and international shorts via their website and in London venues.

First Film Foundation

9 Bourlet Close
London, W1P 7PJ
Tel: 020 7580 2111
Email info@firstfilm.co.uk
Web: www.firstfilm.co.uk

The First Film Foundation supports short filmmakers in their steps towards feature filmmaking. Apart from the funding schemes outlined in chapter 5, an important part of the foundation's programme is to showcase work by emerging filmmakers. The following two schemes aim to facilitate this, and to make the most of the extensive contacts database of UK and US film professionals.

FIRST FILM SHOWCASE

This is an annual event that showcases a selection of short films sent to the foundation by the closing date in March. Films must be no longer than 30 minutes, shot on any format, and must not have been screened at other major events or festivals. The director may apply alone, or with the producer and writer team. Six to eight films will be shown in front of professionals, including development executives, producers, talent agents and financiers.

NEW DIRECTIONS

This annual showcase in the autumn, supports British filmmakers ready to move into feature film production. Selected films are screened to professionals in London, New York and Los Angeles and meetings arranged for the filmmakers with studios, agents, distributors and production companies. Filmmakers will also be given a contacts directory for US professionals, and the opportunity to attend seminars introducing them to the industry in London, New York and Los Angeles. Entry films must have been finished in the last two years, and entrants must have a development slate of two feature films to enable them to make the most of the prize.

Short Circuit

The Workstation
15 Paternoster Row
Sheffield, S1 2BX
Tel: 0114 221 0569
Fax: 0114 249 2293
Email: info@shortcircuitfilms.com
Web: www.shortcircuitfilms.com

Short Circuit was established as a distributor of short films ahead of features at the cinema. They organise bespoke programming to festivals and events and organise their own seminar programme on film marketing and distribution. Currently, they are working with the New Cinema Fund Digital Shorts Scheme, touring the films around the country.

TriggerStreet

www.triggerstreet.com

TriggerStreet.com is Kevin Spacey's forum for upcoming filmmakers. As well as providing a platform where people can upload screenplays and comment on each other's work, TriggerStreet hosts three annual online short film festivals, with judges including Sean Penn, Ed Norton, Mike Myers, Billy Crystal, Cameron Crowe, Danny DeVito, Tim Burton and Bono. Filmmakers upload their shorts for peer feedback before the films are forwarded to the selection panel.

Training and Education

Film Education

21-22 Poland Street
London, W1F 8QQ
Tel: 020 7851 9450
Fax: 020 7439 3218
Email: postbox@filmeducation.org
Web: www.filmeducation.org

Film Education is a film teaching resource for school teachers to improve general knowledge and understanding of filmmaking and film culture. It publishes books, guides, CDROMS and other materials, as well as running training courses and events for teachers. It is a charity supported by the film industry, and the web site is approved by the National Grid for Learning (NGfL).

Media Business School

Velázquez, 14
28001 Madrid
Spain
Tel: +34 91 575 95 83
Fax: +34 91 431 33 03
Email: fbs@mediaschool.org
Web: www.mediaschool.org

The Media Business School, which is
supported by the EU MEDIA Programme,
is a professional training organisation
for European film, television and media
professionals. It caters for a range of
individuals, from those wanting to gain
skills at entry-level, to established and
experienced professionals. There are a range
of courses on offer, from annual seminars to
intensive training programmes in the Film
Business School, the Television Business
School, and the Digital Media Business
School.

National Film & Television School (NFTS)

National Film and Television School
Beaconsfield Studios
Station Road
Beaconsfield
Bucks, HP9 1LG
Tel: 01494 671234
Fax: 01494 674042
Email: admin@nftsfilm-tv.ac.uk
Web: www.nftsfilm-tv.ac.uk

The NFTS is the major professional training
organisation for the screen industries in
the UK offering MA courses, advance
programmes, diplomas and short courses
in a range of screen-based fields. There are
some scholarships and grants available
to support individuals with fees and
maintenance.

Raindance

81 Berwick Street
London, W1F 8TW
Tel: 020 7287 3833
Fax: 020 7439 2243
Email: info@raindance.co.uk
Web: www.raindance.co.uk

RAINDANCE SCOTLAND

3rd Floor
4 Park Gardens
Glasgow, G3 7YE
Tel: 0141 353 6678
Fax: 0141 353 6567
Email: info@raindance.co.uk
Web: www.raindance.co.uk

Raindance is a network that supports and
promotes independent filmmaking in the
UK. It offers a wide range of filmmaking
courses through evening classes and
intensive weekend masterclasses. In addition
the organisation runs the annual festival
for UK independent film and the Raindance
East Festival for films of eastern origin, and
Rawtalent, which aims to be a production
arm. The site also contains information,
guides, bulletins and tips for independent
filmmaking, and publishes a weekly email
magazine called Reelscene. Raindance
hosts the British Independent Film Awards
annually in October.

Skillset

Skillset
The Sector Skills Council for the Audio Visual Industries
Prospect House
80-110 New Oxford Street
London, WC1A 1HB
Tel: 020 7520 5757
Fax: 020 7520 5758
Email: info@skillset.org
Web: www.skillset.org

Skillset is responsible for promoting
and supporting training for the screen
industries, encouraging high standards of
practice, and a wide and fresh skills and
talent base. Skillset provides guidelines
for the professional standards required by

certain jobs in the industry, encouraging training providers to meet them. There is a database of courses and training providers on their website, some of whom work with Skillset to provide the individual with a qualification from Skillset.

There is also a training fund, the Skills Investment Fund (SIF), which supports training providers seeking to train freelancers from the film industry. The SIF is financed by voluntary contributions from film production companies, who are asked to donate 0.5% (up to £39,500) of their production budgets to the Fund. Working in partnership with the fund is the Skills Investment Fund Network, which provides a database of emerging crew and talent to companies that contribute to the SIF.

skillsformedia

Tel: 08080 300 900
Web: www.skillsformedia.com

skillsformedia is run by Skillset and BECTU as a source of careers advice for the screen industries. It aims to be a resource for individuals from all sectors and all levels within the industry, ranging from students to professionals, including those with special needs or facing redundancy. There may be a charge for some of the services.

Further Information

Books

FILMMAKING

"The Beginning Filmmaker's Guide to a Successful First Film" by Renee Harman, James Lawrence and Jim Lawrence (contributor) (Walker & Co)

"The Guerilla Filmmakers Handbook and the Film Producers Toolkit" by Chris Jones & Genevieve Jolliffe (Continuum)

SHORT FILMS

"How To Make Great Short Feature Films: The Making Of Ghosthunter " by Ian Lewis (Focal Press)

"In Short: A guide to Short Filmmaking in the Digital Age" by Eileen Elsey and Andrew Kelly (BFI Publishing)

"Making the Winning Short: How to Write, Direct, Edit and Produce a Short Film" by Edmond Levy (Henry Holt)

CAREER AND TRAINING

"Lights, Camera, Action! Career in Film, Television and Video 2nd Revised Edition" by Josephine Langham (BFI Publishing)

"Listing of Short Courses in Media and Multimedia" by Lavina Orton (BFI Publishing)

REFERENCE

"BFI Film & Television Handbook" edited by Eddie Dyja (BFI Publishing)

"Kays Production Manual" (Kay Media)

"The Knowledge" (Miller Freeman Information Services)

"The Writer's and Artist's Yearbook" by A C Black (A & C Black)

"The PACT directory of independent producers" (PACT)

FUNDING

"The Film Finance Handbook" edited by

Mike Downey (The Media Business School)

"The Art of the Deal" by Dorothy Viljoen (PACT)

"Filmmakers & Financing, Business Plans for Independents" by Louise Levison (Focal Press)

OTHER PUBLICATIONS

"A Guide to Help for Small Business" a free booklet from the Department of Trade & Industry

"A Filmmakers Guide to Distribution & Exhibition" (BFI) free to download from www.bfi.org.uk

"Directory of UK Co-producers 2003-2004" (British Council) free to download from www.britfilms.com

"The Media Business File" by the Media Business School, updated three times a year

Journals

Africa Film and TV, www.africafilmtv.com, African trade journal, focused on African screen industry within International market

Box Office, www.boxoff.com, North American trade journal

Film Journal, www.filmjournal.com, American trade journal with international outlook

Hollywood Reporter, www.hollywoodreporter.com, Hollywood trade journal with an international news section

Le Film Francais, www.lefilmfrancais.com, French trade journal, focused mainly on French and European screen news

Screen Digest, www.screendigest.com, International trade journal for screen business news, research, reference and statistics

Screen Finance, www.informamedia.com, International trade journal about screen finance news and issues

Screen International, www.screendaily.com, English International trade journal with

offices around the globe

Variety, www.variety.com, Hollywood-focused screen trade journal

Indiewire, www.indiewire.com, US independent film news

Useful International Websites

ARGENTINA

AVH	www.avh.com.ar
Gativideo	www.gativideo.com.ar
Hispanolink	www.hispanolink.com/english/Argentina/
LK-Tel	www.lk-tel.com.ar
UIP	www.argenuip.com.ar

AUSTRALIA

ACCC	www.accc.gov.au
Australian Film Commission	www.afc.gov.au
Australian Film Institute	www.cinemedia.net/AFI/
Beyond International	www.beyond.com.au
CEASA	www.geko.net.au/-ceasa
Cinemedia	www.cinemedia.com.au
Disney	www.disney.com.au
Film Australia	www.filmaust.com.au
Fox Movies	www.foxmovies.com.au
Greater Union	www.greaterunion.com.au
Hoyts	www.hoyts.com.au
Palace Cinemas	www.palace.net.au
SAWA	www.sawa.com
Screen Network Australia	www.sna.net.au
SPAA	www.spaa.org.au
Val Morgan	www.valmorgan.com.au
Village Roadshow	www.villageroadshow.com.au

AUSTRIA

Austrian Film Institute	www.filminstitut.at
BMWF	www.bmwfgv.at
Buena Vista	www.buenavista.at
Cine Tirol Filmförderung	www.cinetirol.com
Cinemaxx	www.cinemaxx.at
Constantin Film	www.constantinfilm.at
Europlex	www.europlex.at
Filmladen	www.filmladen.at
Filmfonds Wien	www.filmfonds-wien.at
Hollywood Megaplex	www.hollywood-megaplex.at
Infoscreen	www.infoscreen.at

Metropol	www.metropol-kino.at

BELGIUM

Cinergie	www.cinergie.be
CSA	www.csa.cfwb.be
Kinepolis group	www.kinepolis.be
RMB	www.rmb.be
Vlaams Audiovisueel Fonds	www.vaf.be
Wallimage	www.wallimage.be

BRAZIL

ACNielsen	www.acnielsen.com.br
Cinemark	www.cinemark.com.br
Disney	www.disneycom.br
Fox	www.foxfilm.com.br
Jornal do Video	www.jornaldovideo.com.br
MPAA	www.mpaa.org/mpa-al
Promocine	www.promocine.com.br
UIP	www.uip.com.br
Warner Bros. Brazil	www.warnerbros.com.br

CANADA

Alliance Atlantis	www.allianceatlantis.com
Cinemas Guzzo,	www.cinemasguzzo.com
Cineplex Odeon	www.cineplexodeon.com
CSC	www.csc.ca
Empire Theatres	www.empiretheatres.com
Famous Players	www.famousplayers.com
Imax	www.imax.com
Lions Gate	www.lionsgate-ent.com
NFB	www.nfb.ca
RDS Data	www.rdsdata.com
Statistics Canada	www.statcan.ca

CHINA

China Film	www.chinafilm.com
China Shinco	www.china-shinco.com
Shanghai Paradise	www.paradise.com.cn

CZECH REPUBLIC

Barrandov	www.barrandov.cz
Bontonfilm	www.bonton.cz
Falcon	www.falcon.cz

DENMARK

Danish Film Institute	www.dfi.dk
Danish Novelle Film	www.novellefilm.dk
Metronome	www.metronome.dk
Ministry of Culture	www.kum.dk

Scanbox	www.scanbox.dk
Videoclub	www.videoclub.dk

FINALND

Centre for the Promotion of Audiovisual Culture in Finland	www.kopiosto.fi/avek
Suomen Elokuvasäätiö	www.ses.fi

FRANCE

Agence Culturelle d'Alsace	www.culture-alsace.org/accueil.php
Allocine	www.allocine.fr
Aquitaine Image Cinéma	www.aquitaine-image-cinema.fr
Atelier de Production Centre Val de Loire	www.apcvl.com
Bac Films	www.bacfilms.com
CCRAV	www.ccrav.com
Centre National du Cinema	www.cnc.fr
Cinefil	www.cinefil.com
Circuit A	www.circuita.com
Columbia TriStar	www.columbiatristar.fr
Communauté Urbaine de Strasbourg	www.strasbourg-film.com
CSA	www.csa.fr
Diaphana	www.diaphana.fr
DVD France	www.dvdfr.com
EAO	www.obs.coe.int
Gaumont	www.gaumont.fr
INA	www.ina.fr
Le Film Francais	www.lefilmfrancais.com
Media France	www.mediafrance.org
Mediavision	www.mediavision.fr
Ministère des Affaires Etrangères	www.cinema.diplomatie.fr/medias_soc/cinema/aides
MK2	www.mk2.com
National Film Commission of France	www.filmfrance.com
Pathe	www.pathe.fr
Premiere	www.premiere.fr
Rhône-Alpes Cinéma	www.rhone-alpes-cinema.fr
Région Ile de Franc	www.iledefrance.fr/conseil/action_cinema.asp
Théâtre et Cinéma en Île-de-France	www.thecif.org
Unifrance	www.unifrance.org
USPA	www.uspa.fr

GERMANY

ACNielsen	www.acnielsen.de
Betafilm	www.KirchGruppe.de
Blickpunkt	www.cinebiz.de
Bremer Innovationsagentur	www.bia-bremen.de
Buena Vista International	www.movie.de
Cinecitta	www.cinecitta.de

Cinema online www.cinema.de
Cinemaxx www.cinemaxx.com
Cinemedia www.cinemedia.de
Columbia TriStar www.columbiatristar.de
Constantin www.constantinfilm.de
Deutsches institut fur filmkunde www.filminstitut.de
FilmFernsehFonds Bayern www.fff-bayern.de
Filmboard Berlin-Brandenburg www.filmboard.de
Filmbuero Bremen e.V. www.filmbuero-bremen.de
Filmbüro NW e.V www.filmbuero-nw.de
Filmförderung Hamburg GmbH
www.filmfoerderung-hamburg.de
Filmförderungsanstalt www.ffa.de
Filmstiftung Nord-Rhein Westfalen GmbH
www.filmstiftung.de
Fox Germany www.foxfilm.de
FSK www.fsk.de
GEMA www.gema.de
GVU www.gvu.de
HDF www.kino-hdf.de
Hessische Filmförderung
www.hessische-filmfoerderung.de
Helkon www.helkon.de
Intertainment www.intertainment.de
jugendfilm www.jugendfilm.de
Kieft & Kieft www.cinestar.de
Kinopolis www.kinopolis.de
Kinowelt www.kinowelt.de
Kirch Group www.kirchgruppe.de
Kulturelle Filmförderung Mecklenburg-Vorpommern
www.Film-MV.de
Kulturelle Filmförderung Sachsen
www.smwk.de/index-js.html
Kulturelle Filmförderung Schleswig-Holstein e.V
www.filmbuero-sh.de
MFG www.film.mfg.de
Mitteldeutsche Medienförderung GmbH
www.mdm-foerderung.de
Moviedata www.moviedata.de
MSH www.m-s-h.org
Nordmedia www.nord-media.de
Omniplex www.omniplex.de
Saarland Medien GmbH www.Saarlandmedien.de
Senator Film www.senatorfilm.de
SPIO www.spio.de
Stiftung Kuratorium Junger Deutscher Film
www.kuratorium-junger-film.de
TOBIS www.tobis.de
UCI www.filmab.de
UFA cinemas www.ufakino.de
UIP www.uip.de
Warner Village www.villagekinos.de
Wegra www.wegra.de

GREECE

Greek Film Centre www.gfc.gr

HONG KONG

ACNielsen www.acnielsen.com.hk
Broadway Cinemas www.cinema.com.hk
Chinastar www.chinastarcom.hk
Golden Harvest www.goldenharvest.com
Media Asia Group www.mediaasia.com
Mei Ah www.meiah.com
UA Cinemas www.cityline.com.hk

HUNGARY

Budapest Film www.budapestfilm.hu
Cineplex Odeon www.cineplexodeon.hu
Flamex www.flamex.hu
Intercom www.intercom.hu
MMA www.mma.hu
MOKEP www.mokep.hu

INDIA

Multi Media Frontiers www.multimediafrontiers.com
NFDC www.nfdcindia.com
Zee TV www.zeetelevision.com

IRELAND

Bord Scannan na hEireann www.filmboard.ie
Dept. of Arts, Sport and Tourism
www.arts-sport-tourism.gov.ie
Irish Film & TV Network www.iftn.ie

ITALY

20th Century Fox www.20thfox.it
ACNielsen www.acnielsen.it
AGCM www.agcm.it
AGCOM www.agcom.it
ANICA www.anica.it
Cecchi Gori www.cecchigori.com
Cinema 5 www.cinema5.it
Columbia TriStar www.columbiatristar.it
Direzione Generale per il Cinema
www.spettacolo.beniculturali.it/cinema/cinema.htm
Film Auto www.filmauro.it
Filmexport Group www.filmexport.it
Intrafilms www.intrafilms.it
Istituto Luce www.luce.it
Lucky Red www.luckyred.it
Media Salles www.mediasalles.it
Medusa Film www.medusa.it

Rai	www.raitrade.it
Warner Bros.	www.warnerbros.it

JAPAN

Daiei	www.daiei.tokuma.com
Fox	www.foxjapan.com
TOEI	www.toei.co.jp
Toho	NVWWtoho.co.jp
Shochiku	wwA,.shochiku.co.jp
Sony	www.sonyco.jp
Warner Mycal	www.mycal.co.jp

LUXEMBOURG

National Film Production Fund	www.filmfund.lu

MEXICO

Canacine	www.canacine.org.mx
Cinemark de mexico	www.cinemark.com.mx
Cinemex	www.cinemex.com.mx
Fox	www.foxmexico.com
Ramirez cinemas	www.cinepolis,com.mx

NETHERLANDS

Audiovisuele Federatie Nederland	www.afn.nl
AV-SCENE	www.scene.nl
Commissariaat voor de Media	www.cvdm.nl
Disney	www.disney.nl
The Dutch Co-production Fund for Broadcasting	
Companies	www.cobofonds.nl
Dutch film fund	www.filmfand.nl
Het Rotterdams Fonds voor de Film en Audiovisuele	
Media/	www.rff.rotterdam.nl
Holland Film	www.hollandfilm.nl
Hubert Bals Fund	www.filmfestivalrotterdam.com
Jan Vrijman Fund	www.idfa.nl
Minerva	www.minervagroep.nl
NBF	www.nbf.nl
Nederlands Fonds voor de Film	www.filmfund.nl
RCV	www.rcv.nl
Stimuleringsfonds Nederlandse Culturele	
Omroepproducties	www.Stimuleringsfondsrtv.nl

POLAND

Imperial	www.imperial.com.pl
ITI	www.iticinema.com.pl
Multikino	www.multikino.com.pl
Statistical Office	www.stat.gov.pl/english/
Syrena Entertainment	www.syrena.com

PORTUGAL

Instituto do Cinema, AV e Multimédia	www.icam.pt

RUSSIA

Gemini Film	www.geminifilm.ru
Goskino	www.goskino.ru
Media Most	www.mediamost.ru

SINGAPORE

ACNielsen	www.acnielsen.com.sg
Cathay Organisation	www.cathaycom.sg
Golden Village	www.goldenvillage.com.sg
Mediatech	www.mediatech.com.sg
Min. of Information & the Arts	www.mita.gov.sg
Shaw Organisation	www.shawcom.sg
Singapore Film Commission	www.sfc.org.sg

SOUTH AFRICA

Cinemark	www.cinemark.co.za
Primedia	www.primedia.co.za
Ster-Kinekor	www.sterkinekorcom

SOUTH KOREA

CJ Golden Village	www.cgvco.kr
Daewoo	www.daewoo.co.kr
Hyundai	www.hbs.co.kr
J-Com	www.jcom.co.kr
KOFIC	www.kofic.or.kr
Min. of Culture & Tourism	www.mct.go.kr
Pusan International Film Festival	www.piffor.kr
Seoul Cinema	www.seoulcinema.com

SPAIN

ACEC	vwww.acec.es
Alta Films	www.altafilms.es
CINESA	www.cinesa.es
FAPAE	www.cinespain.com
Golem	www.golem.es
ICAA	www.cinespain.com/ICAA
Lauren Films	www.laurenfilms.es
Movierecord	www.movierecord.com
Madrid Film Promotion Office	www.comadrid.es
Sogepaq	www.sogepaq.es
Yelmo Cineplex	www.yelmocineplex.es

SWEDEN

BVI	www.bionytt.com
Disney	www.disneyse
Film i Dalarna	www.filmidalarna.se

Film i Skaane	www.filmiskane.nu
Film i Sydöst	www.kalmar.regionforbund.se/kultur/film
Film i Väst	www.filmivast.se
FHR	www.fhrse
Fox Film	www.foxfilm.se
Göteborg Film Festival Filmfund	
	www.filmfestival.org/html/eng/filmfonder.html
Metronome	www..metronome.se
Nordic-Baltic Film Fund	www.bmc.dk/guidelines.htm
Nordisk Film- & TV Fond	www.nftf.net
Sandrew	www.sandrews.se
SF Media	www.sf-media.com
Statistiska Centralbyran	www.scb.se
Svensk Filmindustri	www.sfse
Svenska Filminstitutet	www.sfi.se
UIP	www.uip.se

SWITZERLAND

Filmnet	www.filmnet.ch
Fox	www.fox.ch
Metrocine	vwww.metrocine.ch

USA

AFI	www.afionline.org
AFMA	www.afma.com
AMC	www.amctheatres.com
AMPAS	www.ampas.org
Buena Vista	www.movies.com
Carmike	www.carmike.com
Castle Rock	www.castle-rock.com
Cinema Screen Media	www.cinemamedia.com
Cinemark	www.cinemark.com
Cinemark International	www.cinemarkinternational.com
Columbia TriStar	www.spe.sony.com
Digital Theater Systems	www.dtstech.com
Disney	www.disney.com
Dolby	www.dolby.com/movies
EDI	www.entdata.com
Edwards Cinemas	www.edwardscinemas.com
Electronic Industries Alliance	www.eia.org
FCC	www.fcc.gov
Fine Line	www.flf.com
Fox	www.fox.com
Fox Searchlight	www.foxsearchlight.com
General Cinemas	www.generalcinemas.com
Hoyts	www.hoyts.com
IMAX	www.imax.com
Loews Cineplex	www.loewscineplex.com
MGM	www.mgm.com
Miramax	www.miramax.com
MPA	www.mpaa.org
National Amusements	www.nationalamusements.com

National Cinema Network	www.ncninc.com
New Line	www.newline.com
Paramount	www.paramount.com
Pixar	www.pixar.com
PolyGram	www.polygram.com
Regal Theaters	www.regaltheaters.com
Rentrak	www.rentrak.com
Rysher	www.rysher.com
Screenvision Cinema Network	www.screenvision.com
SDDS	www.sdds.com
Sony	www.sony.com
Sony Pictures	www.sonypictures.com
THX	www.thx.com
Technicolor	www.technicolor.com
UIP	www.uipcorp.com
United Artists Theatre Circuit	www.uatc.com
Universal	www.universalstudios.com
Video Software Dealers Association	www.vsda.orgom
Warner Bros.	www.warnerbros.com

Index